Basically Academic

Basically Academic

An Introduction to EAP

Pat Currie
Carleton University

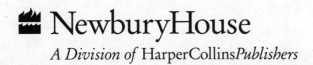
NewburyHouse

A Division of HarperCollins*Publishers*

Director: Laurie E. Likoff
Production Coordinator: Cynthia Funkhouser
Text Design Adaptation and Composition: North 7 Atelier Ltd.
Cover Design: Caliber Design Planning
Printer and Binder: Malloy Lithographing, Inc.

NEWBURY HOUSE
A division of HarperCollins *Publishers*
Language Science
Language Teaching
Language Learning

Basically Academic: **An Introduction to EAP**

ISBN: 0-06-632660-5

94 93 92 91   9 8 7 5 4 3 2

To Raewen and Mike

Contents

Chapter *3* Volcanoes   76

Chapter *4* A Study Skills Manual   101

Chapter *5* Endangered Species   122

Chapter *6* Child Labor   154

To the Instructor

Basically Academic was written for second-language learners who are planning to enter college or university, and who need to make the transition from ESL to more advanced EAP classes. Academic classes require students to accomplish difficult and complex tasks: reading, taking notes in lectures, giving presentations, understanding and integrating required information from several sources, and then selecting, synthesizing, and shaping that information into clear, well-organized text.

As an instructor, I felt there was a large gap between the traditional activities in ESL classes and the far more rigorous demands of EAP and university. I felt that students needed more exposure to academic tasks, more time than that offered by one EAP course, not only to increase their language proficiency, but also to practice the academic skills they would need in content classes. I also felt that they needed to become more independent, less reliant on the teacher.

In academic classes, students are often required to display knowledge through writing. The writing activities in *Basically Academic* are designed to help students develop an independent, effective approach to academic writing. It is important to tell the students that writing will help them clarify and consolidate the subject matter they are required to know, that writing can help them learn.

You may find that students are puzzled by the approach in this book. They may query the lack of focus on grammar, or the absence (with one exception) of essays on personal topics. I have found it helpful to tell my students that research suggests that professors are less concerned with grammatical accuracy than with the content of their writing—the students' ability to respond to the given task.

The Instructor's Manual for *Basically Academic* has been divided into eight sections, which correspond to the student book chapters. Each section begins with a general introduction to the contents of the chapter and continues with an explanation of the activities. The manual contains answer keys to the questions, suggestions for conducting the activities and for each writing task, an authentic student response. Furthermore, it contains an explication of the rationale behind the textbook, because teachers are usually more comfortable using a text when they know the philosophy on which it has been based.

Acknowledgments

First, I would like to thank the students in my classes who used this material while it was being developed, and whose responses were vital in shaping the book.

I would also like to thank my colleagues—Catherine MacNeil, Trudy O'Brien, Lynne Young, Geri Dumouchelle, and Adrienne Soucy—and their students, for field–testing various chapters in their classes.

I would like to express my gratitude to Cindy Funkhouser, Laurie Likoff, Alida Greydanus, and Donna DeBenedictis for their invaluable help, now and in the past, in turning materials into a book.

Finally, I would like to express my appreciation to the reviewers of this book whose comments and suggestions were very helpful:

Jo Anne W. Fischer
Michigan Language Center
Ann Arbor, Michigan

Kevin King
Harvard University
Cambridge, Massachussetts

Melinda Roth Syuvedra
Oregon State University
Corvallis, Oregon

Linda H. Hillman
DePaul University
Chicago, Illinois

To the Student

If you are using *Basically Academic*, you are most likely planning to go on to college or university, where you will face many new demands. You are probably an intermediate language learner; you may now be able to cope quite well with everyday situations in English. In your academic studies, however, you will need more advanced language skills as well as academic skills: You will have to read textbooks, listen to lectures, participate in group discussions, and complete a variety of writing tasks. You will need to study for, and write, examinations.

Basically Academic has been written to take you a large step closer to full-time academic study. It will help you make the transition from ESL to classes in English for Academic Purposes (EAP).

This book is based on the theory that if you practice the kinds of tasks you will be asked to do in your content classes, you will develop the skills necessary to succeed. Thus, the activities in this book match, in many ways, what you will do in academic classes. First, the readings are all authentic: they have been written for native speakers of English and have not been changed in any way. The writing tasks, both the essay topics and the exam questions, are similar to those you could be asked to write at college or university. The book shows you ways to make these tasks more manageable, as well as strategies you can use in your other studies. It will show you, for example, how to analyze, and how to use the clues that textbook writers include to help students find and remember important information. As you do these activities in English, you will be practicing not only your academic skills, but also your English language skills. You will also develop more independence as both a language learner and as a student.

There are eight chapters in this book, each one based on a particular topic, such as heroism or volcanoes. In each chapter, you will find several different readings, which you will use to respond to a final writing task, such as an essay or an examination question. To put it another way, each chapter is similar to an academic course.

In this book, you will discover, perhaps for the first time, that an academic task can be broken down into smaller steps. For example, in your writing, you will learn that you don't have to pay attention to everything at once. If you plan, discuss your plan with a partner, and then write several drafts, you will be able to write more efficiently and effectively.

You may find that this book is different from other ESL texts you have used before. You may find that the material is quite challenging. But if you do the activities here, you will develop both language and academic skills that you can use in academic classes.

Basically Academic

Chapter *1*

Managing Your Own Language Learning

*A*s ESL students, you often spend only a few hours a week in the language classroom. This amount of time isn't enough to effect vast changes in your language proficiency. If, however, you know what you want to achieve and how to go about it, you can practice your language skills all week long. As a result, you will be able to depend less on the teacher and take more responsibility for your own language learning. The activities in the next few classes will help you do this. As you work through them, you'll also be practicing the following skills and strategies:

- outlining
- skimming
- understanding and writing the inform-and-focus section of a text
- reading for specific information
- giving oral presentations
- taking notes in the margin
- selecting relevant information from text, notes, and personal experience
- organizing information to fulfill a specific purpose
- summarizing in your own words

THINK ABOUT THE TOPIC

Current research strongly suggests that before you begin reading about a new topic, you try to recall what you already know about it. Doing this helps you better understand what you read.

To help you think about your own language learning, write point-form answers to the following questions.

1. What languages do you speak / read / write?

2. Approximately how many books did / do you read per year in your own language? in English?

3. What different kinds of writing do you want to be able to do in English?

4. In your earlier English classes, what kinds of activities did you find especially helpful?

5. What opportunities do you have to talk at length to native speakers of English? Do you look for such opportunities? Why or why not?

6. List five things you can *now* do in English that you couldn't do a year ago.

In groups of three or four, discuss your answers.

READING I: "PREFACE"

The readings in this chapter are taken from a book entitled *How to Be a More Successful Language Learner*. The first reading is the "Preface," the introductory section. Read it to find answers to the following questions:

1. Who was the book written for?
2. What is its purpose?
3. What kind of information have the writers included?

Highlight the answers and, in the margin, write one or two key words to help you remember the information. Then check your findings with a partner. Together, discuss why it's important for students to read an introductory section such as this.

Reading I

Preface

If you are presently studying a foreign language or are planning to do so, this book is written for you. In it you will find concrete suggestions to help you become a more effective and successful language learner. You will also become acquainted with a host of time and classroom-tested techniques that will enable you to approach the study of a foreign language in a meaningful and productive way—to derive from your study of a language what *you personally* want from it.

In today's world, contact with speakers of languages other than English is increasingly common; we encounter such people in school, in our travels, in our jobs. As these contacts increase, so does our motivation to study foreign languages. For many the study of a foreign language is a satisfying and truly rewarding experience. Others, however, consider it a frustrating, nearly impossible undertaking. We believe that you can avoid inclusion in the second group if you take the time to learn and understand some basic facts about yourself, about language and communication, and about the way in which languages are learned. We also believe that *now* is the time to do it!

Our purpose in writing this book, therefore, is to share with you, in nontechnical terms, the kinds of insights that will enable you to become a better foreign-language learner. We examine such questions as:

- Why study a foreign language?
- What characterizes a good language learner?
- What is the nature of language and communication?
- Where is a language best learned?
- How does one begin to master a foreign language?

With your help, we also examine you! That is, we ask you to consider what *you* bring to the language-learning process: *your* specific abilities, *your* personality, *your* personal goals, *your* motivation, *your* attitudes. In short, what we do is provide you with the means to become the kind of foreign language learner *you* want to be.

CHAPTER 1 WRITING TASK: ESSAY

As mentioned earlier, part of the purpose of this ESL course is to help you become more independent in language learning. The following writing assignment is the first step in helping you do this:

Write a three- to four-page (double-spaced) essay on the one skill you would most like to improve. Choose from the following: reading, listening, talking, writing. Your essay should include the following information:

an assessment of your current proficiency level in that skill,

your objectives with regard to that skill by the end of the course, and

the two main strategies you'll use in an effort to meet these objectives.

The activities in the rest of the chapter will help you write the essay.

READING II: "PART 1: ABOUT LANGUAGE AND LANGUAGE LEARNING; CHAPTER 1: YOU, THE LANGUAGE LEARNER" (pp. 11–12)

The next reading, the first chapter from *How to Be a More Successful Language Learner*, begins on page 11.

Reading is always easier when you know what information you will find and how it is organized. Good textbook readers can find this out by using the clues good writers provide; for example, titles, headings, and sub-headings. If you use these clues, you can construct an outline of the information in the chapter.

1. Use the titles of Part 1 and Chapter 1 of the text to begin your outline on page 6.
2. Use the headings and subheadings in the rest of the chapter to complete the outline on page 6, writing them in a way that shows which are main sections and which are subsections.

3. Compare your outlines with those of two partners.

_____

(Part 1)

_____

(Chapter 1)

4. Sometimes a sketch can better help you see how ideas are connected. Individually, using the same headings, draw a tree sketch or diagram of the chapter contents. Use a separate sheet of paper.
5. When you finish, put your sketch on display on your desk. Walk around the class, noting other arrangements.
6. With your teacher, discuss the following questions:

  a. What are the advantages of making a sketch *before* you read any chapter in a textbook?
  b. Could you also use sketches to help you take notes ? How?

"INTRODUCTION" (p. 12)

As you work through this chapter, you'll practice skills and strategies to help you read more effectively. You may find that the activities take a lot of time at first, but if you practice them now, you'll be a more efficient, more aggressive reader.

Strategy: Find the Purpose of the Chapter

Read the introduction on page 12 to find out what this chapter will tell you, how you are supposed to use this information, and why the writers want you to do this.

"AGE AND FOREIGN-LANGUAGE LEARNING" (p. 12)

Strategy: Use Headings to Ask Questions; Read to Find the Answers

1. Think about the heading "Age and Foreign-Language Learning." With a partner, write at least two questions you'll likely find answers to in this section.
2. Now read the section to see if your questions are answered. Write key words in the margin to help you remember. Also, note any other important information.
3. As a class, decide how good your questions were. As an adult language learner, what advantages do you have over children learning English?

"INTELLECTUAL PREDISPOSITIONS" (pp. 13–14)

As you read this section, you'll practice three kinds of strategies: those for dealing with unfamiliar vocabulary, those for predicting content, and those for remembering what you read.

Strategy: Use a Variety of Techniques with Unfamiliar Vocabulary

Look at the heading for this section. If you don't understand it, try the following techniques in the order given below:

1. Ask other people in the class.
2. Read the **boldface** summary statement in the text.
3. Read part of the text.
4. Look up the word(s) in a dictionary.

Check your understanding with a partner.

Strategy: Turn the First Sentence into a Question

In a textbook, the first sentence of a paragraph often contains the main point that paragraph will support. If you turn this information into a question, you can actively look for the answer when you read the rest of the paragraph.

1. With a partner, use this technique to read the first sentence of each paragraph in this section. Turn the sentence into a question. Then read the paragraph to find the answer.
2. Write two or three key words in the margin to remind you of the important information.

Strategy: Review the Content in Your Own Words

When you finish the whole section, turn the page face down. With your partner, try to remember what you learned in this section. If you can't state the ideas in your own words, you might not understand them. Read the section again.

"PSYCHOLOGICAL PREDISPOSITIONS" (pp. 14–16)

This part is divided into six sections, each one discussing a particular trait or characteristic important to language learning.

Strategy: Read to Suit Your Purpose

1. Look at the scales on the chart in the box on page 9. Your task is to rate yourself on each psychological predisposition. To do this, read only as much as you need to understand each characteristic (you probably won't need to read the entire text). Then circle the number that best describes you.
2. In groups of three or four, compare and discuss your similarities and differences with regard to these predispositions.
3. Now with straight lines, join the numbers you circled, in order. Compare the resulting *profiles* to see how different you are from the others in your group.
4. What do such differences suggest about your language-learning strategies?

PREDISPOSITION	YOUR PERSONAL RATING				
1. Attitude to English	1 (negative)	2	3	4	5 (positive)
2. Introversion / Extroversion	1 (introverted)	2	3	4	5 (extroverted)
3. Inhibition	1 (inhibited)	2	3	4	5 (uninhibited)
4. Tolerance of Ambiguity	1 (low)	2	3	4	5 (high)
5. Learning Styles	1 (rule-oriented)	2	3	4	5 (risk-oriented)
6. Eye-Ear Learning	1 (eye-oriented)	2	3	4	5 (ear-oriented)

"SOCIOCULTURAL PREDISPOSITIONS" (pp. 17–18)

Strategy: Read for Specific Information

If you know what information you're looking for, you can save yourself a lot of time by looking *only* for that information and ignoring everything else.

1. Use any of your earlier strategies to help you understand the heading "Sociocultural Predispositions".
2. Read the questions below. Then read this section to find the answers. Highlight the information in the text and put the question number in the margin.

   a. What are stereotypes? Why should language learners be aware of them?
   b. How might ethnocentrism interfere with language learning?

3. With a partner, compare the information you highlighted.

"PAST EXPERIENCES" (p. 18)

Strategy: Relate New Information to Your Own Experiences

To help you make new information meaningful, one good strategy is to relate it to your own life. This is what you did when you categorized your psychological predispositions on the scale. Now use the information in this section to help you characterize (briefly) your own past experiences with language learning. Jot down a few key words to help you remember what you want to say. When you finish, discuss your past experiences with one or two partners.

Reading II

Part 1

ABOUT
LANGUAGE
AND
LANGUAGE
LEARNING

Chapter 1

YOU, THE LANGUAGE LEARNER

Everything depends on you.

You, the language learner, are the most important factor in the language-learning process. Success or failure will, in the end, be determined by what you yourself contribute. Many learners tend to blame teachers, circumstances, and teaching materials for their lack of success, when the most important reasons for their success or failure can ultimately be found in themselves. There are several learner traits that are relevant to learning a foreign language, and they usually appear in combination. *A positive combination* of these traits is probably more important than any one alone.

It is important to realize that there is no stereotype of "the good language learner." There are, instead, many individual traits that contribute to success, and there are also many individual ways of learning a foreign language. People can compensate for the absence of one trait by relying more heavily on another, by accentuating their strengths to compensate for their weaknesses. There is no conclusive evidence that any one of the traits described below is more important than another, particularly over long periods of language study. The descriptions in this chapter are intended to help you analyze your predispositions. You will then better understand how to enhance your learning by accentuating your strengths and minimizing the effects of your weaknesses.

AGE AND FOREIGN LANGUAGE LEARNING

Children are not better learners.

Some people think that the best time to begin studying a foreign language is in childhood, and that the younger you are, the easier it is to learn another language. There is little evidence, however, that children in language classrooms learn foreign languages any better than adults (people over age 15) in similar classroom situations. In fact, adults have many advantages over children: better memories, more efficient ways of organizing information, longer attention spans, better study habits, and greater ability to handle complex mental tasks. Adults are often better motivated than children: they see learning a foreign language as necessary for education or career. In addition, adults are particularly sensitive to correctness of grammar and appropriateness of vocabulary, two factors that receive much attention in most language classrooms.

Age does have some disadvantages, however. For instance, adults usually want to learn a foreign language in a hurry, unlike children, who can devote more time to language mastery. Also, adults have complex communication needs that extend beyond the mere ability to carry on a simple conversation. Adults need to be able to argue, persuade, express concern, object, explain, and present information about complex matters that pertain to their work or education. Because most adults do not like to appear foolish, they often deny themselves opportunities to practice for fear of making mistakes, not getting their message across, or appearing ridiculously incompetent. Also adults have more trouble than children in making new friends who speak the foreign language.

One example usually given to support the notion of children's superiority as language learners is their ability to pick up an authentic accent. It is usually observed that children of immigrants learn to speak the language of their adopted country without an accent, whereas their parents rarely do. It is also observed that even adults with high need and motivation, such as diplomats, rarely learn a foreign language without retaining some of their native accent. In a sense, the same is true in sports: to learn well the complex coordination of the hundreds of muscles needed to play tennis, swim, or figure skate, a person has to start young. Most champions begin training at an early age. There are examples of strong competitors who entered their sport after childhood, but they are the exception, not the rule. The same is true of adults who acquire native like accents.

Taken together, the disadvantages of age are clearly offset by advantages. By properly combining positive traits and effective strategies, you *can* indeed master a foreign language—as lots of adults do.

The best time to learn a foreign language, then, is when your need is clearest and you have sufficient time. If you are strongly motivated to study a foreign language and if you have the time to do it, the best time to begin is *now*.

INTELLECTUAL PREDISPOSITIONS

A person's intellectual predisposition to learn a foreign language is commonly referred to as *aptitude*. Aptitude is another way of saying "knack for languages," and like "having a good ear for languages," it is one of those myths people use to explain why some succeed where others fail. Strictly speaking, language-learning aptitude is the intellectual capacity to learn a foreign language, a kind of a foreign language IQ. In a classroom situation, a person with high language aptitude can usually master foreign language material faster and better than someone with lower aptitude. Thus, several studies show a strong relationship between grades and aptitude.

What is your language IQ?

There are several standardized tests that measure language-learning aptitude. They predict how fast and how well an individual can learn foreign languages under formal classroom conditions, when the emphasis is on *grammar* and *memorization*. However, these tests may not be such good predictors of how well a person can learn to *communicate* in a foreign language, especially if he or she has the opportunity to practice in real-life situations. In other words, language aptitude tests may predict ability to learn formally and analytically but they may not be as reliable in measuring ability to learn unconsciously and intuitively.

Remember that language success may ultimately depend not only on ability but on persistence. You may have the potential to be a brilliant language learner, but if you fail to put effort into it, chances are you will not learn much. A good combination of talent and perseverance is ideal. For example, it has been shown that pronunciation accuracy in adult students can be predicted by two traits: aptitude for mimicry, presumably an inherent trait, and strength of concern for pronunciation, a motivational factor. When the two are combined, one can acquire a good foreign accent.

PSYCHOLOGICAL PREDISPOSITIONS

A number of psychological traits appear to be related to successful language learning. One of them, motivation, is so important that it is discussed separately in Chapter 2. In this chapter we examine several other traits that have a significant effect on language mastery.

Attitude

Emotions are important.

If aptitude is an intellectual trait, attitude is an emotional one. On the one hand, it may have to do with the way learners feel about the foreign culture and its people. They may admire them and want to learn more about them by becoming fluent in their language. Or, they may like the people who speak the foreign language and wish to be accepted by them. Research has shown a definite relationship between attitudes and success when foreign-language learners have an opportunity to know people who speak the language they are studying. Such positive attitudes usually help learners to maintain their interest long enough to achieve language mastery. Thus, if you find France and the French people attractive, if you wish to learn more about them or wish to become more like them, you are likely to succeed at learning to speak French well.

Some people are remarkably successful in mastering a language without feeling powerfully drawn to the country or the people who speak it. They may need the language for academic or career purposes, so their attitude is purely pragmatic. These two attitudes are not mutually exclusive: it is entirely possible that a person may want to learn Spanish because he or she wants to understand the Spanish people better *and* wants to study in Spain. More important than specific attitude is that the language learner experience a real need to communicate and make meanings clear.

Extroversion

Practice is important.

It should not be surprising that personality influences the way a person goes about learning a foreign language. Although we cannot, at present, sketch the ideal language-learning personality, several traits appear to be related to success. Of these, extroversion is repeatedly mentioned as a positive trait. When everything else is equal, a sociable person who uses every opportunity to talk with other people may be more successful because by initiating and maintaining more contacts he or she has more occasion to hear and use the new language.

Inhibition

Make yourself comfortable.

People who are painfully aware of their limitations and worry about their ability to use the language are usually less willing to engage in either classroom practice or in real-world communication. Shyness and inhibition can stand in the way of progress in speaking (perhaps less in the way of reading) a foreign language. They can also prevent a person from taking risks or seizing opportunities to practice and learn. Fear of making a mistake or being misunderstood can keep a learner from adopting an open-minded, active, and creative approach to language learning. Everything else being equal, a person who has an open, receptive attitude towards the foreign language, who is not afraid to use it, and who feels at ease in foreign-language situations is more likely to learn from his or her language experiences.

Thus, if you have an open, inquisitive, worry-free approach to learning a foreign language, if you find the whole experience enjoyable and rewarding, you will probably learn better. You may want to review your life situation in general and ask yourself the following questions: Is my self-esteem low in language class? If so, what can I do to raise it? (If your teacher is highly intolerant of errors, you may find it helpful, when you can, to change teachers.) Is there anything wrong with my study habits? Do I expect too much of myself? Do I really have the time to devote to language learning, or do I have too many other pressing matters on my mind?

Tolerance of Ambiguity

Everything is not black and white.

Tolerance of ambiguity allows a person to reconcile and accommodate ideas that may be contradictory or information that may be inconsistent. A person who is tolerant of ambiguity does not see everything in terms of black and white and does not put information in air-tight compartments. Such a person is willing to accept the fact that there are many shades of grey and that uncertainty and inconsistency must be accommodated. Tolerance of ambiguity has been noted as an asset in learning a foreign language because there are so many inconsistencies in language rules that even native speakers cannot always agree on correct usage or explain certain language phenomena. Also, whether a turn of speech is right or wrong may depend on the situation rather than on an ironclad rule. A person who can accept an evasive answer, such as, "Well, I suppose you could say it that way under certain circumstances," is more likely to have an open, flexible system for accommodating new information as knowledge of the language increases.

Learning Style

Rules or risks?

Learning a foreign language is just one form of learning in general; therefore, each individual will employ the approach that he or she usually applies to other learning situations. When it comes to foreign languages, one kind of learner prefers a highly structured approach with much explanation in the mother tongue, graded exercises, constant correction, and careful formulation of rules. This type of learner is very analytical, reflective, and reluctant to say anything in the foreign language that is not grammatically perfect. This person is a rule learner. A second type of learner relies more on intuition, the gathering of examples, and imitation. He or she is willing to take risks. There is no evidence that one type of learner is more successful than the other. What is more important perhaps is that the learner's style be appropriate to the particular task. If the task is to communicate, then risk taking is in order. If the task is to say or write something correctly, than rules should be consulted.

It is important that each learner's preferences be accommodated in the classroom. You may thus wish to examine your own preferences, and communicate them to your teachers. For instance, if you feel that you need rules, you may be quite uncomfortable in a classroom dedicated to imitation and repetition of dialogues and should ask the teacher for more explanations. If, on the other hand, you feel that you learn more from being exposed to the language and from making your own inferences, you may feel ill-at-ease in a classroom where the teacher painstakingly explains the new grammar in English and should ask the teacher for more practice in speaking.

Eye-Ear Learning

When learning a foreign language, some students depend on their eyes; others depend on their ears. Some learners feel that they learn better if they can see the language written out, while others prefer to listen to tapes and records. It is not clear to what extent "eye-mindedness" and "ear-mindedness" are related to foreign-language mastery. You may want to experiment to find out whether a single method or a combination of the two works best for you.

SOCIOCULTURAL PREDISPOSITIONS

Language and culture are inseparably interwoven, so you cannot really learn one without learning something about the other. When you set out to study another language, you also set out to study the culture that gives it life and meaning. Your relationship to the people and their culture is directly relevant to your learning of their language. Let us look at this relationship more closely.

Stereotypes

Are you a cartoonist?

Stereotypes are overgeneralizations, or caricatures, of other people. They can interfere with learning how to understand and communicate with members of other cultures. In a sense, they are defense mechanisms—a way of making the unknown more predictable. The Japanese are "inscrutable," the Russians are "boorish," the French are "snooty," the Arabs are "volatile and unstable." Such oversimplifications impair our objectivity because we then see only those aspects of a foreign culture that we wish to see—that is, the ones that fit the stereotype. Thus, an act of generosity by a Scotsman can be either overlooked or treated as an exception, and an American Peace Corps volunteer may be seen by nationals of the host-country as either a materialist or a misfit.

Once formed, stereotypes are difficult to dispel. But if you realize that your view of Spaniards, Frenchmen, Germans, or Italians is stereotyped, you should examine your views and try to become more objective and open-minded. You will find that there is a difference between a caricature and a real person. It is difficult to learn to communicate with a caricature; you can only do it with a real person.

Ethnocentrism

The grass is always greener on my side.

Ethnocentrism is closely related to reliance on stereotypes. It is the tendency to measure other people against one's own cultural yardstick. Most of us believe that our way of life is the best and most natural one. Thus, when we encounter a different culture, we tend to judge it in terms of our own. Almost invariably, we feel that our culture is superior simply because we feel more comfortable with it and because it gives us a sense of security. Here are a few examples:

Americans like to separate work and private life; Latin Americans socialize a lot with their colleagues. Judged by the Latin American standard, Americans are cold and distant; judged from the American point of view, Latins don't know where to draw the line between work and play. Both feel uncomfortable with each other. This may inhibit the formation of meaningful relationships that would allow members of one group to learn the language and culture of the other.

Similarly, Americans like to pride themselves on their openness, their "telling it like it is." In the Middle East, such candor is seen not as a virtue, but as stupidity or obtuseness. A Middle Easterner uses involved circumlocutions to avoid stating what may be troubling or offensive to a listener. As a result, Americans feel that they cannot believe much of what Middle Easterners may tell them, while Middle Easterners perceive Americans as lacking in finesse. This, of course, can prevent both groups from having personal relationships that would allow them to learn each other's languages and customs.

PAST EXPERIENCES

Is there a foreign language in your past?

Previous experiences with foreign-language study may influence future attempts. If, on the one hand, a person has had a favorable experience studying one language and believes that he or she learned something valuable, that person will be predisposed to study another language and will approach it expecting to achieve success. On the other hand, if an individual's first experiences with a foreign language were not particularly pleasant or successful, he or she will tend to expect the next language-learning experience to be just as stressful and unfruitful as the first. Such a person should examine the reasons for the earlier lack of success. Perhaps it was due to a teacher that the learner did not like, a textbook that was not particularly helpful, a method that clashed with the learner's learning preferences, or perhaps it was due to the learner's own inexperience, absence of motivation, or lack of good reasons for studying the particular language. Chances are that these conditions will not be repeated or can be avoided the second time around. The best approach then is simply to wipe the slate clean and approach the study of the next language as a completely new experience.

Keep in mind, too, that people get better at whatever they do over a long period of time. In other words, based on past experience, they *learn how to learn*. People who have learned several languages usually report that each became successively easier to master, particularly if the languages were related. So don't be surprised when the star performer in your class tells you that it is his or her third or even fourth foreign language.

YOUR CURRENT PROFICIENCY LEVEL

Reread your writing task on page 5.

How many main sections will it have?
What will each one focus on?

Now you'll focus on the part of the writing task that concerns your current level of English proficiency.

1. Think back to the time when you had just begun to learn English. Think about how much you can do now in comparison.
2. Next, look at the table of skills below. In the appropriate spaces, write down things you can already do comfortably in English. This is the time to pat yourself on the back for all your achievements, so focus on the things you *can* do, not on those you can't. Examples have been included to start you thinking.

YOUR ACHIEVEMENTS SO FAR

Reading (for example, read and understand easily most parts of the newspaper)

Listening (for example, understand a native speaker who talks clearly and is willing to repeat or rephrase)

Talking (for example, express ideas about daily life—travel, shopping, family, etc.)

Writing (for example, write a short letter to a friend in English)

YOUR OBJECTIVES FOR ENGLISH

Now you'll consider your goals or objectives. First, however, you will need to think about why you're studying English. Read the purposes below, checking (✔) those that apply to you. You'll likely choose more than one, but put an asterisk (∗) beside the most important reason.

_____ to get a job

_____ to satisfy personal curiosity about the language or culture

_____ to increase the number of languages you already speak

_____ to be able to talk with people in a country you move or travel to

_____ to prepare to study in English

_____ to increase your social status

_____ to be able to communicate with others in the same professional field

_____ to satisfy your parents

_____ other (please specify) _____

In groups of three or four, compare your reasons for studying English.

Setting Your Own English Language Objectives

Now you'll set your own objectives for learning English. You'll do this by thinking of each skill in turn and of the things you want to be able to do by the end of this course. Remember, this isn't a long time, so try to keep your objectives *realistic.* Don't expect, for example, to have perfect pronunciation or to be able to write a full-length novel. Set objectives you have a *reasonable* chance of achieving. Also, be as specific as you can in describing what you want to be able to do. The more realistic and specific you are in setting your objectives, the greater your chances of achieving them.

YOUR OWN PERSONAL OBJECTIVES
Reading
Listening
Talking
Writing

In groups of three or four, compare your objectives, one at a time. You may, if you wish, make changes. When you finish, decide on the one skill you would most like to improve.

MANAGING YOUR OWN LANGUAGE LEARNING: DEVELOPING LEARNING STRATEGIES

This next section focuses on strategies for becoming a more successful language learner. Fortunately, you won't have to do this all alone. You, your teacher, your classmates, and other language learners will pool your knowledge.

READING III: "LANGUAGE-LEARNING STRATEGY 1"

Strategy 1: Find Your Own Way

1. In the section on psychological predispositions, your profiles told you how different you were from your colleagues. This first strategy recognizes your uniqueness and asks you to do what is best for you. It asks you to pay attention first to your own successes, then to those of others. In this way, you'll be able to learn from your own performance as well as from those of other people.

   The first part, "Pay attention to your own successes," presents techniques for improving in three areas—vocabulary, pronunciation, and grammar. As you read through the list of techniques, try to decide how helpful each one might be—very helpful, moderately helpful, or not very helpful at all. Mark each one V, M, or N as appropriate. In groups, compare and discuss your decisions, adding any techniques which you have found helpful but which are not mentioned in the text.

2. In your groups, evaluate the advice in each of the subsequent sections.

Reading III

Language-Learning Strategy 1

Strategy 1
FIND YOUR OWN WAY

Take charge

It is important to remember that unless you can take charge of your own learning you will probably not succeed. You know yourself best and should, therefore, use your self-knowledge to guide your studies regardless of your teacher's methods or what the textbook tells you to do.

As mentioned earlier, people learn in different ways. Some need to be very analytical: they need a rule for everything. Others are more intuitive: they gather examples and imitate. Some need lots of repetition; others require less. In a classroom situation, the teacher cannot tailor the approach to each individual student. Therefore, you cannot rely entirely on your teacher to tell you how to study. You yourself need to experiment to discover what works best for you. Following are some suggestions.

Experiment for yourself.

Pay attention to your own learning successes. Take, for instance, vocabulary learning. A memory technique that helps one person my not help another. Here are some options to try.

1. Put the foreign language words in one column and their translations in another. Study the list from beginning to end; then study it backwards.
2. Put the words and their definitions on individual cards or slips of paper; then study them in varying order.
3. Study the words and their definitions in isolation; then study them in the context of sentences.

4. Say the words aloud as you study them.

5. Write the words over and over again.

6. Tape record the words and their definitions; then listen to the tapes several times.

7. Underline with a colored pencil the words that cause you the most trouble so you can give them extra attention.

8. Group words by subject matter—for example, fruits, vegetables, professions—and study them together.

9. Associate words with pictures or with similar-sounding words in your native language.

10. Associate words with situations—for example, medicines with illnesses.

There are also a number of techniques for studying pronunciation. See which of the following work for you.

1. Listen carefully and repeat aloud after your teacher or a native speaker on tape or in real life.

2. Repeat silently to yourself.

3. Tape record yourself and compare your own pronunciation with that of a native model.

4. Ask native speakers to listen to your pronunciation and comment on your strengths and weaknesses.

5. Ask native speakers how a specific sound is formed and watch when they speak. Then go home and practice in front of a mirror.

6. Practice a sound separately at first; then use it progressively in words, sentences, and, eventually, tongue-twisters.

7. Make a list of words that give you pronunciation trouble and practice them.

8. Listen to native speakers of the foreign language when they speak *your* language and note their pronunciation mistakes.

9. Pretend that you are a native speaker of the language you are studying. For example, pretend you are a Spaniard, Italian, or Japanese speaking English. Sometimes this technique helps people relax.

As for grammar, note whether you retain a rule better when you do specially designed exercises (for instance, filling in blanks or changing word forms) *or* when you are required to communicate a message in speaking or writing. Determine which exercises seem to help you most: translations, mechanical drills, answering questions, compositions, and so forth. Also note whether you find written or oral exercises more helpful and whether you retain a rule better when it is given to you before practice or when you deduce your own rule.

Learn from others.
Pay attention to the learning successes of others. Ask other students how they got the right answers and how they successfully memorized something, and see if their strategies work for you too. For example, if someone guesses a word that you did

not recognize, ask how he or she did it. Sometimes it is helpful to look at how others organize their notes, rules and vocabulary lists. You can also ask other students how they organize their practice, where and how they seek out native speakers to talk to, and the like.

Eye or Ear?

Use both your eyes and your ears. Experiment to see if some tasks are better accomplished through the *eye*, while others are better accomplished through the *ear*. For example, you may find that listening to tapes helps you to improve your oral comprehension and to memorize dialogues; but you may retain vocabulary better if you use flash cards. Remember that applying the same strategy to all tasks does not always work. Try to find strategies that will help you to compensate for your weaknesses.

Continue using the strategies that work for you. Once you have identified the strategies that work best for you, continue to use them, and discard strategies that are ineffective. Don't be afraid to use strategies that work for you even if your teacher says not to.

Be your own master.

Be independent. Follow the goals you have set for yourself even if they differ from those of your teacher or textbook. For instance, if your goal is to develop speaking proficiency, you can work independently on your pronunciation even if your teacher does not stress it in class.

READING IV: "LANGUAGE-LEARNING STRATEGIES 2–10"

Oral Presentations

The next nine strategies will be given as presentations in the class. Their titles are as follows:

Strategy 2: Organize
Strategy 3: Be Creative
Strategy 4: Make Your Own Opportunities
Strategy 5: Learn to Live with Uncertainty
Strategy 6: Make Errors Work
Strategy 7: Use Your Linguistic Knowledge
Strategy 8: Let Context Help You
Strategy 9: Learn to Make Intelligent Guesses
Strategy 10: Learn Some Lines as Wholes

Your teacher will be responsible for Strategy 2. He or she will assign the other strategies. In the next class, each person with a strategy will give a five- to six-minute presentation of that information. During the presentations you'll likely want to take notes so that you'll have a complete set of ten strategies and be able to choose the ones you want to practice.

SPEAKER EVALUATION

In order to work on your presentation skills, you will evaluate other speakers. While your teacher is talking, you will evaluate her presentation. Use the following questions as a guide. You'll discuss the presentation later and establish guidelines for giving talks in class.

Content and Organization

1. How did the speaker introduce the topic?
2. Was there a focus / purpose statement? Did the speaker tell you the subtopics that would be covered in the talk? If so, did the rest of the talk follow this sequence?
3. Could you *easily* identify the main ideas within the lecture / talk? If so, how did the speaker accomplish this?
4. How did the speaker clarify and/or support the ideas (i.e., with examples, statistics, or explanations)?
5. Could you follow the train of thought easily? Why or why not?
6. Was the conclusion helpful for your understanding or memory? How?

Presentation

1. Throughout the talk, did the speaker look at the walls / the ceiling / the back of the room? only certain parts of the group / everyone? How much time did he or she face the chalkboard? If a lot, did this affect the presentation?
2. Did he or she use any visual / audio-visual aids? What, if anything, did they add to the presentation? Explain.
3. Did the speaker talk in a clear, audible voice, or did you have difficulty hearing / understanding?
4. Did the speaker use his or her voice to indicate the importance of the information? If so, explain.
5. Did any of the gestures help you understand better? If so, how?
6. Overall, what was your evaluation of the presentation? Why?

In groups of three or four, discuss your answers.

Assignment

Take these questions to another class on campus or to a talk in your community. Evaluate the speaker as you did your teacher. Bring the results to the next class. You'll share ideas about what makes a good lecture / talk and establish at least five important guidelines for giving presentations. Feel free to add ideas that were not mentioned in the questions. As you prepare your presentations, try to incorporate those features that you feel contribute to good communication.

Share Your Own Strategies

This activity will focus on strategies that have worked for you. For each language skill, write down one strategy that you have found very effective. In groups of seven or eight, present the strategy briefly but in enough detail that it will be useful to your colleagues. When others talk about their strategies, feel free to ask questions. Take any notes.

Talk to the Experts

Language learners who have finished their studies are also likely to have ideas for you to consider. There may be enough time for you to invite several successful language learners to your class to talk about what they did to learn English.

Reading IV

Language-Learning Strategies 2-10

Strategy 2
ORGANIZE

Organization takes two forms in language learning: organizing information about the language and organizing your program of study.

ORGANIZE INFORMATION ABOUT THE LANGUAGE

Learning a new language involves remembering many rules about pronunciation, vocabulary, and grammar. Although your textbook and your teacher will organize this information in certain ways, you will still need to systematize the material for reference and review. The trick is to come to grips with the language as a system and then to devise ways of representing this system for yourself. Below are some hints on how language material can be systematized beyond the textbook.

1. *Organize the study of pronunciation.* Devote a section of your notebook or a separate notebook to pronunciation rules, particularly those that trouble you. For example, if trilled *r*'s give you trouble in Spanish, write out words that contain this sound—*radio, perro, barrio,* etc.—and practice them regularly. Ask a native speaker to record these words for you so you can listen and imitate.

2. *Organize the study of vocabulary.* In dictionaries, words are organized in alphabetical order. This is not the best way to organize words for your own use. A better way is to group them according to some principle. For instance, you can group words by generic categories: furniture, money, foods, verbs of motion, and so forth. Or you can organize them according to the situations in which they occur: under *restaurant,* you can put *waiter, table, menu, eat, bill.* Or you can organize words by function: greeting, parting, thanks, conversation openers, etc. Or, instead

of making a running list, you can put each word on a separate card so you can reorganize them in different ways, for example, color coding for parts of speech.

There are also several kinds of flash cards that are available commercially. On each flash card, write a sentence that illustrates how the word may be used, particularly if it is a verb. If you are studying Chinese, character flash cards are a must.

3. *Organize the study of grammar.* Construct your own grammar tables in the way that makes the best sense to you. When reviewing these tables, add any new information you may have acquired. For instance, you can make a table of verb conjugations in different tenses, noun declensions, prepositions with the cases they require, etc. Each time you learn a new word belonging to a particular category you have set up, enter it in your table. This is especially important if the word is an exception to a rule and needs special attention. Note also that there are various kinds of commercially available study aids for grammar, such as verb wheels.

ORGANIZE YOUR OWN PROGRAM OF STUDY

Effective study habits are one of the key ingredients of language mastery. You need to organize your study habits and follow through on your plans. Here are a few suggestions.

1. *Establish a regular schedule.* Language is learned in small bits, so try to establish a regular schedule for studying and stick to it. You achieve little by cramming only from time to time. After all, you didn't learn your native language all at once. In fact, it took you quite a while to master all its intricacies, so give yourself the same chance when learning a new language. Learning must be continuous. Do some studying every day, even on weekends and when there is no homework assignment. Do your exercises as assigned rather than all together at the last possible minute. They do little good if they don't have time to sink in. Finally, find the best time of day to do your studying. Don't do it when you have many other things on your mind or are exhausted. Your mind has to be receptive for learning to take place.

2. *Learn something new every day.* Set us a schedule for learning something new every day in addition to your classroom assignments. This is particularly true of vocabulary: you need to build your vocabulary on your own. A good idea, therefore, is to learn several new words every day besides those included in your lessons. Try color words one day, vegetables the next, occupations the third day, and so forth. Pretty soon you will impress everyone, including yourself, with the size of your vocabulary.

Strategy 3
BE CREATIVE

Develop a feel for the language.

In order to master another language, you need to be personally involved. You need to play with the language to develop a feeling for how it works. The language must, in some sense, become a part of you rather than remain an external mechanical system that you can manipulate according to a set of instructions. Learning a language is a little like learning to ride a bicycle. One can describe rather precisely what is involved in bicycle riding, but until a learner actually gets on the bike and takes a few spills, no meaningful learning takes place.

Although it's impossible to draw up a precise list of all possible ways to experiment with a new language, the suggestions below should help to get you started.

1. *Experiment with grammar rules.* Often when people are given a rule, they accept it at face value and do not try to use it creatively. Creativity is necessary, however, because most rules have boundaries that must be discovered in order to use language effectively. The way to find the boundaries is to keep applying a rule until you discover that it no longer applies. For example, in English, once you know that words ending in *-x* for their plural by adding *-es*, as in *box—boxes*, you can keep applying the rule until you discover that it is correct to say *fox—foxes*, but not *ox— oxes*. By pushing a rule to its limit you develop a feeling for how it works. It becomes *your* rule instead of an *English* rule.

Don't wait for someone to point out a rule; look for it yourself. Sometimes the rules that you formulate for yourself will be more helpful than those given by your textbook or your teacher because they are organized in ways that are clearer to you. In addition, having found them yourself, you may be better able to remember and apply them.

2. *Experiment with new ways of using words.* For instance, if you have learned a verb in one situation, try to use it in another. If you have learned that in Chinese one uses the verb *kāi* ("to open") with respect to lights, try to use the same verb with other appliances. Or, if you have learned the English word *finish* in the context of *to finish work*, try it in a new context, such as *to finish school*. Watch for a listener's reaction to the new combination. If the new phrase turns out to be unacceptable, ask why. In any case, don't wait for the teacher to provide you will all the contexts for a word; experiment with it yourself.

3. *Experiment with recurring parts.* In most languages, there are certain elements that are used for building words in fairly regular ways. If you notice how these elements are combined, it will help you to build your vocabulary. For instance, in English the element *-er* is often used to describe participants in different occupations or activities, as in *reader* and *rider*. In Russian, you have *chitat´*, "to read," and

chitatel', *"reader."* If *pisat* means "to write," how might Russians say *writer?* In Ka-nuri, a language spoken in Nigeria, we can note the following pattern:

gana	small	*nəmgana*	smallness
kura	big	*nəmkura*	bigness
kuguru	long	*nəmkuguru*	length

Based on this information, how would one say *good* in Kanuri if *goodness* is *nəmnəla*

4. *Experiment with language as art.* You do not have to be very advanced in a foreign language to write a short poem. In fact, you may enjoy the experience and learn something about the way the language rhymes. Try writing plays based on the dialogues you have memorized. Some will be very funny through unexpected juxtapositions. Write foreign-language captions for your favorite cartoons. You may discover that humor is handled differently in another language and culture. Create foreign-language captions for a book of photographs or paintings. You may not be a Shakespeare, but you will enjoy your experience and learn from it in many unexpected ways.

5. *Play games.* An often overlooked way to practice another language is to use it in playing games. Some foreign-language games are available commercially, and many others do not require special equipment. *Scrabble* sets in several European languages are now commercially available. Here are some other kinds of games you can play in a foreign language: *Show and Tell, Tic-Tac-Toe, Twenty Questions, What's My Line? Password, Concentration, Simon Says, Hangman, Celebrity Talk Show, Story Circle, Detectives,* riddles, charades, word mazes, word searches, and crosswords.

Strategy 4
MAKE YOUR OWN OPPORTUNITIES

Don't just sit there.

Language learning must be an active process. Students who make a conscious effort to practice their foreign language, who seek out opportunities to use what they have learned, are more successful than students who assume a passive attitude and rely on the teacher to do the whole job. It is necessary to overcome inhibitions and get into situations where you must speak, read, write, and listen to the foreign language. There is no doubt that exposure to the language in any form leads to increased skill. Below are a few tips on how this can be done.

1. *Perform every classroom activity.* Do every task, even if the teacher does not call on you. For example, if the teacher asks someone else a question, make up your

own answer too. Complete exercises in your head when it is someone else's turn and check your answers against theirs. Listen to the other students and to the teacher as he or she corrects them.

2. *Ask questions in the foreign language.* By asking questions, you invite people to speak directly to you, which provides extra practice. Always try to ask the native speakers in their own language because it predisposes them to answer in their own language as well. As soon as you start studying a foreign language, you should learn how to ask such things as: How do you say that in…?", "Can I say…?", "Is it correct to say…?", "What is the word for…?" Such simple questions offer countless opportunities for learning.

3. *Interact with native and skilled speakers, including your teacher.* Feel free to speak with your teacher outside of class. Together, you can use your new language to discuss a wide variety of topics. Also try to find native speakers on your campus or in your neighborhood. Many colleges have international student programs or clubs that you can join. Many cities have ethnic neighborhoods with stores, restaurants, movies, and sometimes even a newspaper or radio or TV program. Visits to such neighborhoods will give you an opportunity to try out dialogues you have memorized in class. Unlike your fellow students, a native speaker in a store or restaurant will not know the other half of the dialogue and will give you unexpected responses—and this is exactly when learning will take place.

4. *Interact with classmates or other students in your language program.* Talking with your classmates or other students taking the same language can be an easy and enjoyable way to get some practice. You may also find that you feel less inhibited about trying out new things. Many language departments have language clubs. These usually provide an opportunity to meet other students, graduate teaching assistants, and faculty with whom you can practice your newly acquired language. They also offer cultural activities, such as foreign-language movies, music, songs, and informal meetings with interesting people. In addition there are excursions, dances, cooking classes, summer camps, and may other programs that can add to your knowledge of the language and its culture.

If you are living in a country where the language is spoken, put yourself into situations where you will have to communicate. Make phone calls, go shopping, run errands, ask people for directions or help, and so forth. You may have to make an effort to overcome your initial inhibitions.

Best of all, make friends with people who speak the language you are studying. A sustained relationship provides the motivation to communicate and takes away the anxiety involved in speaking to strangers. Friends will also know your language level and will try to tailor their speech to your ability.

5. *Listen to the language regularly.* It is important that you listen to the language on a regular basis. Listening to the language will not only sharpen your comprehension skills, but will also allow you to practice pronunciation and speaking. Depending on how advanced you are, you may select different kinds of listening materials.

If you are a beginner, you will benefit from listening to tapes, based on the materials you use in class. It is usually easier to memorize dialogues when you practice them with a recording. Repeating after the speaker on the tape will improve your pronunciation and fluency. Later, when you are more advanced, listening to taped lectures, stories, and interviews is a good way to improve your comprehension and learn additional vocabulary and grammar. In addition to language tapes especially prepared for your course, try to listen to foreign-language radio broadcasts (a short-wave receiver is required for the Voice of America, which broadcasts in dozens of different languages), watch foreign-language TV, and attend foreign-language movies.

Listening to records of foreign-language songs is also both enjoyable and profitable. Many learners find a song easier to remember than a dialogue. Songs have emotional and artistic appeal that many contrived dialogues do not. In addition, the tune helps in recalling the words.

The first time that you listen to any taped passage in your foreign language, you may not understand a great deal. At first, try only to get the gist of it; then listen again and again. You will find that you will understand more each time. Above all, remember that you need not understand every word you hear.

6. *Read something in the foreign language regularly.* When choosing reading material, look for things that you can understand without relying too much on a dictionary. A page a day is a good way to start. As you advance, you will find that you can increase both the quantity of pages you read and their level of difficulty. To motivate yourself, choose subjects that interest you. Seek out newspapers and magazines as well as books. Find a magazine, for instance, that reflects your personal interests, whether politics, sports, or art. If you enjoy food, buy yourself a cookbook in the language you are studying. Take out a subscription to a foreign-language newspaper or magazine. Many people find that illustrated foreign-language magazines are easier to read because the pictures provide many clues.

7. *Write in the foreign language regularly.* Writing is a good way to practice what you already know while learning how to compose themes in a foreign language. Find your own reason for writing if your teacher does not assign compositions on a regular basis. A pen pal is good motivation. You will learn a lot by trying to communicate with someone who shares your interests but comes from another culture.

Other ways to maintain a regular writing schedule include keeping a diary, writing a story in installments, or summarizing the daily news. If possible, ask a native speaker to comment on your writing to suggest better and more correct ways of expressing your thoughts.

8. *Rehearse silently in the foreign language.* The easiest way to practice is to rehearse silently, since it does not require any particular time, place, equipment, or partner. For instance, you can look at objects and try to name them in your foreign language, or look at persons and try to describe them in detail. For instance you might think: "This is an apple. It is red and shiny. I wish I could eat it. Too bad it is not mine. I wonder if that fellow will let me have his apple. How do I ask him for an apple? What will he answer?"

You can also rehearse everyday situations. For example, after you have conducted a transaction with a salesperson, clerk, or waiter in your own language, pretend that you have to do it in your foreign language. What would the same conversation have sounded like in France, Italy, or Japan? "Two croissants, please. And a cup of black coffee." "Spaghetti with marinara sauce and a bottle of Chianti, please." Two bowls of saimin and don't forget to bring the chopsticks." Then, when you actually need to say these things in a real-life setting, you will be ready.

People who regularly practice silently often find that it becomes a habit. Interestingly, children learning their first language frequently practice with imaginary partners, have conversations with no one in particular, and talk to objects and toys. They endlessly repeat words and sentences and make up nonsense words and phrases. Apparently these activities are an integral part of language learning for children. There is no reason why they should not also help adults.

Strategy 5
LEARN TO LIVE WITH UNCERTAINTY

Learners of a new language often find themselves in ambiguous situations. Ambiguous situations are characterized by complexity, novelty, unexpectedness, or lack of clear-cut solutions. They arise when a person does not understand a sentence, paragraph, or conversation because it contains unfamiliar words or structures. Persons who dislike uncertainty tend to become confused, withdraw from the situation, give up, or avoid further contact with the language. They prefer safe situations in which everything has been rehearsed, drilled, and explained. Such behavior is not constructive because language students must learn to cope with uncertainty. Here are a few suggestions that may prove helpful.

1. *Avoid heavy reliance on a dictionary.* Instead, begin by reading a page and lightly underlining in pencil all the items you do not understand. Then read the page again. The second reading will clear up some of the confusion. Erase the lines under items that you now understand. Repeat the process two or more times, reading through the entire page. After the last reading, look up only those items that really prevent you from getting the gist of what you have read. After doing this for a while, you will find that you do not really need to understand every word in order to glean the basic information. In fact, a bit of uncertainty is not harmful. It happens even in your own language every time you read new information, but you usually continue reading in the hope that things will become clearer. And they usually do. The same happens in a foreign language.

2. *Don't get flustered.* People can really get frustrated when they don't understand what another person is saying to them. Some common reactions are: What did he say? What should I say? I feel stupid! Such responses are, of course, nonproductive.

The easiest solution to such an uncomfortable situation is to play dumb. Lapse into your native language immediately, and tell the other person you did not understand what he said. He will usually respond by translating into your language. The payoff—reduction of anxiety. But what will you have learned? Probably nothing. The conversation will be switched to your language, and you will have missed an opportunity to learn.

Another solution is to take charge of the situation. Using the foreign language, tell the other person that you did not understand and ask him or her to repeat. Your use of the foreign language will show that you wish to continue using it. The person will probably repeat or paraphrase the message and continue the conversation.

Still another, and probably the best, solution is to avoid implying that you did not understand *the whole message* when, in fact, you only failed to understand one or two words. Isolate the words or phrases you didn't comprehend and ask what they mean. This is a very natural approach since we do it all the time in our native language. If you handle such clarifications quickly, the conversation will go on.

Actually, it is really not necessary to understand everything that is said. Try to follow the gist of the message and ask for clarification at the end, if anything remains unclear.

3. *Keep talking.* When speaking, you may feel uncertain about your ability to get your message across, but don't let this stop you. Some people won't say anything unless they are sure that they can say it perfectly. This is a mistake, however, for especially in the beginning, you can't expect to say things perfectly. When your goal is to communicate, you should simply concentrate on producing a normal flow of speech and not be overly worried about individual items. A spoken message at the time it is needed, no matter how imperfect, is worth many unspoken messages, no matter how perfect. It is better to say something promptly rather than say nothing at all or take so long to compose your message that you exhaust your listener's patience and kill interest in further communication.

Strategy 6
MAKE ERRORS WORK

Don't clam up for fear of errors.

Errors are inevitable when you are trying to learn something as complex as a new language. Since most errors result from the learning process itself, try to look on them as a potential source of information and a way of improving your skills. Here are a few suggestions on how to deal with errors.

1. *Don't let errors interfere with your participation.* Some people are so worried about making mistakes that they don't say anything unless they are sure they can say it correctly. This leads to a vicious circle: they make errors because they haven't practiced enough, yet at the same time they deprive themselves of the opportunity to practice for fear of making mistakes. Remember that language learning is a gradual process during which the student moves through successive approximations of skill. This process requires much practice, which includes making errors and being corrected. Don't hold back until that magic future moment when you think you will be able to speak without making errors. Without practice, that moment will never come.

2. *Negotiate with your teacher when you want errors corrected.* Sometimes, with all good intentions, a teacher constantly interrupts to correct students while they are trying to say something. When this happens, the students may become intimidated, lose all interest in speaking, and fail to learn to communicate, although they may learn about grammar. At the same time, the teacher may wonder why all the corrections did not improve the students' speaking skills. The answer, of course, is that the students shouldn't be interrupted while they are speaking. Comments should be made later, and only the most serious errors should be corrected. Serious errors are those that cause misunderstanding or that occur repeatedly.

It is a good idea to let your teacher know how you feel about having your mistakes corrected while you are speaking. Ask the teacher to discuss your mistakes after you have finished speaking rather than interrupt your train of thought. If that does not work, change teachers when you can or find native speakers outside of class to practice with. Most native speakers focus on the message rather that the grammatical forms used to deliver it. They will let you know when they don't understand, but will let you speak without interruption.

3. *Learn from your errors whenever possible.* To make errors a source of learning, you must do several things.

- Distinguish, whenever possible, between a casual slip and a recurring error. Casual slips are not serious; even native speakers have occasional slips of the tongue, and you should not worry about them. Errors that you make consistently, however, show that you have not mastered some aspect of the language. They require additional work.
- Try to understand why you consistently make a certain kind of error. Is it because you are not clear about a rule? Or is it that you have totally misunderstood a rule and are applying a nonexistent version of it? Is it because you have not learned the boundaries of the rule—that is, its exceptions? Check your textbook or ask your teacher for clarification.
- Be sure that you understand your teacher's corrections of your work. Ask for a clarification, if necessary. If you do not study the corrections, both you and your teacher will have wasted your time.
- Incorporate your teacher's corrections into your own system of rules. Your system should constantly expand to accommodate new information.
- When you are doing oral grammar exercises in class, carefully focus on the grammar. At this point, every one of the teacher's corrections should be carefully repeated. Repetition enhances mastery. Many students make it a habit to listen passively to the teacher's corrections without repeating the correct *form*. This is not a good strategy since by repeating the corrected version you give yourself an opportunity to learn it.

• Note whether additional work has any effect on your performance. Sometimes extra formal practice—such as writing grammar exercises—may not improve your grammar skill. Using the language in real-life situations, however, may be very beneficial. Note whether your strategy for eradicating errors is effective. Amount of time spent may not be as important as type of activity.

4. *Treat spoken errors differently from written errors.* Errors often occur in speech because of pressure to respond quickly. Speaking involves many things simultaneously: choosing meaning, correct grammar, appropriate vocabulary, and proper pronunciation. Since meaning is most important, a speaker often concentrates on it and lets other aspects slip. This is natural, and, as a result, you are likely to make a lot more errors in speaking than in writing. Fortunately, listeners are much more tolerant than readers. Listeners don't have time to analyze every mistake you may make, but readers do. Therefore, when speaking, don't let concern with grammar and vocabulary destroy your fluency. On the other hand, when writing, give extra care to correctness.

5. *Note the relative seriousness of your errors.* As mentioned earlier, some mistakes are mere slips of the tongue and will not happen again. Others tend to repeat themselves. But not all recurring errors are equally serious. While some errors provoke strong reactions from listeners, others do not. Often the mistakes that cause the most reaction are sociolinguistic ones, such as using the informal Spanish *tú* to address your elderly teacher. Grammar errors, such as a wrong ending on a noun or verb, are often overlooked. Even among grammar errors, some are more serious that others. For instance, using the Spanish present tense *voy* ("I'm going") instead of the past tense *fui* ("went") can confuse a listener, while lack of agreement between article and noun, such as *un casa* instead of *una casa* ("a house"), is not very serious because it doesn't affect meaning.

Therefore, note the ways in which listeners react to your errors and concentrate more on those that seem to have left the listener offended, laughing, or confused.

6. *Determine how much error is tolerated in a particular language.* Speakers of some languages are less tolerant of errors made by foreigners than are speakers of other languages. Commonly compared extremes are French speakers, who are very intolerant of foreigners' mistakes, and Chinese speakers, who are very permissive.

Try to gauge the amount of error that is tolerated by native speakers of the language you are studying because it can indicate how much attention you should give to quickly developing correct speaking skills.

Strategy 7
USE YOUR LINGUISTIC KNOWLEDGE

Your mind is not blank.

As described in Chapter 3, languages often show similarities in pronunciation, grammar, vocabulary, and idioms. In such cases, you can readily apply what you already know about your own language or other languages you have studied. Such transfer can involve both specific items such as words and expressions, and rules of grammar or word building. Successful language learners rely on what they already know and do not approach a new language as if they knew nothing about it at all. Here are some instances when such an approach will make learning another language easier for you.

1. *Use what you know about pronunciation rules.* If you have studied a language like German, in which final consonants are "devoiced"—that is , *Hund* ("dog") is pronounced with a final *t* instead of a *d*—you can apply the same rule to some other languages, such as Russian, in which the *d* in *rad* ("glad") is also pronounced with a *t* sound. Or, if you have learned how to trill an *r* in Spanish, you can use this skill in Italian, any Slavic language, and even Japanese. But watch out for variations. For instance, the trill may be longer or shorter in some languages.

2. *Use what you know about grammar rules.* If you have studied languages in which nouns have gender, as in Spanish *la casa* ("the house")—feminine; *el libro* ("the book")—masculine, you won't be surprised to find that other languages do the same, although the gender of specific nouns may not coincide. For instance, in French, one has *la maison* ("the house")—feminine; *le livre* ("the book")—masculine, but in German there is *das Haus* ("the house")—neuter; *das Buch* ("the book")—neuter. Rules that apply to verb tenses, word order, and many other grammatical features may be readily transferred from one language to another.

3. *Use what you know about vocabulary.* Many languages are related and contain many of the same words, although they may be pronounced or spelled slightly differently. Words in different languages that come from a common source are called *cognates*. For instance, English *mother*, Spanish *madre*, and German *Mutter* look similar because they all originated from the same parent word. Languages also borrow words from each other, either with or without adjustments to make them conform to grammar rules, as in the Russian verb *parkovat'* ("to park"). Similarities in vocabulary should be noted because they simplify your learning task.

However, beware of differences. Words that look the same but differ in meaning can cause problems. For example, *asistir* in Spanish does not mean "to assist"; it means "to attend." In Russian, *magazin* means "store," not "magazine," and *intelligentnyi* means "educated" not "intelligent."

Sometimes the differences are more subtle, so you have to consider the context in which the similar word is used. For instance, in English the word *class* means both a *lesson* and a *room: I just had an English class*, and *This class is very hot*. In Russian *klass* can only be used in the second sense.

If a language you have already studied has two words that have only one equivalent in your own language, be on the lookout when you study new languages. For example, if you know that the verb *to ask* has two equivalents in Spanish (*preguntar*, "to ask a question," and *pedir*, "to ask for something"), you should not be surprised that there are two equivalents in Russian (*sprashivat'* and *prosit'*), in French (*demander* and *prier*), and in Chinese (*wèn* and *qǐng*).

Thus you can see that experience with one language can help you learn another because languages have many similarities. However, although many things can be transferred from one language to another, great caution is required, particularly when it comes to idioms and special expressions. Whenever you encounter a new idiom, check its meaning in a dictionary or ask a native speaker for an equivalent, but avoid literal translation.

Strategy 8
LET CONTEXT HELP YOU

Not all words mix.

The meaning of a word or phrase is clarified by its use in a specific sentence or social situation. The only real way to understand a speaker's message or intention is to guess the meaning, something we all do routinely in our native languages. By guessing and taking risks, you will be able to confirm your understanding of a conversation. You will then learn to note relationships between words, phrases, and sentences in a conversation or text and among the participants in a discussion and grow to understand them better. In order to identify these important relationships, you should use what you know about your own or other languages and about human relationships in general. Here are some contexts that require attention.

1. *Pay attention to relationships between individual words.* Be on the lookout for words that are used in contexts not found in your own language. For example, in English, the word *handsome* can describe both living and inanimate objects, as in *handsome young man* and *handsome desk*. In other languages, such as Spanish, different words are used to describe the appearance of people and things. Another example is that in English, you can *shoot* both *tigers* and *baskets*, but in Russian and Spanish, you can only *shoot tigers*, not *baskets*. On the other hand, in Russian, *to open* is used not only with regard to books, doors, and windows, but also with regard to appliances, electricity, and water faucets. In English, people are *tall* and buildings can be either *tall* or *high,* but in Russian and Chinese, there is only one word to describe height. You should be aware constantly of new or different combinations of familiar elements in the speech of your teacher, fellow students, and native speakers. Another way to determine the range of a vocabulary item is to ask questions about it: "Can X (a noun) be *handsome?*" Can Y (another noun) be *handsome?*", and so forth.

2. *Use phrase or sentence context to derive meaning.* In most languages, the meaning of a word can only be derived from the context of a sentence. In English, this is true of such verbs as *to take* and *to do.* Look at the variety of meanings associated with these verbs: *to do over* ("to redecorate"), *to do out of* ("cheat"), *to do in* ("to kill"), *what's doing at the office* ("happening"); or *to take ballet* ("to study"), *the vaccination took* ("was effective"), *to take after* ("to resemble").

3. *Use conversational context to derive meaning.* Often you may not be able to understand a particular sentence when you consider it by itself. You need to know how it relates to other sentences in order to really understand it. For example, in Russian, to ask directions to the subway, you would say : *Vy ne skazhete gde tut metro?* ("Can you tell me where the metro is?"). The response—*Ne skazhu* ("I won't tell you")—may strike you as a little annoying or strange. However, a succeeding sentence, such as *Ya ne zdeshniy* ("I'm not local") indicates that the intended meaning of *ne skazhu* is not really "I won't tell you " but rather something like "I don't know," or "I can't tell you." You need the second sentence to determine the meaning of *ne skazhu* and to keep you from misinterpreting it.

4. *Pay attention to social context.* Some words gain their meaning largely from social context. For example, in Russian *sestra* means "sister" in the context of a family, but "nurse" in the context of a hospital. The only way to learn and understand these words is in and with the appropriate social setting.

Strategy 9
LEARN TO MAKE
INTELLIGENT GUESSES

Find the right cue.

In language learning, it is important to constantly try to decipher the message and the speaker's intention. To do this, you must apply what you know about the world and about communication in general. Here are some ways to make intelligent guesses about a message.

1. *Look for the big picture.* In trying to understand a story, conversation, or passage, it always helps to look for the main topic, mood, or setting. This will help you focus your attention and guess other important information. Ask yourself *where* the story or conversation is taking place. Is it in a store? Then there is probably

talk about buying and selling. Does it take place in a restaurant? Then the conversation is probably about food. *Who* is involved in the situation? If it is a doctor and patient, one can assume they are talking about health and medicine. If it is a police officer and a tourist, they may be talking about directions. Use what you know about the world to help you guess.

2. *Focus on the important parts.* A key skill in any learning process is identifying the things that are most important. Look for the main topic or message and don't worry about individual words. In this way, you won't waste your energy, and your learning will move ahead more quickly.

3. *Use probabilities.* Like the parts of a puzzle, the parts of a language are connected, so once you see the overall outline, other things may fall into place. In language, there are certain probabilities of occurrence that will help you understand a sentence. For example, if you hear: "They went to the sports arena to buy some …," there is a good chance that the missing word is *tickets*. It is important to be aware of such probabilities and to play the odds.

4. *Assume that the here and now is relevant.* Assume that what a person says is directly related to something he or she is experiencing at that very minute. Most conversations relate to the present. People commonly talk about the weather, the social setting, their feelings (which are often obvious from their facial expressions), or some action that is under way. So, it is very easy to establish the topic even if you don't know much of the language. Here's an example. A teacher of the Twi language was instructing students how to barter and bargain in an African market. In the process, she said, "I bought an *X* (a Twi word the students had never heard before)." At first, the class was stymied. Then they remembered that they were talking about marketing and began guessing what *X* might be. They asked the teacher: "Is *X* a fruit or a vegetable?" "What color is it?" "What size is it?" They were able to identify the meaning of *X* by assuming that the sentence was directly related to the here and now—that is, to the subject they had just been discussing.

5. *Expect some guesses to be incorrect.* Our assumptions are sometimes mistaken—either our rule is useful or it isn't. Don't be discouraged if your first guess is incorrect. Try another. But try to learn from your mistakes and generate better hypotheses the next time.

Strategy 10
LEARN SOME LINES AS WHOLES

Learn gestalts.

In the course of studying a foreign language, we often run across sentences or phrases that can be understood from context but can't be analyzed word for word. The best way to deal with such expressions, which are sometimes called idioms, is to learn and use them as wholes, without worrying a great deal about their mechanics. In fact, in many cases, an analysis or explanation may be neither available nor helpful. Here are some ways to cope with idiomatic expressions.

1. *Store idioms or expressions for future use.* The meaning of an idiom or expression is often clarified by its context. Recalling the context in which you first saw or heard an idiom will help you remember and use it correctly. For example, suppose you hear one Spanish speaker saying to another when meeting, "Que tal?" (literally: "What such?") with the other answering, "Bien, ¿y tú?". It should not matter too much what *tal* means in this context. The important thing is the whole utterance, the gestalt. Use it next time you have to greet someone. Another example of a gestalt is the Russian combination "vot kak" (literally: "here now") which means "Is that so?". The English word-for-word equivalent, obviously, is nonsensical. Once you find out its meaning, just treat the whole expression as one item or word. Put it away for future use to express amazement.

When using idioms, be sure to watch for the listener's reactions. If the listener does not understand what you said or looks bewildered, you have probably used the phrase inappropriately. Of course, the only way you will learn to use it is by experimenting with it until you find the limits of its use.

2. *Accept some corrections on faith.* Especially in the case of idioms, you may need to accept corrections from your teacher or native speakers without requiring an explanation. Idiomatic expressions may involve grammar or words that you have not yet learned or that are difficult to explain. Adopt each correction, store it, and analyze it later.

3. *Learn proverbs, folk sayings, and the like.* Every language has many proverbs, sayings, and special expressions that are extremely colorful and graphic, although difficult to analyze word for word. If you adopt them, they will make your speech sound more authentic and proficient. For example, in English we say *so-so*, meaning "not particularly good or well"; in Chinese they say *mámǎ húhǔ* ("horse horse tiger tiger"); in Russian one says *tak sebe* ("so to oneself"); and in French they say *comme çi, comme ça* ("like this, like that"). Such phrases can't be analyzed; they must just be used as prefabricated chunks.

4. *Learn parts of songs, poems, commercials, and the like.* Sometimes parts of songs, poems, ads, and commercials are adopted into everyday language. They stick in the mind so easily that people remember them for years. Such turns of speech are most likely to be picked up in informal settings, particularly in the country where spoken. Like other idioms, they defy analysis and must be accepted as self-contained wholes.

5. *Use expressions from textbook dialogues.* Last but not least, don't forget the dialogues that you have learned in class. They can provide ready-made bits of language for use in real-life situations. A line memorized from a dialogue can pop out very quickly because you do not need to construct it yourself. Of course, you can't rely completely on memorized dialogues, but sometimes they can be useful.

WRITING THE ESSAY

Prewriting

As mentioned earlier, part of the purpose of this ESL course is to help you become more independent in your language learning. The writing assignment is the first step in helping you do this. Reread your writing task:

Write a four- to five-page (double-spaced) essay on the one skill you would most like to improve. Choose from the following: reading, listening, talking, writing. Your essay should include the following information:

an assessment of your current proficiency level in that skill,

your objectives with regard to that skill by the end of the course, and

the two main strategies you'll use in an effort to meet these objectives.

You'll complete this essay in stages that ask you to focus on one part of the writing at a time: first, information; then, organization; and finally, language. By not trying to do everything at once, you'll learn to write more efficiently and effectively.

Analyze the Assignment   The first step is to analyze the assignment.

1. Highlight the words in the prompt or instructions that tell you what is expected in the essay. Discuss these with your teacher.
2. Consider the following:

    Your audience: Why has your teacher assigned this particular topic? What information does he or she want to know about you?

    Your purpose: What will you be trying to do with the information in this assignment? Is this also true of your other academic assignments?

    Your information: What information is expected in each part of the essay—both main ideas and support?

3. If you haven't already done so, decide on the skill and the two strategies you want to write about. Write them in the space below.

Gather Your Information   The next step is to collect the information you will need for your essay.

1. Go over your notes and readings. Highlight / circle / box any information you feel you need for your essay.

2. Use a separate page for each main section of your essay. For each one, take key-word or point-form notes of the information you want. Use your *own* words. The following list gives you an example:

> **Current Proficiency**
> can write letter to friend
> can fill out most application forms
> trouble spelling
> like to write in daily journal
> writing introductions difficult
> can summarize stories—not articles
> can't write essays

3. Remember your audience and purpose. Add any information that you need to make sure your reader understands exactly what you mean: details, examples, explanations of terms, etc. For example, it would likely be helpful for your teacher to know what you *can't* do as well as what you *can*.

4. Group those points that are on the same topic or subtopic. As you do this, think about *why* you're grouping them this way. For example, part of your information might look like this:

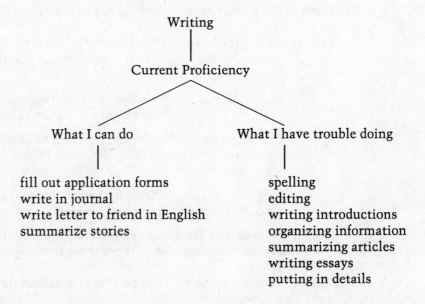

Writing

Current Proficiency

What I can do | What I have trouble doing

fill out application forms | spelling
write in journal | editing
write letter to friend in English | writing introductions
summarize stories | organizing information
 | summarizing articles
 | writing essays
 | putting in details

Sketch and Rehearse What You Want to Say   This next step is very important. It involves seeing how the ideas you have are related to one another.

1. Reread the "What I have trouble doing" section above. Then consider the tree diagram below, which shows how some of those ideas are

related. In the sketch, writing essays is one major problem comprising three other problems. Details and examples are part of "elaborating."

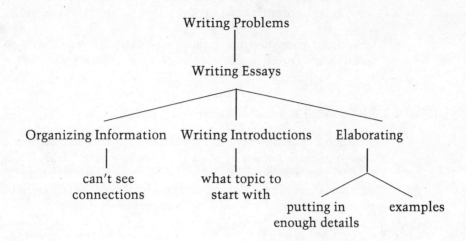

2. Examine your own notes and ideas for relationships. On a separate sheet of paper, draw a sketch using boxes, arrows, etc., to show the information you have chosen to include as well as how you intend to organize it.
3. Work with a partner. Show him or her your sketch. Tell each other what you're going to say in this part of the essay. Listen carefully to each other. Let your partner know if you have any problems understanding.
4. Discuss any problems you have with content or organization. On the basis of this discussion, revise your tree.

Draft One: Focus on Information and Organization

The main purpose of any first draft is to get your ideas down on paper so that you can work with them. Using your tree sketch as a guide, write your first draft of the essay. Double-space your writing. Don't worry about spelling, grammar, or finding the exact word. In later drafts you can focus on language clarity and accuracy. You might want to start with the section you feel you know best. If you get stuck, try rereading the part you just finished to help you start again.

Conference with a Partner When you've finished, find a partner to work with. Read your drafts to each other. As you listen, ask yourself these questions:

1. Is the information complete? Is there enough detail for me to understand what my partner is trying to say? Is all the information in each
section relevant to the main idea of that section?

2. Is the organization easy to follow? Does it help me remember the ideas?

Stop your partner when you can answer "No" to any of these
questions. Together, discuss the problem. When you finish, revise your essay
as you wish.

Draft Two: Organize for Your Reader

Now that you have most of your information, the next step is to ensure
that your reader understands and can follow your ideas. To organize for your
reader, you will need to add to what you've just written. To do this, use a
separate sheet of paper, numbering each piece of text you will later insert. Write
the same number in the appropriate part of your essay.

Write the Focus / Purpose Statement

A. To do this activity, refer to the "Preface" on page 4. Reread until you find
the focus statement, the statement that tells the reader the purpose of that piece
of writing. Check with a partner to see if you agree; then check with your
teacher. As a class, answer the following questions:

1. What words or phrases could be left out without altering the essential
meaning of the statement?

2. What basic structure might a focus / purpose statement take?

3. What words could replace "purpose"?

4. What other kinds of texts are there besides books?

5. In the "Preface," what information follows the purpose statement?
Why have the writers included this information?

B. Write a focus statement for each set of data below. Try to avoid the word
"purpose." Do the first one with your teacher.

1. *Text:* essay
Purpose: Examine similarities and differences in the ways people learn
languages.

2. *Text:* paper
Purpose: a. Review the literature on second language learning.
b. Evaluate current methods of language teaching.

3. *Text:* report
Purpose: a. Examine reasons why foreign student fees have increased
dramatically in the last few years.

       b. Describe the effects on the numbers of foreign students in several countries.

    4. *Text:* essay
       Purpose: a. Discuss problems facing second language learners.
                b. Suggest ways to help them deal with these problems.

Discuss your answers with the rest of the class.

Reread the prompt on page 43. Think about the purpose of *your* essay. Write the focus statement. Then check your essay to ensure that you have kept the promise you made in the focus statement.

Write the Inform Section   The inform section precedes the focus statement. It is the section that (a) gives your readers enough background information on the general topic and (b) leads them into the specific focus of the text.

To write the inform section for this essay, you might want to use the following strategy:

1. Reread your focus statement. Find the nouns. To what general topic group does each noun belong? Think about how you might lead your reader from that general topic to the specific focus of your essay.
2. Discuss your ideas with a partner.
3. Write your inform section.
4. Work with a partner. Read each other's work to see if the essay leads the reader step by step from the general opening topic to the focus statement.

Write the Thesis Statements   Remember that English readers expect writers to prepare them to read. Check your essay to ensure that each main section has a thesis statement that tells your reader the idea that section focuses on.

Write the Transitions   Reread your essay. Concentrate on places where you shift topic. How can you help your reader see how each section relates to the previous one? Add helpful sentences or phrases.

Write the Conclusion   With three or four partners, discuss the purpose of the conclusion in an essay like this. Then write yours.

Put It All Together   Using scissors and tape, add the sections you've just written to what you'd written earlier. You'll need to rewrite any parts that are not legible. What you want in this second draft is a clean copy that a partner can easily read.

Conference with a Partner   Exchange drafts with a partner, reading this time for the flow of the text. You'll want to make sure that you help your reader see how the ideas are related to one another. If there are any problems or gaps, mark the place with an asterisk (*). When you've finished reading, discuss any problems with your partner. Make any necessary revisions.

Draft Three: Focus on Clarity and Accuracy

Edit for Clarity   Before you write the final draft, do the following activity, which focuses on sentence clarity.

1. Read the following paragraph, in which an ESL student discusses her current level of reading proficiency. Find out what she can do well and what she has difficulty doing.

> First I would like to specify my current proficiency level in reading. I can read small stories, small article. On the other hand, if I read a long article or professional article or text books, it is very hard to understand the message of the article or chapter. If I read an article in order to write a summary the main problem is understanding. I understand that, the summary is not a problem but if I don't, I will be in a hard time. For an instance, at the beginning of this course, I got an article to write the summary which was telling about psychology. I was spend more than one hour but I couldn't understand the whole story. So I didn't write a good summary.

2. With a partner, find one sentence in which you have difficulty understanding exactly what the writer meant. Underline any part of the sentence that needs to be clearer. Together, try to figure out what the student was trying to say and what went wrong. With your partner, rewrite the sentence, trying to make the ideas clear.
3. Check your revisions with another pair of students working on the same sentence.
4. As a class, discuss the revisions with your teacher. What advice would you give the writer about improving her writing?

Conference with a Partner   To prepare to write the final draft, go through the following steps with a partner.

1. Read him or her your essay, section by section. Your partner will listen carefully to each sentence and tell you when an idea is not perfectly clear. Mark each one with an asterisk.
2. When you finish, ask your partner to identify the two sentences that were the least clear.   Tell him or her what you were trying to say.
3. Rework each sentence so that it says clearly what you want it to. Then check it out with another pair of students.

4. Try to figure out precisely what the problem was and how you might work on this problem in the future.
5. Alone, revise your essay as you wish. Also edit for spelling and punctuation. Write your final copy. Hand it in.

Note: The next part of becoming a better language learner is more important than writing an essay. In order to improve, you'll need to put into practice the strategies you wrote about. At the end of the course, you might want to assess your effort, your strategies, and your improvement. Keep your essay to reread at the end of the course and again at the end of six months.

Good luck!

Chapter 2
Heroism

*F*or the next few classes, you'll focus on heroism: what it is, its various forms, and who might be called heroic. As you work through the many activities, you'll be practicing the following language skills and strategies:

- using titles, summaries, and introductions to prepare to read
- reading to find specific information
- understanding and writing thesis statements
- using library research skills
- giving oral presentations
- taking notes from a text
- applying a definition to a practical situation
- sequencing information to achieve coherence

Release me!
come on! Baby!
You know it's time to just let go!

THINK ABOUT THE TOPIC

A. In the spaces provided, write the names of five people (living or dead, but not imaginary) that you would consider heroic. To help you start thinking, you might want to consider fields such as politics, science, sports, or service to humanity.

1. Brain Muloney.

2. Prince Charles

3. kelly cooper

4. Wright Brothers

5. _____

B. In groups of three or four, compare your lists. Explain your choices.

READING I: "DEFINING HEROISM: FIGHT, NOT FLIGHT"

Prepare to Read

As you read in Chapter 1, if you can predict what a text will be about, you will have a better chance of understanding the new information. The next few activities help you do this.

1. a. Read the title of the article and the summary statement below. Highlight the words that tell you what the article will be about.

<u>Defining Heroism: Fight, not Flight</u>

Each of us may have a different idea of <u>heroism</u>. Contributing Editor Charles A. White defines the word and looks at some of the <u>forms</u> heroism can take.

1. b. With a partner, use this information to predict what you'll likely find in this article. Below, write brief notes about your predictions. Then discuss them with your teacher.

2. Another part of the text that prepares you to read is the introduction. You will remember that in Chapter 1, the introduction had two parts: the *inform section* and the *focus statement*. Not all texts, however, have a focus statement. Some have a *thesis statement*—a complete idea that the rest of the essay will attempt to prove. The introduction to "Defining Heroism: Fight, not Flight" has such a statement.

Below you will find the six sentences that form the introduction. Unfortunately, they're not in the right sequence.

a. First, find the thesis statement that the rest of the essay will support. Put a "6" in the blank. Check your decision first with a partner; then with your teacher. Next, read the other five sentences that precede this thesis statement, numbering them 1 to 5 to show their correct order. To do all this, you have approximately ten minutes.

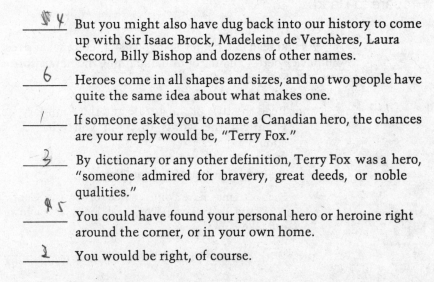

_____ But you might also have dug back into our history to come up with Sir Isaac Brock, Madeleine de Verchères, Laura Secord, Billy Bishop and dozens of other names.

___6___ Heroes come in all shapes and sizes, and no two people have quite the same idea about what makes one.

___/___ If someone asked you to name a Canadian hero, the chances are your reply would be, "Terry Fox."

___3___ By dictionary or any other definition, Terry Fox was a hero, "someone admired for bravery, great deeds, or noble qualities."

_____ You could have found your personal hero or heroine right around the corner, or in your own home.

___2___ You would be right, of course.

b. In groups of three or four, compare your sequencing. Try to agree. Discuss your answers with your teacher.

3. What do you suppose was the writer's purpose in including such names as Billy Bishop and Laura Secord? How helpful did *you* find this information? What advice would you now give to anyone writing for an international audience?

Read for Specific Information

You already know that the article will focus on the author's definition of heroism, including some different forms or kinds of heroism. Now read the rest of the article looking for this information. As you read, write key-word notes in the margin of the text.

Reading I

Defining Heroism

Fight, not Flight

Each of us may have a different idea of heroism. Contributing Editor *Charles A. White* defines the word and looks at some of the forms heroism can take.

1   If someone asked you to name a Canadian hero, the chances are your reply would be, "Terry Fox." You would be right, of course. By dictionary or any other definition, Terry Fox was a hero, "someone admired for bravery, great deeds, or noble qualities."

2   But you might also have dug back into our history to come up with Sir Isaac Brock, Madeleine de Verchères, Laura Secord, Billy Bishop and dozens of other names. You could have found your personal hero or heroine right around the corner, or in your own home. Heroes come in all shapes and sizes, and no two people have quite the same idea about what makes one.

3   There are some common factors. All heroism, most agree, involves the idea of sacrifice for the sake of others. One sacrifices health, another is willing to sacrifice life, a third sacrifices material comforts to serve people, a fourth sacrifices career for a cause.

4   If we think about it a little more, we find another quality in most heroism. The heroic people have a choice. They can turn their backs on a challenge but instead choose to accept it. That voluntary decision to take the route of risk, danger and sacrifice distinguishes the hero from more ordinary folk.

5   Some heroic acts are spectacular and brief; others are of the enduring kind. There is no better example of this second kind than Terry Fox's "Marathon of Hope." Terry's run from St. John's to Thunder Bay has inspired thousands of Canadians to pick up where he left off in the fight against cancer. Last September's ten-kilometre run in his memory, held from coast to coast, is likely to become an annual event.

6   People with all kinds of disabilities

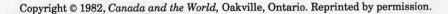

have caught the Fox inspiration. There is Richard Beecroft of Ottawa, a victim of multiple sclerosis. He took four months to ride from Vancouver to St. John's on a specially designed tricycle. And there's Newfoundland marathoner, Wayne Morris. He also arrived in St. John's after running across his home province to raise money for a brain scanning machine. Morris was saying thank you for the brain surgery he underwent three years ago.

7   In this kind of thing we find a fairly common effect of heroism. The noble quality in the hero strikes a spark in others and they take on challenges which would have been unthinkable before.

8   A more obvious kind of heroism is the daring act of special courage which risks life and sometimes loses it. Canada has three awards to mark such deeds: the Cross of Valour, the Star of Courage, and the Medal of Bravery.

9   The Cross of Valour has been awarded only 11 times since 1972, and four of the recipients received it posthumously (after death). Three Newfoundland fishermen, Lester Fudge, Harold Miller and Martin Sceviour were presented with this highest award by Governor-General Edward Schreyer in June 1981. They rescued 12 crewmen from the trawler *Remoy* in hurricane force winds and Arctic seas. In the words of a news report, "The cold was so severe that night that no one could have survived even one minute if they had fallen into the sea."

10   Search the records of the Star of Courage and the Medal of Bravery awards and you find in each of them that common element of voluntary sacrifice for others. Sylvain Fillion, 22, of Chicoutimi-Nord, Quebec was awarded the Star of Courage posthumously. An inexperienced swimmer, he drowned

after rescuing his four-year-old niece. Constables John Robins and Ian Haimes of the Winnipeg Police Department received their Stars for saving a 70-year-old woman from a fire that destroyed her home. John Barnett and Owen Jones (posthumous) were Star of Courage recipients in the rescue of a boy cleaning a fume-filled well in Kirkfield, Ontario.

11   Medals of Bravery are awarded for a level of heroism only marginally below that required for the two top honours. Donald Irwin and Constable William Willis of the Edmonton Police received their medals for saving Steven Smyth from drowning in the North Saskatchewan River. Both men had to be hospitalized after their battle against the river's strong current. John Hiram, 17, and RCMP Constable Reinhard Krenz saved Paul Erickson from drowning near Squamish, British Columbia. Erickson was the sole survivor of a light aircraft crash in Howe Sound and was in extreme difficulties when the two men risked their lives to rescue him. Helicopter pilot Robert Carter and Flight Engineer Ralph Hemphill of the Coast Guard got their medals for landing their 'copter on the deck of a half-submerged barge near Low Point, Nova Scotia. In "very heavy seas and high winds" the flight engineer then crawled toward three men stranded on the barge and guided them one at a time to the waiting helicopter. All got off safely.

12   As one reads the bulletins announcing the awards one is struck time and again by such phrases as "without a thought for himself," "without the slightest hesitation." The idea of instant, positive action runs like a thread through all these tales of heroism. It may give us another clue to just what makes the hero tick.

13   Heroes of the medal-winning sort tend to act rather than think about acting. To think, nine times out of ten, is to reason that the feat is impossible. <u>Logic tells you it can't be done</u>, so you turn away. For the <u>heroes</u>, adrenalin flow moves them to <u>fight, not flight</u>.

14   Another kind of hero draws little attention. The quiet heroes in this group advertise their courage only in the way they live. We don't have to look that far for quiet heroism. All of us know unsung heroes or heroines who, by the example of their lives, inspire admiration. A young mother is widowed or deserted. Instead of giving up, she puts her life together again by sheer strength of character and, year after year, makes sacrifices to give her children a good start in life. A father's alcoholism is bringing his family to the edge of financial and emotional ruin. He has a choice to make. Keep on at the bottle and watch everything fall apart, or make the supreme effort needed to beat his disease. To follow the second route takes guts. The person who wins has fought an inner battle just as heroic, many would say, as more visible forms of courage.

15   One person's villain is sometimes another's hero. There's no doubt that Palestine Liberation Organization or Irish Republican Army terrorists fall into this category. To many Palestinians and Irish these people are heroes.

16   There are also "<u>grey</u>" areas of <u>heroism</u>. Most Canadians and Americans give Ken Taylor hero status for his decision to hide six U.S. hostages in his Iranian embassy. Taylor doesn't agree. He argues that he really didn't have any choice, that the decision was simply in line of duty, made, as he says, "professionally, instinctively."

17   His <u>attitude</u> is the soldier's: "I only did what had to be done." But there are soldiers and soldiers. Most are normally courageous, but few rise to the bravest heights. When does doing one's job stop being routine and start being heroic?

18   There is no choice, either, in terminal <u>disease</u>. One way or another, the person sentenced by the doctor's verdict must deal with the fact of death. One whines about fate. Another suffers in grim silence. A third tries to live every remaining minute to the full. While fatal illness gives no choice, the decision to override pain and live your last days positively is a voluntary one. Is there heroism here or not?

19   These few examples show that heroism is many different things. It is bravery, but more than bravery. It is sacrifice, but more than sacrifice. It is often in plain sight, but just as often hidden somewhere inside us. It can explode in one flashing deed or go on for most of a lifetime. What is routine for the fearless can be heroic for the timid.

20   Heroism, in fact, is a very personal thing. What we look for in our heroes depends on the kind of people we are ourselves.

Record Important Information

1. Use your notes to compile a list of the qualities or characteristics by which White defines heroism. What is meant by each one?

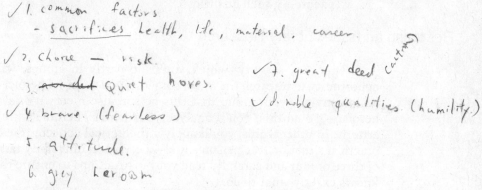

✓ 1. common factors
   - sacrifices health, life, material, career.

✓ 2. Chance — risk.

3. ~~avoided~~ Quiet heroes.

✓ 4. brave. (fearless)

5. attitude.

6. grey heroism

✓ 7. great deed (military)

✓ d. noble qualities (humility.)

2. Complete the list of White's categories of heroism.

a. Brief and spectacular

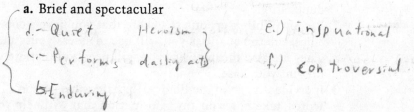

d. - Quiet   Heroism
c. - Performs daily acts
b. Enduring

e.) inspirational

f.) controversial.

3. Discuss your answers with two partners. Use the text to help you reach a consensus.

Questions for Discussion

In your groups, discuss the following five questions. You don't need to write answers.

1. What does "fight, not flight" mean?
2. Have you ever known a "quiet hero"? If you have, tell your group about her or him.
3. Together, reread paragraph 15.
   a. What does this paragraph tell you about the author's personal view of heroes?
   b. Try to think of at least three other controversial heroes. Be prepared to explain to the class why they would fit into the category of "controversial."
4. Can the following be heroes:
   a. someone who protests against oppression in his or her country?

b. someone who works toward the overthrow of the government in his or her country?

5. Are there any heroic qualities you feel the writer neglected to mention? If so, what are they? Can you think of any people who would exemplify such qualities?

Resolving an Issue: Library Research

This next activity, which you'll do partly in groups, will give you an opportunity to research the life of someone *you* consider heroic. Your task will be to convince your group that this person also meets *White's* definition for heroism. To do this, you'll analyze your hero's / heroine's life using White's criteria. In other words, you'll apply a theoretical concept (the definition) to a practical situation (the person's life)—a common university task. Form groups of three or four and carefully read your instructions to ensure that each person knows exactly what to do.

1. Each of you will choose one person to research. There should be no duplication.
2. Review White's criteria to ensure that you have a complete list. These are the qualities you will use to assess your "hero / heroine." They are also the qualities you will need to illustrate when you present your case.
3. Individually, go to the library. Research this person's life. In your own words, take notes on any information that will help you convince your group that this person is or was truly heroic. Make sure you have enough detailed supporting information to prove your conclusion about each part of the definition.
4. Next, prepare a five- to seven-minute talk about this person for presentation in class the next day. Make sure you organize the talk so that it proves each of your points individually; it's not enough merely to tell about the person's life.
5. Your talk should contain an inform-and-focus-section that introduces your group to your hero / heroine and then focuses on your purpose for the presentation. You should also state your decision about each criterion before you support it. That way your listeners will be able to link the support to your decision.
6. Remember not to read your information, but rather to *talk* to your group.

READING II: "MARY SHADD: PREJUDICE FIGHTER" (pp. 60–61)

This reading presents the story of a woman named Mary Shadd. Read the title and summary statement. What do you now know about her?

You will read the article to resolve the following issue: *Does Mary Shadd meet Charles White's criteria for heroism?* To resolve the issue, you'll use the same steps as for your presentations.

Carefully read your instructions. You have forty-five minutes to complete all six steps. Stay within your time limits.

Step 1   To help you view all the relevant information, set up one page with four columns as indicated below.

A HEROIC QUALITIES	B EVIDENCE FOR	C EVIDENCE AGAINST	D CONCLUSION YES/NO

Step 2   Refer to White's list of heroic qualities.List them in Column A, leaving enough space for notes. These criteria will be the theory you apply in the next part of the task.

Step 3   Now read the article on Mary Shadd. As you read, look for evidence for or against each quality or criterion. If you find such evidence, make brief, keyword notes in the margin. Next, note down these ideas on the table you set up, in either column B or C.

Step 4   In small groups, discuss the evidence for or against each criterion, one at a time. For each one, decide whether or not she meets that criterion. In Column D, write "Yes" or "No," depending on your conclusion. It is not necessary to reach a unanimous decision.

Step 5   Then decide whether or not, all things considered, you consider her heroic.

Step 6   Discuss your decisions with your teacher.

Reading II

Mary Shadd

Prejudice Fighter

Freelance writer **Carol Sevitt** looked into Canada's past and found one woman who certainly qualifies as heroic.

Mary Shadd, a beautiful and brilliant black woman, lived in a society where being black was one strike against you, and being female was another. Born in Delaware in 1823 to free blacks in a slave state, Mary could never accept the prejudice and intolerance around her. She became a teacher in the hope of educating her people, who still had a slave mentality.

In 1850, the Fugitive Slave Law was passed in the United States. It gave slaveowners the right to hunt down and reclaim runaway slaves. This law endangered freed slaves too, as a slaveowner didn't have to prove his claim on a black person to anyone. Many blacks looked to Canada for refuge because once on British soil, they were free.

Mary Shadd joined this "Canada Venture" with the idea of setting up a school to teach young and unschooled blacks how to read and write. She went to Windsor, then a tiny place of about 200. The only building she could use as a school was a cold, unfurnished barracks. She received very little payment, because the fugitives were destitute and couldn't afford the luxury of paying a teacher.

Although life was difficult in Canada, blacks had no "masters" and could build a new life here. Mary believed that instead of living an oppressed life in the United States, both fugitives and freed slaves should come to Canada where they had a greater chance for a life of dignity. A talented writer, she produced a tract "Notes on Canada West" containing information about schooling, climate, religious practices, the law, elections and currency.

While in Windsor she became embroiled in a political controversy surrounding an organization called the Refugee Home Society. Run by Henry Bibb, this organization collected money from people all over the United States to buy land in the Windsor area for fugitives. However, very few fugitives actually settled on this land, and the money collected made Mr. Bibb a wealthy and powerful man. Mary was very critical of the organization. This enraged the community leaders involved with it and led to her dismissal as a teacher. A corrupt and self-serving man, Henry Bibb ran the only black newspaper, *Voice of the Fugitive,* using it as a vehicle to attack Mary.

Always a fighter, she decided the only way to defend her name and spread the truth was to publish her own newspaper. It was an extremely radical thing for a young woman to do in the middle of the 19th century. In those days, women didn't have the right to vote and were considered intellectually inferior to men.

The Provincial Freeman was intended to be "anti-slavery, pro-temperance, and devoted to the elevation of the (black) race . . . ." Mary desperately needed paid subscriptions to keep her newspaper alive, so she went on many speaking tours, both inside and outside Canada, trying to make sales. Usually, she travelled alone, at a time when women risked a riot by daring to address a public meeting. Encountering physical hardships and prejudice wherever she went, Mary often became disheartened, but never gave up.

Through Mary's subscription tours, the paper developed a wide circulation, but few people knew the editor, M.A. Shadd, was a woman. When she gained confi-

dence in the paper's success, she began signing her full name, Mary A. Shadd, Editor. The public was outraged that a woman was doing an editor's job, and this threatened the paper's existence. Eventually, a male editor was found and Mary gave up her position.

She continued to work for *The Provincial Freeman* as a travelling agent, and wherever she went her good looks and personal charm drew people to her. In 1856, she married Thomas Cary but, unlike most women of her day, did not settle down to a quiet domestic life. She retained her job with the paper and when the editor became ill, Mary was once again called upon to be co-editor. She bore two children over the next few years and then, tragically, her husband died.

South of the border, continuing tensions between the North and South erupted into civil war. At first, black men were not welcome to join the troops, but a few years later when they were permitted to fight, Mary became involved in recruiting. She was the only woman to be commissioned as a recruiting officer in the American Civil War.

After the war, about two thirds of the blacks who had settled in Canada, including Mary Shadd, returned to their former homes and roots in the United States. In her later life Mary studied law, the first woman to do so at Howard University. She did not graduate until she was 60, and had a flourishing law career until her death.

Oral Presentations

You have about forty-five minutes for this activity. Stay within your time limits.

1. In your groups, you will take turns giving your presentations on your own candidates for heroism. As each person talks, you will come to a conclusion about each candidate. To help you decide, you may wish to set up your notes as indicated below.

CANDIDATE	QUALITIES					CONCLUSION
	Bravery					

2. In the left column, write the name of each person's candidate. At the top of each of the other columns, write in one of White's criteria.
3. At the end of each talk, come to your own conclusion about the candidate in terms of each criterion (you may wish to question the presenter further). Write "Yes" or "No" in each box, depending on the support presented. Come to your own conclusion about his or her overall heroism. Write "Yes" or "No" in the last column, as appropriate.
4. Compare your decisions and discuss your reasons.

CHAPTER 2 WRITING TASK: RESOLVING AN ISSUE AND JUSTIFYING YOUR DECISION

The task you have just practiced—resolving an issue—is also what your writing task asks you to do.

Situation You're a student in an introductory sociology course. Each week you submit a short (two-page) assignment based on the concepts and theories that you have studied in class. These aren't essays, but rather short, analytic assignments that are to be concise and to the point.

The assignment for this week focuses on Charles White's definition of heroism. The professor has given you the task of applying his definition to the life of a man named Chico Mendes. You will resolve the following issue:

According to Charles White's definition, should Mendes be considered a hero? Why or why not?

You'll work on this task both in class and at home over the next few days.

WRITING THE ASSIGNMENT

Prewriting

This assignment, like much of the writing you do at university, requires that you know the answer *before* you write about it so that you can argue concisely. The next few activities will help you do this.

Resolve the Issue   There are seven steps in this activity. You have one hour to complete them all.

Step1   If necessary, reread White's definition, noting his criteria for heroism.

Step 2   Read the article on Mendes on pages 65–67, highlighting information relevant to any of those qualities. Look for any information that indicates he did *not* meet one or more qualities. Write brief notes in the margin.

Step 3   With two or three other people, compare your margin notes.

Step 4   Use these notes to help you collect the information you will need to resolve the issue. Use a separate page for *each* criterion in White's definition and set it up as follows:

CRITERION	EVIDENCE FOR	EVIDENCE AGAINST	DECISION/ CONCLUSION

Take notes *in your own words*, putting relevant information in the appropriate place.

Step 5 Next, weigh the information you have on each quality and come to a conclusion for each one. Write your conclusion in the last column.

Step 6 Finally, considering all the evidence for and against the established criteria, decide whether or not Mendes was a hero.

Step 7 In groups, discuss your decisions. Remember, in this issue as in many others, your justification is more important than your conclusions.

Reading III

Strength from a Stillness Within

Brazilian rubber tapper and environmentalist Chico Mendes died trying to protect the forest he loved.

By Kristin Helmore

Chico Mendes was a gentle man—very different from the rough, "macho" stereotypes of what a leader of Brazilian rubber tappers might be like. The strength he exuded came from a stillness within him. It came from the love he freely demonstrated for his people and for the beautiful, fragile rain forests they live in and depend on. And it came from his calm conviction that the cause he was living for—the preservation of those forests—was also worth dying for.

For an internationally acclaimed activist, Mr. Mendes was extremely modest, unassuming—even, at first, a little shy. Yet he liked to laugh and joke with the exuberance of a true Brazilian.

One day last September, Mendes and his cousin Miguel took two journalists on a walk through the jungle. He showed us the towering rubber trees he loved as if they were human, the diagonal incisions in their bark carved by rubber tappers like himself, and the milky latex that drips out into cups made from another forest product—sturdy, thick Brazil nut shells.

After a while, as we wandered down a rubber tappers' path, marveling at the beauty and power of the forest, we came to a mysterious barrier: long filaments of springy rubber tied from tree to tree blocked our way like the beginnings of a giant cobweb. Suddenly we realized Mendes had disappeared and the forest was still. Well, not quite. Laughter was coming from somewhere deep among the trees.

Mendes was shot to death at his home in the little jungle town of Xapurí in the state of Acre on Dec. 22 by a hired gunman. His death is an immeasurable loss to those who knew and loved him, and, because of the scope and impact of his work, to millions who have never even heard of him.

His full name was Francisco Mendes Filho, but everyone in Acre knew him as Chico Mendes. For 10 years, he had been the leader of the National Council of Rubber Tappers (CNS), representing some 150,000 people who live in, and off, the rain forests that cover 87 percent of Acre.

In 1987, he received the Global 500 Award from the United Nations Environmental Program for his nonviolent, yet remarkably effective, efforts to halt the destruction of the rain forest. Twelve percent of all Brazil's rain forests have already been destroyed, mostly in the last decade, by cattle ranchers, small-scale farmers, and speculators.

Mendes helped to increase in Acre's rubber tappers a self-awareness, solidarity, and a determination to defend their rights. But his greatest practical achievement was the creation, through negotiations with the Brazilian government, multilateral development banks, US congressmen, and environmental agencies, of four "extractive reserves" in Acre and eight in other Amazon states. These reserves, more than 5 million acres, are protected for the extraction of rubber, nuts, resins, and other forest products.

It was Mendes' hope that 40 percent of Acre will eventually be classified as reserves. But he was also concerned that, in areas without a strong rubber tappers' union, the extractive reserve movement might fail.

The forest where Mendes walked with the journalists is in a reserve called Cachoeira. Sixty-seven families live there, including Mendes' aunt and uncle. A cattle rancher named Darly Alves claims part of Cachoeira as his own land. In recent months, Mr. Alves had repeatedly threatened Mendes' life, to the point where the governor of the state assigned him two bodyguards. These guards were in his house when Mendes walked out his back door and was shot. Alves' son Darcy admitted guilt a few days after the murder, but police continued to search for his father. He was found hiding in the forest last week and is now in police custody, pending the investigation of his alleged responsibility for this and other killings.

The entire world needs the rain forests Mendes died trying to protect. Yet it should be understood that in Brazil, which contains 30 percent of the earth's remaining tropical forests, inequities of land distribution are a major cause of the increasing destruction of these forests. Small farms, half of all rural properties in Brazil, cover only 3 percent of occupied rural land, while large estates, owned by less than 1 percent of the landholders, occupy 43 percent of the land. And an estimated 335 million hectares are being held, unused, for speculative purposes.

A key role in many violent land disputes in Brazil is played by a landowners' association, the Rural Democratic Union (UDR) whose leaders admit to having stockpiled 70,000 weapons. UDR defends large landholdings and cattle ranches against peasants' attempts to implement existing land reform laws. According to Amnesty International, the organization is responsible for the deaths, disappearance, and torture of hundreds of Brazilian peasants, priests, and union leaders. The day after Mendes' murder, the UDR leader in Acre, Joao Branco, left the country and is now reported to be in Paris.

Stephan Schwartzman of the Environmental Defense Fund in Washington says that, judging from the international outrage over Mendes' murder, the Brazilian government may finally take action against UDR. "This could be the straw that breaks the camel's back," he says. "Maybe this time the people responsible will go to jail, and it may discredit and even dismantle UDR. The final responsibility for this [killing] rests with UDR for promoting an atmosphere of terror in rural Brazil and using violence to stop any kind of agrarian reform."

When interviewed by phone, Brazilian Vice President Ulysses Guimaraes stated emphatically that "the government is acting with much determination to punish those responsible [for the murder]." However, he said just as emphatically that he knows nothing at all about possible UDR involvement with the case.

"Chico Mendes taught the international environmental community something of crucial importance," says Schwartzman. "Environmental protection in the Amazon, and in the developing world in general, can't be separated from social justice for the people who live there. His death is unfortunately the most terrible kind of proof of that fact."

The world will always owe a huge debt to Mendes, for his work will continue. Those who knew him can be grateful they did, and treasure him in their memories.

I keep thinking of his tiny son who looks so much like him, beside himself with joy when his father came home at the end of the day. Monitor photographer Neal Menschel remembers a moment in the home of Mendes' uncle, when Mendes said goodbye to his aunt. He picked up her two hands, worn and wrinkled from a lifetime of hard work, gently turned them over, and kissed her upturned palms.

Kristin Helmore writes about the third world for the Monitor.

Thesis Statements

In this assignment, you will need to write clear thesis statements or conclusions. The following activities will help you do this.

claim

Understanding Thesis Statements For each thesis statement below, check the diagram that best illustrates its meaning.

1. "Some heroic acts are spectacular and brief; others are of the enduring kind."

   compare : different

   a. *Same*
   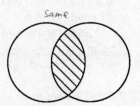

   c. *not comparing*
   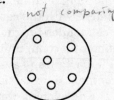

   b. *no comparing*
   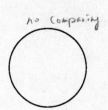

   d. *different*
   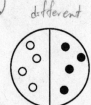

2. "Another kind of hero draws little attention." *(including)*

   a. *Same*
   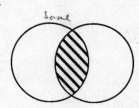

   c.

   b. *two stuffs*

   d. *not little*

3. "One person's villain is sometimes another's hero."

a. not same

c. trending

b. nothing

(d.)

4. "All heroism involves the idea of sacrifice for the sake of others." trending. ⌃ idea.

a. doesn't involves

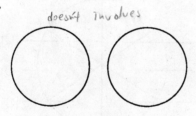

c. not trending

b. doesn't involve

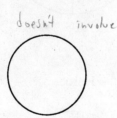

(d)

In groups, compare your answers, justifying your choices. Try to reach a consensus.

Writing Thesis Statements Each diagram below represents a thesis statement. Write what you think it says.

1.

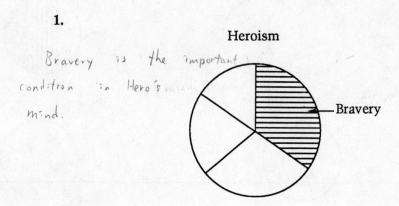

Bravery is the important condition in Hero's mind.

2.

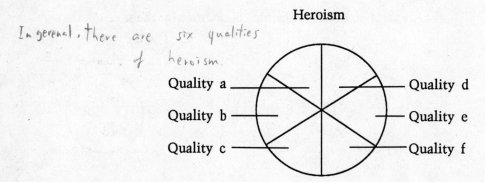

In general, there are six qualities of heroism.

3.

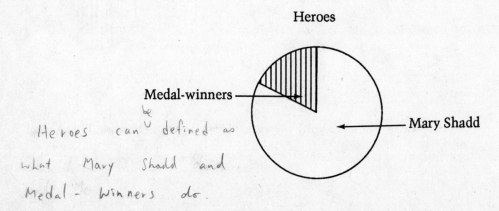

Heroes can be defined as what Mary Shadd and Medal - winners do.

In groups, compare your answers.

Select and Organize Your Information

Now that you've resolved the issue, you can concentrate on writing your answer. In groups of three or four, consider these questions:

1. How many main sections will your assignment contain? 4
2. How should each one begin? Why?
3. What kind of information should follow? *evidence*
4. What should you do about any evidence that contradicts your conclusion? Why?
5. What do you need to state at the beginning of the assignment? Why?
6. How will this affect the sequencing of the main sections?

① For each criterion in the definition, write your <u>conclusion</u> *or* <del>on</del> the thesis statement about Mendes at the top of a <u>separate page</u>. Check each one with a partner to ensure that it says what you want it to.

Go over the reading about Mendes and your notes, <u>highlighting</u> or boxing all the evidence you <u>weighed</u> in arriving at each <u>conclusion</u>. Consider how you will sequence the information in each section.

On the page with the conclusion, draw a <u>tree sketch</u> showing your information as well as how it should be <u>organized</u>. Use enough <u>key words</u> to enable you to write the assignment using only <u>your sketch</u>. If you don't have the original text in front of you when you write, you are less likely to copy from it.

Write your opening paragraph. Arrange the pages to correspond with what you say there.

Rehearse Your Assignment   Work with a partner. Using your sketches, talk him or her through your assignment. Your partner will listen to make sure that your argument about each quality is complete and clear. If your partner feels there is anything you should add, explain, or delete, he or she will tell you. Then revise your sketch as necessary.

Draft One: Focus on Information and Organization

Using only your sketch for reference, write your first draft. Double-space your writing; you'll need room to make changes. As before, don't worry about spelling, punctuation, or finding the right word. Just keep writing to get your ideas down on paper in a fairly organized way. As in Chapter 1, you might want to start with the part you feel the most confident about.

Conference with a Partner   When you finish, work with a different partner.

Read your assignment to your partner. He or she will listen carefully, making sure that you

have included the information required to support your conclusion, and to convince your professor that you understand the ideas;

have organized the ideas in a way that enables your reader easily to follow them; and

have included only relevant information in each section.

Discuss any problems and revise your assignment as necessary. If you don't have room on the page, put the revision on a separate page and indicate where it should be inserted.

Draft Two: Organize for Your Reader

Coherence: The Ordering of Old and New Information   One quality important in good writing is coherence, the smooth flow of ideas from one sentence or paragraph to the next. One way to help guide your reader through your text is to sequence the information so that it moves from the known to the unknown; that is, from the old to the new.

Read paragraph 6 from "Fight, not Flight":

People with all kinds of disabilities have caught the Fox inspiration. There is Richard Beecroft of Ottawa, a victim of multiple sclerosis. He took four months to ride from Vancouver to St. John's on a specially designed tricycle. And there's Newfoundland marathoner, Wayne Morris. He also arrived in St. John's after running across his home province to raise money for a brain scanning machine. Morris was saying thank you for the brain surgery he underwent three years ago.

Now read statements (a) and (b) to answer the questions below.

a. We find a fairly common effect of heroism in this kind of thing.
b. In this kind of thing we find a fairly common effect of heroism.

1. Which sentence—(a) or (b)—do you prefer as the logical follow-up to paragraph 6? Why?   (b)

2. Which one did Charles White prefer? How does White's choice help the reader proceed from the known information to the unknown?

3. Read the following paragraph. Then choose the best sentence below (a), (b), or (c) for the blank.

Although life was difficult in Canada, blacks had no "masters" and

could build a new life here. _____

_____

_____

_____. To encourage such

a move, she produced a tract "Notes on Canada West" containing

information about schooling, climate, religious practices, the law,

elections, and currency.

   a. Shadd believed that both fugitives and freed slaves should come to
      Canada where they had a greater chance for a life of dignity, instead
      of living an oppressed life in the United States.
   b. Shadd believed that, instead of living an oppressed life in the United
      States, both fugitives and freed slaves should come to Canada where
      they had a greater chance for a life of dignity.
   c. Shadd believed that both fugitives and freed slaves should come to
      Canada. Doing so would give them a greater chance for a life of
      dignity instead of living an oppressed life in the United States.

In groups of three of four, compare and discuss your choices. Be prepared to justify your final decision.

Reread your assignment on Mendes, ensuring that your ideas flow logically from one to the next. Revise as necessary.

The Conclusion   With your teacher, discuss what information you think your professor expects in the conclusion of the assignment. Write your conclusion.

Conference with a Partner   When you've finished, exchange papers with a partner. Read each other's papers to ensure that each section consists of a thesis statement followed by clear, detailed support, and that you can follow the ideas easily from one to the next.

Draft Three: Focus on Language Clarity

You will now edit for clarity and correctness. Work in groups of three. Exchange assignments. Read the one you have for any parts that are not absolutely clear or for any problems with spelling, punctuation, and grammar. Together, try to resolve any problems. Revise as you feel necessary.

EVALUATE YOUR ASSIGNMENTS

When she or he evaluates your papers, the professor often considers several criteria: information, organization, and language.

1. Information

    Completeness—specific and detailed enough for the idea to be absolutely clear and to convince the professor of your understanding

    Relevance—all the information in the section on that topic should be directly connected to that topic

    Support—specific details justify your decisions

2. Organization

    The introduction states both the definition and your general conclusion.

    Each section begins with a thesis statement or conclusion about that part.

3. Language

    Clarity is crucial. Minor errors will usually be forgiven, but your professor does not want to have to interpret what you have written. The more work *he or she* does, the less *you* appear to have done, and the less you appear to have understood the concepts.

Now you'll outline expectations using all three criteria.

Information (15 points)   With your teacher establish a point-form list of the information necessary for a complete answer. Consider details and examples as well as main points.

Organization (5 points)   Discuss the following questions with your teacher:

1. What introduction does your assignment require?
2. What does each section require?
3. What conclusion does your answer need?

Language and Clarity of Expression (0 to –5 points)   It is possible that language affects your grades the most when it makes your assignment difficult to follow. The grading scheme below reflects the amount of interpreting the professor must do to get meaning out of the text.

Work with a partner. Read each other's papers three times, once focusing on content; once, on organization; and the last time, on language. Assign points, depending on the level within each category. In marking for clarity, deduct points according to the amount of interpretation you have to do.

	Excellent	Good	Adequate	Poor
Content	15–13	12–10	9–8	7–0
Organization	5	4	3–2	1–0
Clarity	0	–1	–2 / –3	–4 / –5

Assign a total grade out of 20. Return the paper, discussing your evaluation with your partner.

Chapter *3*

Volcanoes

*T*he topic of this chapter is volcanoes. Its main purpose, however, is to acquaint you with academic textbooks. Because there is so much reading to do at college or university, you need to learn to read efficiently and effectively. Textbook writers often help you do this by providing support such as a list of student objectives, a summary of important information, and questions for thought and review. The text you'll read is a complete chapter taken from a university textbook. Activities you do in this chapter will help you develop reading strategies that you can use with other texts.

At the end of the chapter you'll predict questions for a test on the information in the chapter. This is a useful way to prepare for the tests and examinations that you'll face at college or university.

As you do the activities in this chapter, you'll be practicing a number of other skills and strategies necesssary for academic study:

- predicting the content of a section of text
- deciding what information is important in a text
- taking notes in tabular form
- understanding and writing definitions
- giving oral presentations
- understanding and writing compounds

THINK ABOUT THE TOPIC

The first activity will help you develop some background information on volcanoes. Do the questions below. Don't worry if you can't get many of the answers. At college or university it's often true that you don't know much about the new topic before you study it. As you work through this chapter, you'll gradually learn a great deal, just as you would in academic study.

1. Match the names of volcanoes in column A with their countries in column B:

-A-	-B-
Vesuvius	The United States
Mount Etna	Japan
Krakatoa	Hawaii
Mount St. Helen's	Italy
Mount Fuji	Indonesia
Mauna Loa	Italy

2. In groups, compare your answers. Share any information you have on these volcanoes.
3. As a class, think of any terms associated with volcanoes that you already know. Make a list on the board and pool your knowledge.

READING: "VOLCANOES"

The Outline of Chapter Contents (p. 88)

One kind of support writers often provide is an outline of the topics to be covered in the chapter. This helps you get an overview of the topics you will be reading about.

1. Do this question with a partner. Read the outline of chapter contents on page 88. Predict the content of each section.
2. Decide which sections focus on volcanoes and which are there as supports to help students use the text efficiently and effectively.
3. Discuss your answers with your teacher.

Support Sections

You have forty minutes to complete the following six questions. Read your instructions carefully.

1. Below, in the left column of the table, write the names of the five student support sections.

SUPPORT SECTION	KIND OF SUPPORT PROVIDED

2. With a partner, look over each section, noting the kind of information in each one.
3. In the right column, write brief notes to indicate the kind of support provided in that section.
4. Compare your information with that of another pair of students.
5. In your group of four, discuss the following questions:
   a. Of what use might the Student Objectives be?
   b. In the Outline, put a star beside each section you think will be important. Which sections will you be able to read quickly?
   c. Read the Summary on page 100. In an introductory text, why do you think there is so much emphasis on definitions?
   d. Read over Questions for Thought and Review on page 100. Of what use might this section be to you now? later?
   e. Consider the Selected Readings on page 100. When might these be useful?
6. You'll likely have noticed the number of definitions in this chapter. Individually, set up a "Definitions" page in your notebook. As you read the chapter, highlight any important terms and define them on this page.

"The Birth of Vesuvius" (p. 89)

Do these questions with a partner.

1. Quickly read over the support sections to determine how important this section is going to be. Explain.
2. Read the title. What kind of information will you likely find here? Why do you think the authors included this section?
3. Read the section to find out whether your predictions were accurate and to understand what happens when a volcano is "born."
4. Discuss your answers to question 3 with another pair of students.

"Volcanism" (pp. 90–91)

1. According to the support sections, how important is this part of the text? What information should you pay special attention to as you read?
2. Read this section carefully. As you read, do the following:

   highlight any new terms you consider important, and be prepared to say why you think so,

   put key words in the margin to help you remember the important information,

   decide what other labels you could add to Figure 3-1,

   consider why Table 3-1 was presented as a table rather than in paragraphs.

3. Discuss your answers to question 2, first with two partners, then with your teacher.
4. Add any new and important terms to your list of definitions.

"Products of Volcanism" (pp. 91–93)

Do the six questions below. You have twenty-five minutes.

1. Read the title; then look over the support sections. Will this section contain important information? How do you know? What information should you focus on here?
2. Read the introductory paragraph. What main parts are there in this section? How did the writers organize the rest of the section? How might this advance organization help you read more effectively?
3. Use the information in this section to complete the sketch on page 80. Add any other information you consider important.

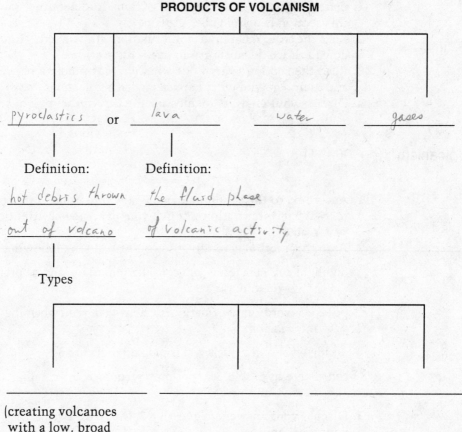

PRODUCTS OF VOLCANISM

pyroclastics   or   lava   water   gases

Definition: Definition:

hot debris thrown   the fluid phase

out of volcano   of volcanic activity

Types

(creating volcanoes
with a low, broad
profile)

4. Compare your sketches with those of two other people.   Add any information you feel you should have.
5. You may be wondering about the term "igneous." Try to figure it out using two other "ign-" words you may know. When you light a match, you *ignite* it. And to start up your car, you put your key in the *ignition*. What, then, might "igneous" materials be?
6. What definitions should you add to your notes? How did the writers signal important terms?

"Types of Volcanoes and Craters" (pp. 93–96)

You have twenty minutes to do this activity. Some of the questions are to be done in groups; some, individually. Read your instructions carefully and stay within your time limits.

1. Do questions 1 and 2 with two or three partners. Check the support sections. How important is this topic? What information will you need to concentrate on?
2. Together, read paragraphs 1 and 2. What two possible ways are there of classifying volcanoes? Which one do the authors prefer? Why? What other bases for comparison are linked to the *forms* of volcanoes?
3. Do this question by yourself. Read the last sentence in paragraph two. What is missing from the text? Individually, construct a clear and complete Table 3–3 using the information in the rest of this section. Your table should include the following headings: Type, Form, Kind of Material Ejected, Type of Activity, and Examples. (Before you begin, decide whether or not to include "caldera" in your table.)
4. Like any notes, tables are helpful if they're complete and clear. In your original groups, compare your tables for completeness and clarity. Decide who has the best table and why.

"Some Spectacular Examples" (pp. 96–99)

Read the title. Predict the information you will find in this part. Judging from the Student Objectives and the Questions for Thought and Review, how important are the examples? Why do you think the writer included them?

1. To learn about the spectacular volcanoes, share the workload. Form groups of three and distribute the examples among you.
2. Individually, read your story, highlighting important information. Turn the text face down and tell yourself the story of the eruption. Then prepare a seven- to eight-minute presentation on the information. You'll need to elaborate in enough detail so that your partners will understand and appreciate how spectacular the event was. Make *brief* notes on 3" x 5" cards. Put only two or three words on each card. Rehearse your presentation quietly to yourself. Remember, *don't read* your presentation; *talk* it.
3. Reform your groups. Take turns giving your presentations.

"Volcanoes in Space and Time" (p. 99)

Do these questions with two or three partners.

1. According to the support sections, what information should you focus on here?
2. Read the first sentence in both paragraphs. Then, in as much detail as you can, predict what information you'll find here.
3. Read the section to check your predictions. Highlight any important information you didn't already know.

"A Good Word About Volcanoes" (pp. 99–100)

Do these questions with a partner.

1. Judging from the title, what kind of information will this section contain?
2. How do the first two sentences reinforce this impression?
3. Individually, read the whole section. Take brief margin notes. Then turn your paper over. With a partner, try to remember the benefits. (*Don't peek.*)

PREPARE FOR THE TEST

Draw a Concept Map

One way to study is to use a concept map—a sketch showing the important topics in the chapter and how they're related to one another. On a separate sheet, turned sideways, draw a detailed concept map of important information about volcanoes. The map has been begun for you below. When you finish, compare maps with two partners. Add any information your partners have that you think would help you study, and reorganize, if necessary, to show connections between topics.

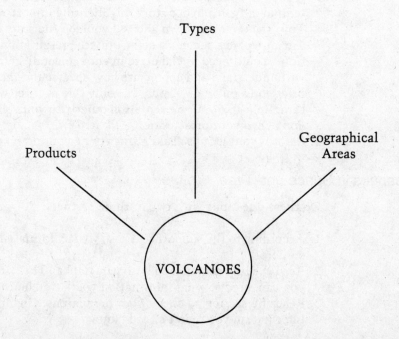

Predicting Questions

One way to prepare for tests and exams is to try to predict the questions you will be asked. The purpose of this next activity is to help you do this. Form groups of three and carefully read your instructions for this activity. You have one hour to do all five questions and hand in your one exam question to your teacher.

1. What important instructional verbs (e.g. Discuss, List) do you often find in exam questions? List at least six or seven below in Column A.

A	B
1./ discuss 10./ draw 11./ Define	1./ benefit
2./ list 12./ show	2./ product
3./ state 13./ Name	3./ Type
4./ summarize 14./ classify	4./ form
5./ provide 15./ argue	5./ examples
6./ support 16./ compare/ (both) contrast (difference)	6./ activity
7./ answer	7./ summary
8./ distinguish	
9./ explain (with reason)	

2. What topics or ideas were important in this chapter on volcanoes? List at least six in Column B.
3. Together, use the verbs and concepts above to help you think of three questions you might be asked on a test or exam about volcanoes. Write them on a separate page. Also, discuss what the professor would expect as an answer to each one.
4. Select one question. Decide what information should be in the best answer and how it should be organized.
5. Use key words to draw a detailed tree diagram of the best answer. Sign your names at the bottom of the sheet, and submit it to your teacher.

Next day, you'll consider the questions and select those you and your teacher feel would be most likely to appear on a test.

Compounds

This activity will help you write concise answers to test questions.

English uses adjectives to describe nouns, to answer the question "What kind of . . . ?" In English, adjectives are placed before the noun; for example, *poisonous* gases, *violent* explosions, *volcanic* ash, *agricultural* benefits, *powdery* substance, *igneous* material, and *quiescent* activity. But because it doesn't have enough adjectives to express every idea, English often uses nouns, making them behave like adjectives. The resulting phrase is called a *compound*.

Examples

Original Phrase		Compound
level of the sea	→	sea level
cone made from cinders	→	cinder cone
extrusions of lava	→	lava extrusions

Why do you think English speakers often prefer compounds to prepositional phrases? *more concise*

1. With a partner, use the examples above to form rules for the construction of compounds in English. Make sure your rules can answer the following questions:

   • Which words are used to make the compound? *first and last words.*
   • What is the new order of the words?
   • What change might be needed when the second noun is moved?

2. Listen to your teacher read the compounds above. Which word in the pair is emphasized when you say the compound aloud?
3. Compare your rules with those of another group of three. Together, test their accuracy by using them to form compounds from the following phrases:

   a. a release of energy   *energy release*
   b. volcanoes that resemble a shield   *shield volcanoes.*
   c. the floor of the sea   *sea floor*
   d. walls of a crater   *crater walls.*
   e. lakes of lava   *lava lakes*
   f. migrations of plants and animals   *plant and animal migrations*

Discuss any problems with your teacher.

3. Other common compounds found in English are derived from the phrases below. Individually, see how many you can form. You probably already know many of them.

a. a table for a computer *computer table*
b. tickets for the bus *bus trickets*
c. trays for making ice cubes *ice - cubes trays*
d. laces that go in shoes *shoes laces*
e. an opener for cans *can opener*
f. a punch that makes three holes *three - holes punch*

Check your answers with your teacher.

4. As a class, consider how a knowledge of compound formation might be useful in both reading and writing.

Definitions

In any introductory course, one of the principal objectives is for the students to learn the language they'll need to discuss the concepts in that field. This is why an introductory textbook usually has so many definitions. Many times in your academic study you, too, will need to define terms, either in test questions to display your knowledge, or in essays to clarify ideas for your reader. This activity will help you understand and write definitions

A. Read the definition of lava:

Lava is the fluid phase of volcanic activity.

1. In what order do you find the following information?

_____ *1* the term being defined

_____ *4* the ideas which clarify or limit the generality of this group

_____ *3* the general group this term belongs to

_____ *2* the main verb

2. What is the main verb? *is*

B. Compare your answers with a partner's.

C. Use these questions to formulate rules about the order of information in definitions. Together, test your hypotheses on the following definitions:

1. "A volcano is the accumulated pile of igneous debris around the point of exit."
2. "Volcanism is the general term referring to all the activity resulting from a transferral of igneous products to the surface of the earth."

Discuss your answers with your teacher.

D. In your text, look up the first time these definitions occurred. Why did the writers choose to put them there?

E. Below, you will find scrambled definitions. Unscramble them, writing the definition in the space provided. Delete any unnecessary commas.

1. Volcanic ash, occurring during the eruptive process, a substance, of lava, light gray, powdery, resulting from the pulverization, is.

Volcanic ash is a light gray powdery substance resulting from the pulverization of lava occurring during the eruptive process.

2. Volcanic bombs, thrown out of a volcano, pieces of igneous material, consist of, while still in a soft plastic condition.

Volcanic bombs consist of pieces of igneous material thrown out of a volcan while still in a soft condition.

WRITE THE TEST

Your next task is to write the exam your teacher gives you.

EVALUATION

Organizing to Answer the Question   One frequent complaint of professors is that while their students may have the information, it is not organized to address the question. Failure to organize to answer the question may tell the grader that you haven't really understood the question. It may also increase the effort she or he has to make to grade your paper. If so, your mark could suffer. Before you grade the essay question, do the following activity.

A. Describe   On the test, you might have been asked the following question:

Describe stratovolcanoes and shield volcanoes in terms of their form, products, and the type of activity.

Below you will find nine sentences that could form the answer. The sentences, however, are not in the correct order. Use the numbers 1 to 9 to sequence them correctly.

act 8 ____8 4____ The activity of shield volcanoes is termed quiescent, or relatively quiet.

Form 5 ____1____ Shield volcanoes have a profile that is low and broad.

act. 3 ____8 8____ In terms of activity, stratovolcanoes alternate between periods of quiet and periods of noise.

9 ____5____ One example of a shield volcano is Mauna Loa, a volcano in Hawaii.

Prod. 2 ____8 7____ Stratovolcanoes produce both lava and pyroclastics.

4 ____8 9____ One example of a stratovolcano is Mount Fuji.

Form. 1 ____6____ Stratovolcanoes have the form of a symmetrical cone which is made up of alternating layers of its products.

Prod: 6 ____8 2____ Shield volcanoes produce only highly fluid basaltic lava.

7 ____8 3____ This lava builds up around the base to produce the characteristic profile.

In groups of three or four, discuss your answers.

B. Compare   Now use these same sentences to answer the following question:

Compare stratovolcanoes and shield volcanoes in terms of their form, products, and type of activity. Give examples.

Discuss your answers with your teacher. How do your answers illustrate the point made by the professors? *GENERAL STATEMENT OF Comparison.*

Evaluate Your Answers

1. In groups, decide what information needs to be in each answer. You'll likely want to use some of the notes you made earlier. Write point-form notes.
2. Exchange papers with a partner. Using your notes and the grading scheme on the test, mark each other's answers. Add the marks up to find the total.
3. Return each other's papers. Explain your marks.

Reading

Volcanoes

STUDENT OBJECTIVES

At the conclusion of this chapter the student should:

1. know what a volcano is and the kinds of material it ejects

2. recognize various types of volcanoes and the nature of their activity

3. know about the distribution of volcanoes on the earth, both in the present and in the past

4. appreciate both the positive and negative aspects of the relationships between volcanoes and human beings

THE BIRTH OF VESUVIUS

When faint tremors and groanings within the earth were noticed by the 20,000 inhabitants of Pompeii on the morning of August 24, A.D. 79, few believed that a violent volcanic eruption was imminent. Perhaps an earthquake, yes, because the town was still rebuilding from an earthquake that shook it and nearby Herculaneum 16 years before. Small shocks and tremors had been commonplace since then. While it was true that Monte Somma to the north was a volcano, it had not erupted within the memory of anyone living and was thought to be extinct. Monte Somma's crater walls had been crumbling from the onslaught of erosion for centuries, and within the enlarged crater itself wolves and boars roamed in a thick tangle of brushwood and wild vines.

On that day in August this complacency was abruptly dispelled by a series of thunderous explosions. A column of smoke, gases, and steam rose into the air above the crater of Monte Somma and blew out part of its ancient walls. A dense rain of volcanic ash and glowing debris turned day into night over the towns of Pompeii, Herculaneum, and Stabiae. Vesuvius was born.

Most of the population of these towns escaped; many did not. A number sought safety within their villas, carrying food and water with them into lower rooms. They are still there, huddled in corners where they were suffocated by poisonous gases. A few in the act of flight died on the streets. Pliny the Elder, captain of the Roman fleet at Naples, engaged in rescue operations. In attempting to get a closer view of the eruption, he perished at the town of Stabiae. His nephew, Pliny the Younger, later described the tragedy in two letters to his friend Tacitus. These documents, still extant, provide us with details of what happened. In the several hours since the onset of the eruption, Pompeii became buried under 20 ft (6 m) of volcanic ash, with roofs of houses collapsing and finally disappearing in the inundation. Herculaneum, closer to the base of Vesuvius, received 50 ft (17 m) of water-saturated flows of volcanic ash. Ironically, the city of Pompeii was built originally on the site of an old lava flow.

In the centuries following this eruption, the location of these towns was forgotten. Their location remained unknown until excavations in the eighteenth century accidentally brought them to light. Since that time systematic digging has uncovered 60% of Pompeii and a good portion of Herculaneum, resurrecting well-preserved art treasures and a magnificently detailed glimpse into Greco-Roman life of the first century,

Paintings, mosaics, statues, temples, and private houses have been exhumed. On the mundane side, scribblings on walls (graffiti), chariot ruts in the streets, and ring marks from wine glasses on counters have been preserved. Loaves of bread with the baker's name engraved, medicinal pills, olives, almonds, and fish roe have also been found.

Vesuvius continued to be active in the intervening centuries since A.D. 79, erupting 50 times. A major outburst in 1631 sent torrents of lava and mud over several villages, and a conspicuous eruption occurred in 1944.

VOLCANISM

As we saw in Chapter 6, igneous activity takes place extensively beneath the surface of the earth. When igneous material reaches the surface, one of the most spectacular events in nature occurs: volcanic action. As the account of Vesuvius suggests, the erruption of volcanoes has a vital effect on human activities.

The term *volcanism* includes all activity associated with the expulsion of igneous material from the interior of the earth to the surface. This transferral is accomplished by means of a conduit or *fissure* that penetrates deeply into the earth, tapping a supply of superheated fluids and gases. A *volcano* is the accumulated pile of igneous debris around the point of exit, usually called the *vent*. Volcanoes form when pressure buildup from below rends the overlying rocks. In some cases a slight upward bulging will appear in the region of a volcano prior to its eruption, as sensitive tiltmeters on Hawaii have shown. One main conduit usually feeds the volcano from below, but vents may be numerous. Offshoots from the main conduit may result in *parasitic cones* on the flanks of a volcano (Figure 3–1).

Expanding water vapor plays an important role in helping to propel magma up along fissures, especially in the more explosive volcanoes. Steam is plentiful in volcanic emissions. During a phase of eruption at Mount Etna in Sicily, it was estimated that 460 million gallons of water (as steam) escaped from one vent. On Hawaii, an average water content of nearly 80% has been found in magmatic gases issuing from volcanoes there (Table 3-1) .

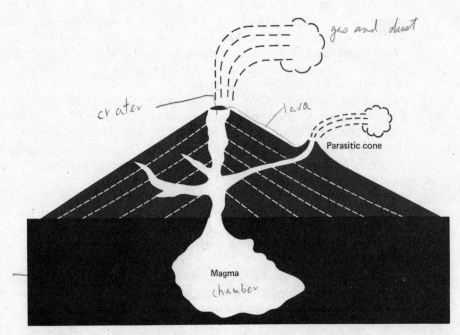

FIGURE 3–1. Cross section through a volcano shows possible structure.

TABLE 3-1. Typical composition of magmatic
            gases in Hawaii

Substance	Percentage
Water	79.31
Carbon dioxide	11.61
Sulfur dioxide	6.48
Nitrogen	1.29
Hydrogen	0.58
Carbon monoxide	0.37
Sulfur	0.24
Chlorine	0.05
Argon	0.04

Source: J. F. White, ed., © 1962, p. 90, *The Study of the Earth*. Reprinted by permission of Prentice-Hall, Inc., Englewood Cliffs, N. J.

PRODUCTS OF VOLCANISM

Igneous material emitted by volcanoes can be classified into two groups: (1) *lava* and (2) *pyroclastics*. Lava is the fluid phase of volcanic activity. Pyroclastics (also called *tephra*) are various-sized, discrete particles of hot debris thrown out of a volcano. Whether lava or pyroclastics are being ejected, the eruption is normally accompanied by the expulsion of water and other gases.

Lava

Lava usually expresses itself as elongate flows or, literally, rivers of molten rock, moving down and outward from the slopes of a volcano. In composition, lava is basaltic, andesitic, or rhyolitic (see Chapter 6); but basaltic flows are the most common. When congealed, many lavas still display flowage features. *Pahoehoe* or ropy-looking lava is one such type (Figure 3–2). Sometimes a lava flow cools and becomes sluggish and forms an outer crust. When the still-fluid lava beneath the crust starts to move again, it breaks the crust into jagged chunks and blocks. The final product of such a flow is called *aa* (pronounced ah-ah)).

Basaltic lavas are known for their low viscosity and are capable of spreading out over wide distances from vents to form volcanoes with a low, broad profile. In the earth's distant past, crustal instability has produced fissures of regional extent from which many cubic miles (kilometers) of basalt have upwelled to form *basalt plateaus* thousands of square miles (square kilometers) in area. Rhyolitic lava is much more viscous. Because of this high viscosity it does not spread widely from its vent and is more restricted in areal extent.

Pyroclastics

Pyroclastics are fragmentary materials that are ejected from volcanoes and fall in solid form to the ground. Some common types are shown in Table 3-2. The

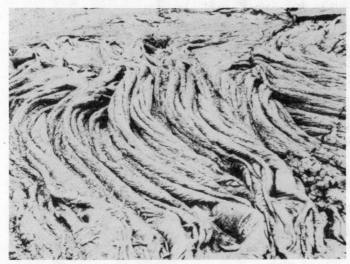

FIGURE 3–2. Congealed flow of pahoehoe or ropy lava.
(Photo by John S. King.)

finest particles are called volcanic *ash*. Typically a light gray powdery substance representing the pulverization of lava during the eruptive process, ash can be swept by winds over vast distances before it settles. When volcanic ash forms solidified layers, the term *tuff* applies. *Cinders* or *lapilli* range from the size of a pea to that of a golf ball and are irregular in shape. They consist of either solid or cellular lava fragments. *Pumice* is essentially a solidified volcanic froth with many watertight voids within it. Lapilli-sized lumps of pumice have fallen into the sea and, instead of sinking, have floated on the surface. So much of this debris floated on the sea near Krakatoa (following its eruption in 1883) that ships were not able to push through it.

Volcanic *bombs* consist of pieces of igneous material thrown out of a volcano while still in a soft, plastic condition. As the bombs rotate and solidify in flight, they may take on an elliptical or rounded shape and may exhibit contorted surface markings (Figure 3–3). *Blocks* are solid, angular pieces of debris of varying size,

TABLE 3-2. Pyroclastic materials ejected
during volcanic eruption

Type of material	Size range (diameter)
Blocks	Greater than 32 mm up to several meters
Bombs	4 mm up to several meters
Cinders	4–32 mm
Ash	Less than 4 mm

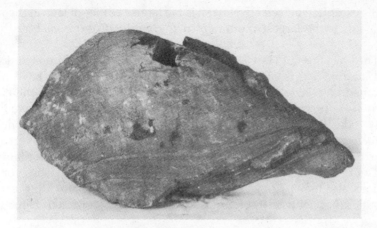

FIGURE 3–3. A volcanic bomb. (Courtesy of Jan Patterson-Wittstrom.)

some weighing several tons. Blocks do not necessarily have to be of igneous material; blocks of limestone or other country rock lining the vent wall may be torn off and carried up along the fissure and expelled.

TYPES OF VOLCANOES AND CRATERS

Volcanoes can be classified according to the nature of their activity, that is, *quiescent* or *explosive*. Quiescent activity involves the relatively gentle extrusion of quantities of lava, usually basaltic in composition. Explosive activity is associated with the production of pyroclastics, including cinders, bombs, and blocks. The sudden release of pressures long contained shatters magmatic materials and catapults discrete particles over wide areas. A single volcano often displays both explosive and quiescent phases during its eruptive history and may change from quiet to explosive during a single eruption.

A more precise way to classify volcanoes is on the basis of their *form*, which bears a strong relationship to the kind of igneous material ejected from them. And this, in turn, may relate to the quiescent or explosive type of activity exhibited. Table 3-3 lists some common types of volcanoes and their characteristics.

Shield volcanoes

The low, broad profile of the *shield volcano* is the result of great outpourings of highly fluid basalt, which spreads over wide areas. The fluidity of basalt prevents it from building up any volcanic cone with sides much steeper than 7°. Hawaii is a typical locality for the shield volcano. This group of islands is the result of eruptions of basaltic lava that originally poured out onto the sea floor and built up through about 3 mi (5 km) of water to reach sea level. Continued eruptions of basalt created the present land area of 6,424 mi² (10,360 km²), with such peaks as Mauna Loa and Mauna Kea rising to more than 13,600 ft (4,125 m) above sea level.

With the exception of Iceland, Hawaii is the largest edifice of lava in the world; and Mauna Loa is the largest mountain in the world in terms of both height and volume.

The volcanoes of Hawaii are so characteristic of quiescent eruption that the term *Hawaiian type* is often used instead. Craters on Hawaii have in the past maintained lava lakes so large that waves of lava slosh against the crater walls (Figure 3–4). In such volcanoes pyroclastics are relatively minor, and explosive activity of the Vesuvian type is normally absent. But it should not be concluded that Hawaiian eruptions are harmless. Swiftly moving lava flows have overrun villages. Mild explosive phases occurred in 1790, when part of the Hawaiian army was wiped out, and later in 1924, when Kilauea spewed pyroclastics for ten days. Eruptions also took place in 1955 and in the early 1960s, providing excellent opportunities for scientists and tourists to observe and record their behavior.

Stratovolcanoes

A *stratovolcono*, the most common type of volcano, alternates between explosive expulsions of pyroclastics and relatively quiet extrusions of lava. The resulting volcanic cone is made up of alternating layers of each kind of material. (For this reason stratovolcanoes are known also as *composite* volcanoes.) Such volcanic action constructs the beautifully symmetrical cones exemplified by Mayon in the Philippines, Fujiyama in Japan (Figure 3–5), and Mount Shasta in the United States.

FIGURE 3–4. Lava lake in crater of Pauahi, Hawaii. (Photo by John S. King.)

FIGURE 3–5. Fujiyama, Japan, is a stratovolcano.
(Courtesty of Japan Airlines.)

Alternation of activity results when a quiescent lava-ejection phase concludes and forms an effectlve seal of solidified lava within the conduit of the volcano, permitting gradual pressure buildup below and setting the stage for a violent blast of pyroclastics. The cycle then repeats itself. Stratovolcanoes such as Vesuvius gain a reputation for explosivity, because during such phases the greatest destruction occurs.

Cinder cones

A *cinder cone* is a conical hill of pyroclastics, most of which lie within the cinder-size range. These volcanoes tend to be explosive, but extrusions of lava are not unknown. Cinder cones are numerous, occur in all sizes, and tend to be steep sided. Paricutín, a cinder cone in Mexico, began in a cornfield on February 20, 1943, as a hole in the ground throwing out dense smoke. Within 24 hours a cone of cinders had risen to more than 100 ft (30 m), and the cornfield was no more. In ten days Paricutín was 400 ft (120 m) high. Lava started to flow, spreading out 3 mi (5 km) from the crater and invading two villages. After a year Paricutín was more than 1000 ft (300 m) high. It continued to erupt until 1953, when it lapsed into inactivity.

Calderas

The term *caldera* refers not so much to a particular type of volcano as it does to the crater that results. A caldera is essentially a very large crater that may form in different ways. Calderas can result from massive collapse or subsidence during

FIGURE 3–6. Crater Lake, Oregon, a caldera. (Oregon State Highway Division, photo #26639. Courtesy of the Oregon State Archives.)

volcanic activity, or later from erosion during dormancy. Some calderas may result from unusually violent explosions (Figure 3–6).

SOME SPECTACULAR EXAMPLES

Mt. Pelée

Certainly the people of St. Pierre on the island of Martinique in the West Indies had ample warning that Pelée was about to erupt. In the 2 weeks prior to May 8, 1902, Pelée announced its revival (after 50 years of dormancy) with loud hissings of steam, boiling of lake waters within the crater, and discharges of flourlike ash that spread over the surrounding countryside to despoil crops and affect cattle. At night a strange glowing could be seen near the summit. As May 8 approached, the pent-up forces within the earth intensified, and detonations like distant artillery could be heard.

The population of St. Pierre was about 30,000. Vowing to avoid a panicky exodus, the governor posted troops on roads leading out of the city, and they turned many people back. The crater rim of Pelée was several hundred feet (meters) high but was breached on the side facing St. Pierre by the erosional activity of a stream, the Rivière Blanche, which had carved a valley down the slope of Pelée to the edge of the town. Thus the gash in the crater was like the muzzle of a gun pointed at St. Pierre, 4 mi (6 km) away.

Eighteen ships rode at anchor in the harbor at St. Pierre at about 8:00 A.M. on May 8. Sailors aboard the *Roddam* heard a deafening explosion, and the ship lurched. A gigantic dark cloud appeared at the summit of Pelée and, glowing with increasing intensity, hurtled down and across the town and into the harbor. Ships burst into flames and sank. The *Roddam* managed to get under way and luckily escaped beyond the so-called "singe area." In a matter of minutes, 30,000 people had died, most of them either roasted alive or suffocated by incandescent dust. Only one man, imprisoned below ground in a dungeon, survived. The fiery avalanche of gas, ashes, and cinders that engulfed and destroyed St. Pierre later was named a *nuée ardente,* or glowing cloud. The eruption of Pelée was not accompanied by significant lava flows, although mudflows were common.

Krakatoa

Krakatoa is situated in the Sunda Strait between Java and Sumatra, a region of numerous volcanoes. In 1883 it recorded one of the most violent eruptions in history. Like Vesuvius, Krakatoa had been the scene of volcanic activity in the remote past. The remnants of a large caldera lay submerged beneath the sea. Resumption of volcanism centuries before had produced three small coalesced cones protruding above sea level. Beginning in May 1883 and throughout the summer months, these three cones emitted smoke and steam. More vents appeared below the water's surface. If any people lived on the island, they left.

On August 26, loud explosions were heard 100 mi (160 km) away, and dense clouds of ash and pumice shot 17 mi (27 km) into the air. Along the coast of Java and Sumatra, darkness fell as volcanic clouds shut out the sun. This darkness lasted two and a half days. Torrential ash-laden rains added to the turmoil. On August 27, Krakatoa reached its peak of explosivity. The sounds of a series of detonations were heard in Australia, 3000 mi (4840 km) away. At the same time, volcanic debris was thrown many miles (kilometers) into the sky. The finer particles, riding on stratospheric winds, encircled the earth and took two years to settle. It is estimated that 4–5 mi^3 (6-8 km^3) of rock debris were blown into the air during the paroxysms that pulverized Krakatoa, with an energy release matching that of the most powerful hydrogen bomb.

Had Krakatoa erupted in a densely populated area, millions of lives might have been lost. As it was, the reverberations of Krakatoa unleashed a *tsunami,* a large sea wave that attained a height of 120 ft (38 m) from base to crest as it crashed against the coasts of Java and Sumatra and swept 36,000 people to their deaths. The force of the tsunami can be appreciated by the fact that it carried a large ship 1 $^1/_2$ mi (2 $^1/_2$ km) inland and stranded it there 30 ft (10 m) above sea level.

Rocks weighing up to 50 tons were transported even further. Krakatoa is not dead. A new cone rose above the sea in 1928 and was named Anak Krakatoa (child of Krakatoa). By 1953 the child had grown to a height of 360 ft (108 m).

Surtsey

Surtsey appeared in the North Atlantic south of Iceland on November 14, 1963. By the second day it was 33 ft (10 m) high. Scientists and other observers kept the new volcano under close watch. The basaltic intrusions had built up from the ocean floor 425 ft (128 m) below. Loud explosions accompanied a towering cloud of pyroclastic debris that rose thousands of feet (meters) into the air. The cloud could be seen from the capital city of Reykjavik, 75 mi (120 km) to the north. By the end of a week the infant island had grown to 200 ft (60 m) in height and 2000 ft (600 m) in length. The abrupt contact of red-hot magma with cold seawater caused a continuous display of explosions. Blocks up to 3 ft (1 m) in diameter were hurled hundreds of feet (meters) into the air, to fall whistling like bombs.

Between November and April the effusives from Surtsey were pyroclastic. But the survival of the new island was questionable, because the loose particles of ash and cinders would not he able to withstand the pounding of ocean waves, and the island would be washed away. In April, however, flows of basalt created a solid rock barrier to protect the island from excessive wave erosion. Lava continued to extrude until, in June 1967, Surtsey had grown to a height of 570 ft (171 m).

VOLCANOES IN SPACE AND TIME

Volcanoes are not scattered at random over the earth. They are more abundant in certain areas of the world. The zone of greatest volcanic activity (called the *ring of fire*) encircles the Pacific Ocean basin. In the Mediterranean region, another area of conspicuous volcanism, the earliest observations of volcanoes were made by Greeks and Romans. The question arises, Why only certain zones of volcanic activity? The question cannot be answered with utmost certainty but these areas coincide with those of greatest earthquake activity. Advocates of plate tectonics theory believe that these are areas of plate contact where energy release takes place. This subject will be considered in more detail in Chapter 20.

Volcanoes are not unique to the present. Geologists, probing among the rocks of past geologic periods, find abundant evidence of continued volcanism throughout earth history. For example, in Pennsylvania and Virginia, extensive thin layers of *bentonite*, an altered volcanic ash, attest to protracted volcanic activity in the eastern United States hundreds of millions of years ago. In Canada hundreds of cubic miles (cubic kilometers) are present. In fact, virtually every period in earth history yields evidence of volcanism somewhere in the world.

A GOOD WORD ABOUT VOLCANOES

It would seem that, so far in this chapter, we have portrayed the volcano as a villain: erupting and sending thousands to their deaths by roasting, gassing, or—

equally insensitively—by spawning tsunamis to drown them. However, volcanoes do have positive aspects. From the scientist's point of view, close study of active volcanoes such as those on Hawaii afford us an appreciation of the forces of nature and a knowledge of the internal condition of the earth, laying the groundwork for possible predictions of volcanic eruptions.

If this is small comfort, then consider that it has been through volcanic eruption, according to most scientists, that the hydrosphere and much of the atmosphere came into existence. Volcanism has resulted in the creation of new land (such as Surtsey) available for settlement by many life forms, including humans (such as Hawaii). Volcanic islands may have served as steppingstones for migrations of life to continents and island areas. Another benefit has been the creation of fertile volcanic soils for raising coffee beans in South America, grapes in the Mediterranean area (that make exceptionally good wines), and pineapples in Hawaii.

SUMMARY

Volcanoes can erupt explosively at the earth's surface, taking a heavy toll in lives and property. A volcano is the accumulation of igneous material around a vent, or exit from the interior. Volcanism is a general term that refers to all the activity resulting from the transferral of igneous products to the surface. These igneous products include lava, which produces relatively quiet eruptions, and pyroclastics, which include various-sized fragments of hot debris ejected in an explosive manner.

Three types of volcanoes include: (l) shield volcanoes, having a low, broad profile and emitting fluid basalts like the volcanoes of Hawaii; (2) stratovolcanoes, which alternate between quiescent and explosive activity and build up a composite cone of alternating lavas and pyroclastics reflecting this activity; and (3) cinder cones, composed chiefly of pyroclastic material such as Paricutín in Mexico. A caldera is an unusually large crater produced by collapse, protracted erosion, or exceptional explosivity.

Mount Pelée, Krakatoa, and Surtsey are vivid examples of volcanic eruption. Such volcanic activity has been going on extensively and continuously since the earliest days of the earth, but today the greatest concentration of volcanic activity is in the ring of fire around the borders of the Pacific. Volcanoes are not all bad, despite their threat to humankind. Through volcanism the hydrosphere and atmosphere probably have been produced. Volcanoes provide new land for settlement and may have served as steppingstones in the migration of plants and animals. Rich productive soils also result from volcanic debris.

Questions for thought and review

1. What is a volcano?
2. What is the role of water in a volcanic eruption?
3. Might you find a shield volcano composed of rhyolite? If not, why not?

4. Why can some volcanic ejecta float in water?
5. During the eruption of Krakatoa it was estimated (afterwards) that 4–5 mi³ (10–11 km³) of rock debris were blown into the air. Could you speculate on how scientists arrived at this estimate?

Selected Readings

Bullard, F. M., 1962, *Volcanoes in History, in Theory and in Eruption*, University of Texas Press, Austin.

Maiuri, Amedeo, 1958, Pompeii, *Scientific American*, vol. 198, no. 4, pp. 68–82.

Williams, Howel, 1951, Volcanoes, *Scientific American*, vol. 185, no. 5, pp. 45–53.

Chapter 4

A Study
Skills Manual

This chapter will focus on your success as a student. It will discuss ways to deal with academic problems common at college or university.

The writing task for this chapter is a resource booklet containing strategies and techniques for effective study—that is, a study skills manual. You will distribute the resource booklet to your class. As you prepare to write the manual, you will also practice the following language skills and strategies:

- reading for specific information
- interviewing
- listening and note-taking
- note-taking from texts
- asking questions for clarification and repetition
- doing research in the library
- practicing the writing skills you have developed to this point
- working in groups to accomplish a writing task

THINK ABOUT THE TOPIC

One problem many students have is time management. The purpose of the following activity is to help you assess your use of your time.

1. In the space below, write down any tasks / jobs you want to do on the three days specified by your teacher. For example, you'll have school-related tasks such as classes, assignments, and studying; errands such as grocery shopping or doing laundry; and leisure activities such as going to a movie or having coffee with friends.

    * – write the first draft for the project.
    * – write my parents a letter.
    – grocery shopping.
    * – doing laundry
    – having coffee with friend.
    * – studying maths.
    – go downtown with friend
    – cooking supper
    – phone to my friend

2. Next, decide which tasks are essential and put an asterisk beside them.

3. On pages 103–104, you will find a Time Plan. At the top, fill in the three days specified. In the "Planned" column, write in the activities from question 2. Then, schedule the other activities around these, writing them in the Time Plan, too.
    A few words of caution are in order here. Do not forget the time for traveling to classes. Also, be realistic: There are only 168 hours in a week. Leave yourself time to get enough sleep. Remember to be flexible: buses can be late, and grocery lines can be long.

4. As the three days go by, fill in the column labelled "Actual." This column is a record of how you actually spend your time. Its purpose is to show you how closely you kept to your schedule, or how much you deviated from your original plan.

5. Bring the completed plan to class with you on the day your teacher specifies. Discuss your ability to manage your time efficiently and effectively.

TIME PLAN

Day	Thursday		Friday		Saturday	
Time	Planned	Actual	Planned	Actual	Planned	Actual
7:00						
8:00						
9:00	English class		get up, first draft		get up, final draft	
10:00	↓		↓		↓	
11:00			↓			
12:00	↓		grocery shopping		cooking lunch	
1:00	first draft		doing laundry		↓ having coffee with friend	
2:00			↓			
3:00	↓		write my parents a letter		↓ studying	
4:00	Maths. class		↓		Maths. ↓	

(continued)

TIME PLAN (continued)

Day	Thursday		Friday		Saturday	
Time	Planned	Actual	Planned	Actual	Planned	Actual
5:00	Maths class		go down-town			
6:00	go home					
7:00	cooking supper				cooking supper	
8:00	studying Maths				watch T.V	
9:00	phone to friend					

READING I: "THE BASIC ACADEMIC COMPETENCIES"

1. The first reading on page 105 focuses on the Basic Academic Competencies—the fundamental skills you'll need to succeed at college or university. The reading names these competencies and explains their importance. As you read, look for this information. Take key-word notes in the margin.
2. Check your answers with two partners.

Reading I

The Basic Academic Competencies

The Basic Academic Competencies are the broad intellectual skills essential to effective work in all fields of college study. They provide a link across the disciplines of knowledge although they are not specific to any particular discipline. *[join information]*

The Basic Academic Competencies are reading, writing, speaking and listening, mathematics, reasoning, and studying. These competencies are interrelated to and interdependent with the Basic Academic Subjects. Without such competencies, knowledge of history, science, language, and all other subjects is unattainable. *[of those are very important]*

The Basic Academic Competencies are developed abilities, the outcomes of learning and intellectual discourse. There are different levels of competency; they can be defined in measurable terms.

Although the Basic Academic Competencies are not always identified explicitly, spelling them out provides a way to tell students what is expected of them. Knowledge of what is expected is crucial to effective learning.

In order to do effective work in college, it is essential that all students have the following academic competencies.

READING II: "FIVE BASIC ACADEMIC COMPETENCIES: READING, WRITING, SPEAKING AND LISTENING, MATHEMATICS, AND REASONING"

The purpose of this activity is to enable you to determine your own level in each basic competency. You have thirty minutes to complete the three steps.

1. Reading II, which begins on page 107, describes five academic competencies—reading, writing, speaking and listening, mathematics, and reasoning—in terms of their subskills. Read to find out what each competecy involves.
2. Below you'll find a rating scale for each competency. Read the key carefully. For each competency, circle the number that best describes your current overall level in that skill.
3. When you finish, form groups of four or five. Compare and discuss your answers. Be sure to give details and examples to explain why you gave yourself those ratings.

YOUR OWN PERSONAL INVENTORY OF COMPETENCIES

Key

1 Poor
2 Fair
3 Good
4 Very Good
5 Excellent

Competency	Your Present Level				
Reading	1	2	3	(4)	5
Writing	1	(2)	3	4	5
Speaking and Listening	1	2	3	(4)	5
Mathematics	1	2	3	(4)	5
Reasoning	1	(2)	(3)	4	5

Reading II

Five Basic Academic Competencies: Reading, Writing, Speaking and Listening, Mathematics, and Reasoning

READING

- The ability to identify and comprehend the main and subordinate ideas in a written work and to summarize the ideas in one's own words.
- The ability to recognize different purposes and methods of writing, to identify a writer's point of view and tone, and to interpret a writer's meaning inferentially as well as literally.
- The ability to separate one's personal opinions and assumptions from a writer's.
- The ability to vary one's reading speed and method (survey, skim, review, question, and master) according to the type of material and one's purpose for reading.
- The ability to use the features of books and other reference materials, such as table of contents, preface, introduction, titles and subtitles, index, glossary, appendix, bibliography.
- The ability to define unfamiliar words by decoding, using contextual clues, or by using a dictionary.

Reprinted with permission from *Academic Preparation for College: What Students Need to Know and Be Able to Do*, copyright © 1983 by College Entrance Examination Board, New York.

WRITING

- The ability to conceive ideas about a topic for the purpose of writing.
- The ability to organize, select, and relate ideas and to outline and develop them in coherent paragraphs.
- The ability to write Standard English sentences with correct:

  – sentence structure;
  – verb forms;
  – punctuation, capitalization, possessives, plural forms, and other matters of mechanics;
  – word choice and spelling.

- The ability to vary one's writing style, including vocabulary and sentence structure, for different readers and purposes.
- The ability to improve one's own writing by restructuring, correcting errors, and rewriting.
- The ability to gather information from primary and secondary sources; to write a report using this research; to quote, paraphrase, and summarize accurately; and to cite sources properly.

SPEAKING AND LISTENING

- The ability to engage critically and constructively in the exchange of ideas, particularly during class discussions and conferences with instructors.
- The ability to answer and ask questions coherently and concisely, and to follow spoken instructions.
- The ability to identify and comprehend the main and subordinate ideas in lectures and discussions, and to report accurately what others have said.
- The ability to conceive and develop ideas about a topic for the purpose of speaking to a group; to choose and organize related ideas; to present them clearly in Standard English; and to evaluate similar presentations by others.
- The ability to vary one's use of spoken language to suit different situations.

MATHEMATICS

- The ability to perform, with reasonable accuracy, the computations of addition, subtraction, multiplication, and division using natural numbers, fractions, decimals, and integers.
- The ability to make and use measurements in both traditional and metric units.

- The ability to use effectively the mathematics of:

  - integers, fractions, and decimals;
  - ratios, proportions, and percentages;
  - roots and powers;
  - algebra;
  - geometry.

- The ability to make estimates and approximations, and to judge the reasonableness of a result.
- The ability to formulate and solve a problem in mathematical terms.
- The ability to select and use appropriate approaches and tools in solving problems (mental computation, trial and error, paper-and-pencil techniques, calculator, and computer).
- The ability to use elementary concepts of probability and statistics.

REASONING

- The ability to identify and formulate problems, as well as the ability to propose and evaluate ways to solve them.
- The ability to recognize and use inductive and deductive reasoning and to recognize fallacies in reasoning.
- The ability to draw reasonable conclusions from information found in various sources, whether written, spoken, or displayed in tables and graphs, and to defend one's conclusions rationally.
- The ability to comprehend, develop, and use concepts and generalizations.
- The ability to distinguish between fact and opinion.

READING III: "STUDYING"

This final competency, "Studying," will be considered separately because of its unique nature.

1. Read the description of each subskill on page 111.
2. Assess your own level in each study skill. Rank the six abilities in an order that shows your strengths and weaknesses: in the margin, put the number 1 beside the ability you feel the most confident about and the number 6 beside the one you are least confident about.
3. In your groups, compare your answers, discussing your similarities and differences.

Reading III

Studying

This set of abilities is different in kind from those that precede it. They are set forth here because they constitute the key abilities in learning how to learn. Successful study skills are necessary for acquiring the other five competencies as well as for achieving the desired outcomes in the Basic Academic Subjects. Students are unlikely to be efficient in any part of their work without these study skills.

- The ability to set study goals and priorities consistent with stated course objectives and one's own progress, to establish surroundings and habits conducive to learning independently or with others, and to follow a schedule that accounts for both short- and long-term projects.
- The ability to locate and use resources external to the classroom (for example, libraries, computers, interviews, and direct observation), and to incorporate knowledge from such sources into the learning process.
- The ability to develop and use general and specialized vocabularies, and to use them for reading, writing, speaking, listening, computing, and studying.
- The ability to understand and to follow customary instructions for academic work in order to recall, comprehend, analyze, summarize, and report the main ideas from reading, lectures, and other academic experiences; and to synthesize knowledge and apply it to new situations.
- The ability to prepare for various types of examinations and to devise strategies for pacing, attempting or omitting questions, thinking, writing, and editing according to the type of examination; to satisfy other assessments of learning in meeting course objectives such as laboratory performance, class participation, simulation, and students' evaluations.
- The ability to accept constructive criticism and learn from it.

CHAPTER 4 WRITING TASK: STUDY SKILLS MANUAL

As you learned at the beginning of this chapter, your writing task for this unit is a Study Skills Manual designed to help students manage their studying problems. The manual will describe techniques to help them improve their study skills. You will distribute this manual to your own class and possibly to other students who want to study at college or university. You'll complete the manual in stages.

A. Read the list of study difficulties below. Check (✔) areas in which you've had problems as a student. Also, add any other difficulties you've had but which are not on the list.

- time management
- examination anxiety
- remembering what you've read
- taking notes in lectures
- inability to focus when trying to work
- studying effectively
- non-understanging what lecturer is talking about because of vocab.
-
-

In groups of four or five, compare and discuss your answers.

B. As a class, do the following:

1. Decide on the problems you wish to work on for the manual. Choose four or five that are the most common in the class.
2. Form groups of equal size. Each group will choose a different problem to focus on. That problem will be your topic for the manual.

The next few activities will help you gather information for the manual.

READING IV: "THE SURVEY Q3R METHOD"

Your next reading describes a technique for improving your reading abilities.

1. Read about the method. Then, reread it, following the advice in the article.
2. With two partners, discuss how helpful you consider this technique.

Reading IV

The Survey
Q3R Method

The title for this higher-level study skill is abbreviated in the current fashion to make it easier to remember and to make reference to it more simple. The symbols Survey Q3R stand for the steps which the student follows in using the method; a description of each of these steps is given below:

SURVEY 1.　Glance over the headings in the chapter to see the main points which will be developed. Also read the final summary paragraph if the chapter has one. This survey should not take more than a minute and will show the three to six core ideas around which the discussion will cluster . This orientation will help you organize the ideas as you read them later.

QUESTION 2.　Now begin to work. Turn the first heading into a question. This will arouse your curiosity and so increase comprehension. It will bring to mind information already known, thus helping you to understand that section more quickly. And the question will make important points stand out while explanatory detail is recognized as such. Turning a heading into a question can be done instantly upon reading the heading, but it demands a conscious effort on the part of the reader to make this a query for which he must read to find the answer.

READ 3.　Read to answer that question, i.e., to the end of the first headed section. This is not a passive plodding along each line, but an active search for the answer.

RECITE 4.　Having read the first section, look away from the book and try briefly to recite the answer to your question. Use your own words and include an example. If you can do this you know what is in the book; if you can't, glance over the section again. An excellent way to do this

Reprinted from Robinson, F. P. (1962). *Effective Reading*. New York: Harper & Row, Publishers, Inc.

reciting from memory is to jot down cue phrases in outline form on a sheet of paper. Make these notes very brief!

Now repeat steps 2, 3, and 4 on each subsequent headed section. That is, turn the next heading into a question, read to answer that question, and recite the answer by jotting down cue phrases in your outline. Read in this way until the entire lesson is completed.

REVIEW 5.   When the lesson has thus been completely read, look over your notes to get a bird's-eye view of the points and their relationship and check your memory as to the content by reciting the major subpoints under each heading. This checking of memory can be done by covering up the notes and trying to recall the main points. Then expose each major point and try to recall the subpoints listed under it.

These five steps of the Survey Q3R Method—Survey, Question, Read, Recite, and Review—when polished into a smooth and efficient method should result in the student reading faster, picking out the important points, and fixing them in memory. The student will find one other worthwhile outcome: Quiz questions will seem happily familiar because the headings turned into questions are usually the points emphasized in quizzes. In predicting actual quiz questions and looking up the answers beforehand, the student feels that he is effectively studying the material considered important in a course.

Exam and Study Strategies

Below you will find a list of techniques for dealing with exams and studying. Individually, decide how helpful each technique would be: Very (V), Quite (Q), Not Very (NV), and Virtually Useless (VU). Put the appropriate abbreviation in the margin. This is your own personal opinion, so wait until you finish before you consult anyone else.

V **1.** Early in the course, design a "concept map" or a "global map" of the information in the course. This map allows you to see the logical structure of the information—how the various ideas are related. Continue to build your map throughout the course.

NV **2.** In plenty of time before the exams, prepare a master calendar, breaking down the term's work into manageable units. Allow time for ongoing review as well as for last-minute cramming.

NV **3.** Plan your study, work, and review sessions for short periods. Give yourself small, realistic goals to achieve.

Q **4.** Just before an exam, ensure that you take time for important physical needs such as eating, sleeping, and exercise.

V **5.** In the essay exam, survey the questions first. Beside each question, jot down any ideas that come to you. Expand this list as you work through the exam.

Q **6.** Right before a test or exam, concentrate on what you *know*, not on what you don't know.

Q **7.** With other students in the class, form a study group. You can meet regularly to work on assignments, do readings, and prepare for exams.

V **8.** Whenever a teacher returns a paper, make sure that you get feedback that will enable you to do that type of assignment better the next time.

V **9.** If you're anxious about an oral examination, practice by having as many short, nonthreatening conversations with the instructor as you can.

V **10.** Before a test or exam, meet with the instructor to resolve any problems you're still having with the course material.

Compare and discuss your answers with three or four other people. If you've tried any of these strategies before, tell about your experiences.

READING V: "RECORDING NOTES IN LECTURES"

This reading focuses on a very common problem in academic studies—taking lecture notes. It will also help you take notes from textbooks. The reading is divided into three sections: "Selecting," "Organizing Layout," and "Ways to Organize Material in Notes." To do the activity, work with two partners. You have thirty minutes.

1. In groups of three, read the advice in the first section, "Selecting." As you read, examine the margin notes. What can you tell about how the writers made notes?
2. Look at the second section, "Organizing Layout." Cover up the margin notes on the left. As you read, make your own margin notes on the right side of the text. When you finish, compare your notes with those the writers included to see if you got the main ideas.
3. Individually, read the last section, "Ways to Organize Material in Notes." Write your own notes in the margin on the left. Compare your notes with those of your two partners and evaluate what you wrote.

Reading V

Recording Notes in Lectures

Selecting what to record

- Main ideas
- Use abbrev. & incompl. sentences
- Keep in mind Selection
- Framework!

Strategies

a. Be early → catch outline

b. Written notes

c. Emphasis & Repetition

Why Organize Layout?

1. Learn more

2. Easier to read & use

SELECTING

Since it is not usually possible to write down everything, it is necessary to pick out main ideas while the lecturer is speaking and to make notes. You will find that you need to use abbreviations and incomplete sentences at times to be an efficient note-taker. You will not need to write down everything that is said but only the key information.

Strategies which aid selection are:

a) Getting to class early to take down any outline that the lecturer may put on the blackboard or overhead.
b) Paying particular attention to the notes that the lecturer writes down in class.
c) Watching for the lecturer's use of emphasis and repetition.

ORGANIZING LAYOUT

You can improve your learning efficiency if you focus on making your notes as organized and as meaningful as possible when you are actually in the lecture. This focus on organization and meaning in the lecture has two benefits: 1) you will learn far more in the lecture itself and thus have much less to do on your own and 2) your notes will be much easier to read, edit and review after class.

Strategies which help are:

Overall Organization of Notes

a) Using clear lecture title headings and dates or numbers on each page.

b) Writing on only one side of the paper. You can then use the other side of the page to add information from the text, additional examples, or review questions.

c) Leaving a 2-3 inch margin on your notetaking paper and using it to keynote main ideas when you edit notes after class.

d) Storing lecture notes in loose leaf binders (as opposed to copybooks) so that you can add hand-outs, etc.

Ways to Organize Material in Notes

a) Leave lots of white space so that you can add comments later. Also the notes look better.

b) Select and set out headings and subheadings throughout the material by underlining, indenting, circling, etc., likely headings and subheadings. Otherwise the notes look like paragraphs or prose where little stands out.

c) Under headings and subheadings list important details with 'bullets' or numbers or letters.

d) Make graphs and diagrams *big* and *label* them sell so that they will be meaningful to you later on.

e) Decide on alternate notetaking structures for different kinds of material. For example when ideas are compared you can draw a line down the middle and collect the relevant details on each side. Another example would be branching 'flowcharts' for step-by-step decision making.

Strategies
a. Headings, dates, page #'s
b. one side only
c. Margin for keynotes
d. Loose leaf binder

a) leave space for comments.
b) select heading and subheading
c) list important details
d) Make graphs and diagram
e) decide notetaking structure

Interview Classroom Guests

To get more information for your study skills manual, you'll interview people with practical, tested advice about succeeding at college or university. While they're visiting your classroom, you'll also have an opportunity to ask them questions about your own suggestions.

1. Individually, prepare two or three questions you'll want to ask them. Check your questions with a classmate to make sure they're clear.
2. Remember to ask for clarification or explanation if necessary. With your teacher, discuss how to do this.
3. During the interviews, if you hear any good ideas, jot down key words to help you remember them. Don't try to write down everything, but do listen carefully, so that after the class, you can fill in your notes.

Research the Topic in the Library

As a final step in gathering information, each member of your group will use the library resources to research other strategies for the manual. In your own words, take notes on one valuable strategy and be prepared to explain it in detail to your group members.

WRITING THE MANUAL

Prewriting

Evaluate and Select Your Information Work with your group members to plan the manual.

1. List as many techniques as you can think of. Don't evaluate them now.
2. Discuss each one; ensure that everyone in the group understands how each technique is carried out. Decide which ones you want to include in the manual.
3. Decide who will be responsible for which technique or techniques. Make sure you understand precisely what each one involves.

Consider Your Audience and Your Purpose

1. Before you begin to write, consider who you're writing for and why you're writing. With your teacher, consider the following questions:

   a. Who will use the manual?
   b. For what purpose?

2. Consider how the answers to these questions will affect

   a. the kind of information you should include,
   b. the amount of information you should include,

c. how you should organize it, and

d. the kind of language necessary to make your suggestions clear to your readers.

Plan and Rehearse What You Want to Say

1. Individually, write point-form notes of the suggestions you will include in your part of the manual. Each technique should include the suggestion itself and the supporting detail.
2. In your group, decide how you will sequence the individual techniques as well as the support.
3. Individually, draw a tree sketch showing the information you wish to include and how you intend to organize it.
4. With a partner in your group, talk through your sketch. Discuss any gaps or problems in either the content or the organization.

Draft One: Focus on Information and Organization

Info — clarity
— completeness
— relivance

As you know, the purpose of the first draft is to get the important information on paper.

Write the first draft of your part of the manual. Double space. You might want to start with the part you know the best.

Conference with a Partner in Your Group   Read your partner's draft twice: once for information, and once for organization. Ask the following questions as you read:

Information
• Is everything relevant?
• Is there enough detail there so that readers will understand what to do and how to do it?

Organization
• Will readers be able to follow the ideas easily?
• Why or why not?

Discuss any problems. Then revise—add, delete, or reorder—as you wish. You might want to use arrows, boxes, scissors, and tape.

Draft Two: Organize for Your Reader

As a class, do the following:

1. Decide how you want to sequence the sections.
2. Decide how you want to use headings and different kinds of print to help your reader through your manual.

3. Develop an inform-and-focus section that introduces your readers to the manual and tells them precisely what to expect.
4. Write a conclusion that will encourage them to try the techniques you've included.

You now have a complete second draft.

Draft Three: Focus on Clarity and Accuracy

1. Read your own section aloud to help you find places that may confuse your reader. Listen and read to make sure that your ideas are coherently expressed. Revise any sections that you feel are unclear.
2. Work with a partner. Read each other your drafts, sentence by sentence, listening for clarity and coherence. Discuss any problems and revise as necessary. Make sure that you have a legible copy.
3. As a group, ensure that the sections are in the correct order and that the headings are consistent.
4. Rewrite each section neatly and legibly.
5. Assemble your manual. Arrange to have it copied and distributed to your class and any other designated recipients.

Chapter 5

Endangered Species

Animals are important for a variety of reasons: food, clothing, and maintaining the balance of nature to name but a few. A country might demonstrate this importance by having an animal as its national symbol. Canada, for example, is symbolized by the beaver; the United States, by the bald eagle; and the Soviet Union, by the standing bear. Another place we see the importance of animals is in children's literature. Aesop's fables tell about many different animals. One fable concerns a fox who can't reach the grapes because they're too high and then claims that they're probably sour anyway. We also have Aesop to thank for the story of the famous race between the tortoise and the hare.

This chapter will focus on animals, particularly *endangered animals*—those species that are declining in number to the point where their very existence is threatened. You'll consider the following areas:

which species are threatened with extinction,

the causes of the endangerment, and

what might be done to increase their chances of survival.

As you do the activities in this chapter, you'll have a chance to review and practice the following language skills and strategies:

- finding relevant information and ignoring the irrelevant
- summarizing
- recording information in tabular form
- giving oral presentations
- understanding and writing sentences containing causal relationships
- using library resources

THINK ABOUT THE TOPIC

Write brief, key-word answers to the questions below.

1. Does your country have an animal for its national symbol? If so, which one? Why do you think this particular animal was chosen?

2. What animal stories do you remember from your childhood?

3. In your country, what animals provide clothing?

4. Which animals do you eat? Are there any animals that you may not eat? If so, which ones? Why are you not allowed to eat them?

5. List any other contributions animals make to our lives, both directly and indirectly. Include both domestic and wild animals.

B. In groups of four or five, share and discuss your answers. Take turns, answering one question at a time.

Animals, then, are extremely important to people. And yet, many species of wild animals are in danger of decreasing drastically in number, even to the point of extinction. The result is that many countries are now concerned about preserving their wildlife—both plants and animals—what we call flora and fauna.

READING I: "ENDANGERED WILDLIFE—MAMMALS"

Your first reading, which begins on page 126, is an article from a booklet entitled *Endangered Wildlife in Canada*. To prepare to read it, write brief, key-word answers to the four questions below.

1. Use the titles of the booklet and the reading to predict what the article will be about.

2. Read the first and last paragraphs, adding to your predictions.

3a. Read sentence 1 of paragraph 2—the thesis statement of the paragraph. What will you read about in this paragraph?

b. Read the rest of the paragraph to check your predictions.
c. Draw a tree sketch of the information in the paragraph.

4. Read paragraph 3 to find the specific focus of this article.

In groups of three or four, check your answers. At the same time, clear up problems with new vocabulary.

Read the Text for Specific Information

1. For each endangered animal discussed in paragraphs 4 to 15, decide if the animal has become endangered *naturally*, or *as a result of human interference*. If the endangerment is attributable to *human* influence, decide if such influence has been *direct* because of outright killing or *indirect* as a result of people's actions on the environment. Then write the name of the animal in the appropriate column below. If you can't tell from the article, put the name in the last column, "Can't Tell."

SOURCES OF ENDANGERMENT			
NATURAL	HUMAN		CAN'T TELL
	DIRECT	INDIRECT	

2. In groups of three or four, share and discuss your answers. If necessary, use the text to help you reach a consensus.

Reading I

Endangered Wildlife—Mammals

by N. S. Novakowski
Staff Specialist (Mammalogy)
Canadian Wildlife Service

1   In Canada there has generally been little concern, except by local conservation organizations, for animals which are in danger of extinction. Historically we have the classic example of the prairie buffalo, which with the exception of one or two concerned individuals might have become extinct. Although the buffalo is a well-known example there are many others, smaller forms generally, which also had the same fate as the buffalo. However, rather than to dwell in the historic past it is important that we outline what the situation is with numerous of our present living forms and try to make the necessary and important decisions for their preservation.

2   An animal becomes endangered or actually becomes extinct in two important ways. Firstly, there is an evolutionary type of extinction or reduction in numbers in which animals either adapt to a changing environment or become so specialized in their requirements that they cannot contend with the changing environment. Thus the environment and the animal populations living in it in a natural state are in a constant state of evolution. Secondly, there is human influence. In many instances, human habitation and human requirements have utilized habitat which was at one time the natural range of many species. When these animals became competitive or interfered with the pastoral or industrial pursuits of the human population they were either eliminated or forced to seek new habitat, much of which has been marginal to their needs. As a case in point, the bighorn sheep ranged from the Rocky Mountains east to the Black Hills of South Dakota. Now the sheep exist in isolated pockets generally in national parks in Canada and in limited numbers in the United States. Their former range on the prairies has been usurped by agricultural pursuits, both farming and ranching. It goes without saying that areas such as national parks and wildlife sanctuaries play an important part in the preservation of rare or endangered species.

3   Generally, small mammals such as various subspecies of rodents are difficult to categorize as endangered. These

animals commonly have very little mobility and exist in very restricted habitats which might be endangered by some natural catastrophe or human error or ignorance. Instead of trying to deal with them, I will concern myself with the larger mammals in Canada that might be classed as endangered.

4   Roosevelt's elk exists in a small area in British Columbia on Vancouver Island. It has been completely eliminated in mainland British Columbia. Huntable populations remain in the three northwestern states in the United States. Numbers in Canada are small, however, and require total protection for some time to come.

5   Although the Rocky Mountain bighorn is now restricted in its distribution because of the encroachment of habitation, sufficient populations exist in the American and Canadian national parks so the species is not entirely endangered. Furthermore, there have been some attempts by United States wildlife authorities to transplant the Rocky Mountain bighorn into parts of the range it formerly occupied in the Rocky Mountain chain.

6   The California bighorn is in a different situation, however, as it is restricted in distribution to the southern parts of British Columbia and to parts of the State of California in the United States. Attempts are being made to isolate the known populations into protected sanctuaries. The biggest danger to their survival in British Columbia is the use of California bighorn sheep range by cattle. This problem is being slowly solved.

7   The wood bison is a very rare subspecies and relative of the plains bison. When recently rediscovered, the total population of wood bison was in the neighbourhood of 200 animals. Two groups of animals have been removed from Wood Buffalo National Park and one of these has been transplanted on their historic range west of Great Slave Lake where they are thriving. As this subspecies once ranged from the Great Slave Lake and Wood Buffalo National Park areas west to the Mackenzie Mountains and along the Rocky Mountain chain to Colorado, it is anticipated that future transplants may be made in many areas of this historic range.

8   The northern kit fox is probably extinct in Canada but has not entirely vanished from some of the northern states in the United States bordering on the Great Central Plains. Rehabilitation appears to be still possible, but some form of sanctuary must be provided for this species if it is to thrive in Canada. At present none exists.

9   The Vancouver Island wolf is very near extinction. It is holding its own at the present time and indications are that it will probably not increase further in numbers because of encroaching civilization. Protection in parks and sanctuaries is a necessity.

10   The eastern cougar is so secretive that only unconfirmed sightings from scattered points throughout eastern Canada and especially from New Brunswick indicate that it may still exist. In case the eastern cougar has survived civilization's advances, only immediate and effective conservation efforts can keep it from becoming extinct.

11   The Newfoundland pine marten was once well distributed throughout Newfoundland but was subjected to heavy trapping pressure and is now restricted to isolated areas throughout the island. Marten are almost always vulnerable to any trapping because they fall victim to traps set for squirrels or other members of the weasel family.

12   The black-footed ferret is generally associated with the black-tailed prairie dog in the most southerly areas of

Saskatchewan and Alberta. Only a few prairie dog colonies are protected and the black-footed ferret suffers the same fate as the prairie dog as a result of poisoning campaigns to destroy the latter. The black-footed ferret is now nearly extinct in Canada.

13   The barren ground grizzly is now generally protected but sparsely distributed on the barrens.

14   The Arctic hare once ranged throughout Newfoundland. But the varying hare, introduced by man to the island in 1864 and again around 1900, increased greatly in numbers and became a serious competitor of the Arctic hare. The moose, introduced in 1904, further depleted food supplies, and the Arctic hare ultimately was reduced to low populations in interior highlands. Indiscriminate logging practices, however, are said to be creating much ideal Arctic hare habitat. It may be that this exploitation of Newfoundland's forests will allow the Arctic hare to expand both in numbers and range.

15   The sea otter was exterminated in Canadian waters by fur hunters near the turn of the century. In July, 1969, about 30 sea otters from Alaska were released off the northwestern coast of Vancouver Island in an attempt to reestablish the species in Canada.

16   The precarious situation of most of the species mentioned above has been caused by excessive exploitation by trapping or by the demands of an uninformed public exerting pressure for "control" programs on government agencies. Hopefully this is now a part of history and we can look forward to more enlightened management. In the meantime, research on these valuable and interesting species will be accelerated.

17   In general Canada has been singularly lucky in that few of its major species have been lost and it has not been deluged with unwanted and unneeded exotic species. It is obvious that our native wildlife requires space and habitat to maintain itself. We cannot long expect to persecute those animals which we selfishly designate as harmful to our economic interests and expect the natural environment to remain healthy. As a civilized nation we should be capable of more than passing platitudes about the animals that share this country with us. At the same time, whatever methods required to rehabilitate the animals now in danger of extinction should receive the full support of all people. There is undoubtedly a certain level beyond which animals that are hunted or persecuted will not recover. At the same time, there is also a level at which animals given full protection and wise management can recover to stages where they can be more readily seen, appreciated or otherwise utilized. Unfortunately, there is very little legislation to protect the animals that I have discussed here. This appears to be a first step in the rehabilitation of many of these animals. Public awareness is also another important step before legislation is produced, and each individual must decide for himself that these steps are necessary and desirable.

CHAPTER 5 WRITING TASK: MAGAZINE ARTICLE

Because the topic of endangered species is so vast, your writing task will focus only on how people have jeopardized the existence of various animal species.

You are a writer for an international nature magazine for high school students. Because of your concern for the environment, you've decided to write an article on the ways people have endangered animals. The article should include the major human causes of this endangerment and their effects on particular species. Since this is an international magazine, the article should also include examples from various parts of the world. Remember, your purpose is to inform your readers of the situation and convince them of its seriousness.

READING II: "COMING SOON: MASS EXTINCTIONS"

Prepare to Read

The following reading, which is really an interview, was taken from *International WILDLIFE*, a magazine "dedicated to the wise use of the earth's resources." The interviewer is Robert Brock; the interviewee, Peter Raven, an internationally renowned botanist—a scientist who studies plants.

Below you'll find the title, summary statement, and introduction. With a partner, use these three sections of the text to predict as much as you can about what the article will say. Also, determine the attitude of the person interviewed. Make key-word notes in the margin. You have five minutes. When you finish, discuss your notes with another pair of students; then, with your teacher.

Reading II

Coming Soon: Mass Extinctions

Botanist Peter Raven looks into his crystal ball and sees the greatest animal die-off since the dinosaurs—all in our lifetime.

Inside a huge geodesic dome in St. Louis, a computer controls conditions to simulate almost every climate on Earth. The structure is a sophisticated green-house—the centerpiece of the Missouri Botanical Garden—and plants inside represent ecosystems from around the world. Only a small sample of the Earth's flora can be contained in these protected environs, but the garden's director, botanist Peter Raven, has emerged as one of the world's most articulate authorities on protecting all plants—in their natural environment. Recently, *International WILDLIFE* interviewer Robert G. Brock asked Raven about the destruction of tropical forests and the extinction of species they contain. The resulting look into the future paints a disturbing picture.

Reprinted by permission of the National Wildlife Federation, from *International WILDLIFE*, Ottawa, 1985.

Read to Get the General Idea: Match Questions and Answers

The purpose of this next activity is to help you practice getting the general idea before looking for specific information.

Below are the six questions Brock asked Raven. They are followed by Raven's answers. Read the questions. Then read the answers to find out which one belongs to each question. Do not read the entire answer carefully; instead, try reading only the first sentence or two to get the general idea.

Put the appropriate question number on the line beside the answer. You have fifteen minutes to complete this task. Then compare your answers with others in the class.

1. *Q:* You have warned that by the year 2010 our world will change drastically. What specifically do you foresee?
2. *Q:* Are you suggesting that the rain forests will be gone sometime early in the next century?
3. *Q:* In your estimation, where can we expect this destruction to occur?
4. Q: As these small and medium-sized forests disappear, what will we lose?
5. Q: What can we do? Intensify conservation efforts? Protect areas of the forest with parks?
6. **Q:** What role do the growing populations of poor people in the tropics play?

Answers

_____ Trying to save species by putting aside parks and reserves is worthwhile on the short-term, but on the long-term it simply won't work. With current populations and the very poor lot of most of the people, they will go right on using up whatever is available regardless of whether you call it a park or not. Fifty-two percent of the world's people—2.4 billion people—will be added to the world population according to the Population Reference Bureau. That increase alone equals the entire world population for the year 1950, and most of them will be added in tropical countries. By the year 2000, three out of five people in the world—60 percent of the total population—will live in the less-developed countries.

Perhaps even more profoundly significant is the distribution of poverty. In order for those people to get anything at all for their families, whether it's simply food or the basis to advance themselves, they have to take something from the forests. A single man with an axe can clear a hectare of forest in twelve days and there are waves of people doing just that.

_____ As the deforestation of the tropics accelerates, an event will occur within our lifetimes whose parallel can only be found some 65 million years ago with the extinction of the dinosaurs. We're talking about an extinction of that magnitude or greater, involving plants, animals, fish and microorganisms. We don't really know how many kinds of organisms there actually are in the tropics. We think that the 500,000 tropical organisms we have named or have knowledge of represent less than a sixth of what's there.

_____ A major portion of the diversity of the tropics. On the island of Madagascar, only 7 percent of the land is still left in natural vegetation. But 6,000 to 7,000 plants and perhaps 125,000 living things live nowhere else on Earth except in that small area. Lemurs, for example, a group of primitive primates of considerable interest to us, currently exist only in Madagascar, and they are in immediate danger. In fact, nearly all of the world's primates, those animals most closely related to ourselves, live in the tropical regions of Earth and all are seeing their habitats diminished.

_____ Not exactly. It may take a little longer. In 1975 the area of existing tropical lowland moist forest was estimated by the Food and Agriculture Organization (F.A.O.) of the United Nations at 9.35 million square kilometers, about half of its original extent worldwide. The F.A.O. further estimated in 1982 that 100,000 square kilometers was being deforested each year. But the National Research Council Committee on Research Priorities in Tropical Biology, which I chaired, estimated in 1980 that the *total* rate of disturbance is 250,000 to 300,000 square kilometers—an area roughly the size of Great Britain—each year. At that rate the world's tropical forests would be disturbed or destroyed in something like 36 years. Both of these predictions, however, assume no acceleration, which is false.

_____ Small and medium-sized forests in vast areas of the world—most of Africa, all of Southeast Asia and bordering islands like the Philippines, Indonesia, New Guinea, Central America, the West Indies, and much of South America—will be totally destroyed by very early in the next century, even though relatively large blocks in the western Amazon basin in South America and the Congo basin of Africa may be persisting for another 50 years if they are lucky.

_____ About two-thirds of the destruction of the rain forests is attributable to slash-and-burn agriculture, where poor people use the land for a while and then move on when it is depleted. The forests themselves are productive only because the trees have the ability to lock up nutrients. The soils are actually relatively poor. When the trees are cut, nutrients are depleted rapidly by annual crops. We should learn to clear only the most fertile land. In other places we should learn to harvest from the forest itself or to use agroforestry to mix tree growth and agriculture. In this way, we can sustain the land's usefulness.

We need to immediately address the legitimate claims of extremely poor people in order to slow down the degree to which they are destroying the whole works. We would be well advised to link our foreign aid directly to the very poor, truly needy nations to alleviate the worst problems. It is not only the humane thing to do. It is the single most important thing to do in terms of saving species immediately. We must get the tropical countries into a mode of stable, sustainable productivity based on their own resources. Until and unless we are able to do that, we're losing the whole game, not only in terms of species survival, but also in terms of the economic survival of America and the rest of the developed world as well.

Read for Specific Information

A. Now reread the interview to answer the following six questions. (The question numbers correspond to the numbers in the question-and-answer matching.) Write brief notes in the spaces provided.

1. Which groups will suffer because of deforestation in the tropics?

2. In this paragraph, Raven compares the total size of the area of tropical forest being harmed each year to the area the size of Great Britain. Why do you think he did this?

3. Using the map on page 134, mark the following:

- those areas that will be destroyed early in the twenty-first century
- those areas that will be destroyed later in that century

Use a different way of marking each.

4a. Which large group of animals inhabits the tropical areas of the earth?

b. Which subgroup of these animals is severely endangered even now?

5a. What short-term solution is offered in paragraph 5?

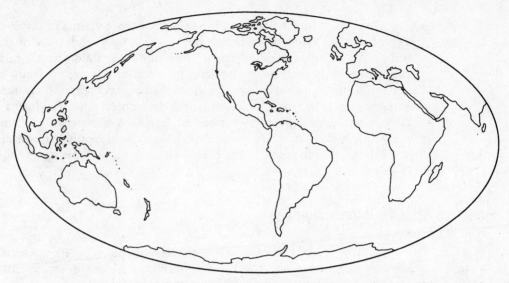

Reprinted from *Nelson's Canadian School Atlas*, copyright 1958 by Nelson Canada, a Division of International Thomson Limited, Scarborough, Canada. Reprinted with permission from the publisher.

b. In your own words, briefly explain why it won't work as a long-term solution.

c. What factor makes the situation even worse? How?

6a. What, in your own words, is "slash-and-burn agriculture"?

b. Complete the diagram below showing how this kind of farming **harms** the forest.

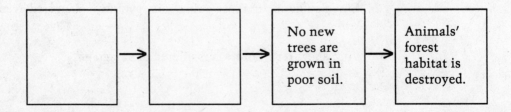

c. What long-term solution does Raven propose?

B. In groups of three or four, compare your answers. Resolve difficulties by referring to the text.

READING III: "OUR GARBAGE IS KILLING THE GIANT TURTLES"

You will now consider some of these endangered species in more detail. The first article you'll read concerns the giant turtle. As you read, look for and highlight the following information:

- where it's found,
- the extent of the decrease in population,
- past and present reasons for the decline,
- possible rehabilitative measures and outlook for the future.

There may be some information you cannot find. You have ten minutes.

Take Notes in Your Own Words

1. With your teacher, take point-form notes on this information. To do this, create a chart using the headings below, and put the information in the appropriate spaces.

ANIMAL	LOCATION	DECLINE IN POPULATION	CAUSES	POSSIBLE REHABILITATIVE MEASURES AND PROGNOSIS

2. Mark the giant turtle and its habitat on your map on page 134.

Reading III

Our Garbage Is Killing the Giant Turtles

Popular name
   Leatherback turtle
Formal name
   Dermochelys coriacea
Population
   An estimated 40,000 reproducing
   females world-wide
Habitat
   All the world's oceans except the
   Antarctic
Adult size
   2.5 metres long, 2.7 metres reach,
   680 kg in weight
Size at birth
   5 cm (2 inches) long, 33 grams
   (1 ounce) in weight
Diet
   Jellyfish

By JACK MILLER
Toronto Star

There are little turtles, medium-sized turtles, big turtles and a few huge turtles.

And then there's the leatherback turtle, which makes all the others look like pikers by growing to 2.5 metres (well over 8 feet) from nose to tail. It measures even longer sideways—2.7 metres from flipper tip to flipper tip.

More amazing still is its weight: up to 680 kilograms (almost 1,400 pounds).

The leatherback is more than twice the size of the giant tortoises found on the Galapagos Islands, which most people think of when anyone mentions huge shelled creatures than can walk on land. If this were a fish, people would call it a small whale.

The leatherback is not only the biggest but also the rarest of all the great sea turtles. It's almost like a look at the most ancient of history. Turtles are reptiles and back when the biggest reptiles—the dinosaurs—were roaming the earth, turtles were roaming the seas. That was more than 100 million years ago and the great sea turtles, with the leatherbacks by far the greatest, now are one of the last available glimpses of what life probably was like in pre-caveman days.

Mature females

This last look may be lost soon. It's hard to know how many of these elusive creatures survive but the latest estimate, made after the discovery of a major nesting area in French Guiana, is that there are 40,000 mature females in all the world's oceans. Only mature females are seen as a rule, because they have to come ashore to lay their eggs. The males, and females who are too young to mate, stay in the water and sometimes travel amazing distances. One that was spotted laying eggs was found to have been tagged earlier at a spot 2,896 kilometres (1,800 miles) away.

The turtle is called the leatherback because this describes it fairly well. Its shell is not bone-hard or horn-hard like those of other turtles. Instead, it's made up of a leathery skin over a 5-cm-thick (2-inch) layer of a tough, oily, cartilage-like substance that has small plates of bone embedded in it.

The leatherback is different from other turtles in another key way— its head grows so big that the creature can't pull it back inside its shell when threatened.

But despite the softer shell and unguarded head, the leatherback does not seem to be threatened much by anything living in the world's oceans. It's simply so huge that few creatures care to tangle with it.

Occasionally, a shark may take a bite. Even more rarely, a killer whale may make a meal of one. And, occasionally, jaguars have been known to attack the great females when they're most vulnerable—making their laborious way across nesting beaches on South America's ocean coasts, where they scratch out nests in the sand to lay eggs.

But modern times have created a peril for the leatherback that no one could have predicted. The turtles are mistaking a certain type of human garbage for their special brand of turtle food, and it's causing them a lot of trouble.

These turtles spend most of their life on or near the surface of the world's oceans, usually in the warm areas near the equator, and they find dinner is served almost non-stop there by nature.

Dinner is jellyfish, which float along the ocean surface, sometimes packed so closely together that they look like a lace tablecloth.

That's the reason you won't see a leatherback turtle in the Metro Zoo. "Jellyfish are poison to people," explains zoo spokesman Toby Stiles. "They sting, and badly, so it's not practical to expect our staff to handle them every day to feed one of our residents."

However, clear plastic bags—which civilized people use by the millions now—can look a lot like jellyfish floating in the ocean. And plastic bags get tossed out of ships with other garbage dumped at sea. And leatherback turtles have been eating them.

Again and again, dead leatherbacks have been examined and found to have their digestive tracts clogged with such plastic. It's been estimated up to 44 percent of all today's adult leatherbacks are suffering or dying from this.

They can also find other trouble. They become entangled in fishing nets at sea and occasionally a fisherman will harpoon one, either out of ignorance or neglect. This is against the law almost everywhere, however, so it doesn't happen often.

Leatherbacks are different in another way. Other turtles are cold-blooded, but these giants maintain a body temperature of 25.5 degrees Celsius (77 F). This makes it possible for them to swim in cold water as well as warm, so they're seen all the way from the coasts of Alaska and Norway and the Soviet Union in the north to Chile and Argentina in the south. They've been seen along Canada's maritime provinces and off British Columbia, but never in winter.

Thousands of eggs

These living bits of the planet's history have survived all these eons mainly because the few that made it to adulthood were big and tough enough to be safe from almost any predator. This let the females live for years so they could lay thousands of eggs apiece.

But baby leatherbacks face terrible odds. They hatch from eggs laid in nests dug as much as a metre deep in the beach sand, and when they push their way out, they scurry madly for the water—hundreds at a time in a desperate stampede. But at that stage, they're only 5 cm long, and they run a deadly gamut through dogs, birds and crabs that feast wildly on them. Very few make it, but those few have been enough to sustain the population once they became adults.

Now plastic bags, of all things, may decimate the adult population and unhinge a balance of nature that has lasted more than 100 million years.

READING IV: "SEA OTTER'S BEAUTY WAS ALMOST ITS DEMISE" (pp. 139–140)

READING V: "LOGGING CREWS THREATEN ORANGUTANS" (pp. 141–142)

READING VI: "SANCTUARIES MAY BE RHINO'S LAST HOPE" (pp. 143–144)

The next activity, which involves reading, extracting relevant information, and summarizing it for your group, will give you more information for your magazine article. There are three readings, focusing on three endangered animals: the sea otter, the orangutan, and the great Indian rhinoceros. Form groups of three and distribute the readings. Then carry out the steps below. You have approximately fifty minutes to complete the entire activity. Stay within your time limits.

1. In the text, find and highlight the same kind of information about these animals that you found out about the giant turtle. (10 minutes)
2. In your own words, take point-form notes on this information. Put it in the appropriate spaces in the chart you used before. Begin a new one if necessary. Indicate its habitat on the map. Add any other information you think would be useful for your writing task. (10 minutes)
3. Regroup and take turns telling your partners about your animal. Talk rather than dictate the information to them. Answer any questions. (15 to 20 minutes)
4. Go over your notes, making sure that you have the information you need for your writing task. (5 to 10 minutes)

Remember who your partners are. You'll regroup later.

Reading IV

Sea Otter's Beauty Was Almost Its Demise

Name:
 Sea otter
Formal name:
 Enhydra lutris
Population:
 350-plus in Canadian waters
Habitat:
 Shallow North Pacific coastal
 waters
Diet:
 Shellfish, abalone and sea urchins
Size:
 Up to 1.5 metres (5 feet) long,
 weighing 28 kilograms (more
 than 60 pounds)

By JACK MILLER
Toronto Star

Alive, the sea otter is as cute as a button, but dead, he's beautiful. That means he's worth more dead than alive, which explains why there aren't many still living.

The beauty in question is only skin deep, but that's all it takes to wipe out one of the brightest beasts of the sea.

It's their fur that's special. People used to kill them for it. Both the fresh-water and salt-water otters are relatives of the weasel, putting them in the family that produces mink and ermine, which are great furs. But the sea otter hide is what you might call super-mink.

Once these jokers of the ocean coast were as thick as fleas (which they don't have) all around the Pacific's rim, from southern California up to British Columbia and around Alaska and the Aleutian Islands and down along Siberia to the south tip of Japan.

But their fur was so magnificent—thick, silky and warm—that wealthy Chinese mandarins, in particular, paid top dollar for it. So from the middle of the 18th century to the beginning of this one, an estimated half million sea otters were slaughtered and their skins sold to Russian, European and American fur traders, who then sold them to the mandarins.

At the peak of the killing, the sea otter was the most expensive fur in the world.

At the start of this century, the entire surviving population of the breed was estimated at between 1,000 and 2,000.

In 1929, at Checleset Bay, near the village of Kyuquot on the sea side of Vancouver Island near its north tip, the last known sea otter in Canadian waters was shot and killed—for money.

What a shame. They are so bright. They use tools—the only mammals in all the world's oceans to do that. Their diet is shellfish, and while they have developed big back teeth to break open shells, they are smart enough to figure out an easier way. An otter will get, for instance, an oyster or a spiny sea urchin and, while floating on its back in shallow water, place a flat rock on its chest. The otter then puts the shellfish on the rock and smashes it with another rock—just like a human hammering a walnut out of its shell.

Then the otter floats on its back, using its chest like a table, nibbling its newly uncovered dinner delicately, a bit at a time.

That floating-on-the-back posture has always been a favorite of the sea otter. They can be seen clutching babies on their chests to keep them up out of the ocean's chill. Sometimes they'll swim into a kelp field and wrap some of the seaweed around themselves. Experts assume they do this to keep from drifting out to sea once they drifted off to sleep, but it really looks like humans pulling up the covers under their chins for the night.

They're playful, too. Lots of animals play as babies, but otters keep doing it through their adult lives, as well.

And they can show deeper human-style feelings. When frightened or hurt or sad, they'll let out a cry of distress so high-pitched and powerful you can hear it a kilometre away. And when a baby dies, sea otter mothers are known to grieve so deeply that they'll keep the little body clutched on their chests for weeks, trying vainly to coax it back to life.

No matter—they were slaughtered anyway for that beautiful fur.

It's a remarkable fur—it has to be, to keep them alive. The breed had evolved somewhat from its fresh-water cousins by growing bigger, and by changing its hind feet into a form of flippers (which let it swim better but made it awkward on land, so it stayed almost full-time in the water). But it never developed a layer of fat or blubber under its skin to keep it warm, the way the dolphins and whales did, so it needs that fur to keep from getting a chill and dying in frigid water.

The insulation is achieved by air trapped between the strands of the fur, but this works only if the fur was clean. If it becomes soiled or oily, the hairs mat together, leaving no air between them, providing too little warmth for survival. So the sea otter spends a lot of time preening and cleaning its coat, which keeps the coat gleaming clean and glossy thick—the kind a wealthy human would pay a fortune for.

Abandons coast

And so by the end of 1929, when there were only a few sea otters left in the world, there were none at all left along Canada's Pacific coast.

Yet oddly, almost half a century later, another human activity that many considered far worse was to start to compensate for Canada's loss. The United States decided to carry out a test nuclear explosion on Amchitka Island off Alaska in the early 1970s and the state government, knowing some surviving sea otters were there, suggested a few be caught and moved down to Vancouver Island's Checleset Bay, the breeds's one-time haven. Twenty-nine came to Canada this way in 1969, protected from people by law at last. Alaska sent another 14 from its own waters in 1970 and another 46 in 1972.

No one hunts the sea otter here now, except for the occasional killer whale or shark if they swim too far from their home shallows. About the only threat left from man would be an accident like an oil spill, which could mat their fur and cause them to freeze.

Spots faces

Guarded by law everywhere, the sea otter has come back strongly in other places—there are 2,000 now in California, maybe 15,000 in Russia, and as many as 160,000 in Alaska.

In Canada, they're still scarce, but the signs are hopeful. Observers, careful to hide in the woods and not startle them, have more and more often been able to spot the beaver-like faces, described by one expert as "80 per cent whiskers, 20 per cent nose," poking out of the water.

The estimated numbers in Canada, after some lean and worrisome seasons, climbed past the 350 mark this season. They may start moving out from Checleset Bay soon, fanning up and down the coast, just like the old days— barring any oil spills.

Reading V

Logging Crews Threaten Orangutans

Popular name:
  Orangutan
Formal name:
  Pongo pygmaeus
Adult size:
  Males 4.5 feet tall, 160 pounds;
  females 80 pounds
Reach:
  Eight feet, fingertip to fingertip
Diet:
  Fruit, great variety
Home:
  Treetops in rain forests of Borneo
  and Sumatra
Surviving numbers:
  Estimated 150,000, shrinking fast
  as forests cut

By JACK MILLER
Toronto Star

Don't think of the orangutan as a "species" of "animal" that's endangered and needs saving: Think of it as an ancestor who deserves respect for making the human race possible.

Even the name does not denote an animal. "Orang" means "man" and "Utan" means "of the woods."

The latest theory (admittedly controversial) is that man did not evolve from a family of great apes that included gorillas, chimpanzees and orangutans. Instead, it says two evolving families branched off from the orangutan long ago. One of them included the gorillas and chimps, the other included the caucasians, blacks and orientals—in a word, us.

This would make the chimps and gorillas something like hairy cousins to people instead of forefathers, with the orangutan the grandaddy of us all.

But if logging crews on Sumatra and Borneo don't slow down, such talk will be just academic rambling. There won't be any more long-armed redheads using their amazing 2.4 metre (8-foot) reach to sweep from branch to branch under the dark canopy of the great rain forests; no more living shadows swinging like prehistoric Tarzans, 20 metres (70 feet) above the ground. What's being done there to the big trees could cut the trunk out from under humanity's family tree.

Each day on those huge islands north of Australia, the lumber industry's snarling chainsaws rip bare another swath of countryside the size of Massachusetts. The part of the world where orangutans can live as they did in the pre-people era is shrinking fast.

Hopes for this solitary simian have been on a roller coaster in the past few years, riding up and down. At one point, it was believed there were no more than 2,000 left in the wild, hidden by the treetops from prying eyes. Then better search methods found the woods were full of them and the population estimate rocketed to 150,000. But this brought no great glee to naturalists, because they could see the woods were being hacked away—specialized woods in a specialized climate, the only place in the world (except zoos) where orangutans are found.

While naturalists worry about keeping the race alive, they marvel as well at how many ways these creatures are like people (or perhaps, how many habits we have inherited from our most distant living ancestors).

Orangutans may be the smartest of all animals, with an intelligence rated equal to that of a 5-year-old child. They use tools. They learn by doing. They rustle up material and weave themselves a new nest in a new treetop each night (no permanent homes for them). They

---

make faces: bemused, happy, sad, curious, disgusted, sometimes obviously bored stiff. They spoil their kids.

As with people, no two orangutans look alike and each has its own personality. And you can tell the males from the females at a glance—the men are taller (up to 4.5 feet) and up to twice as heavy (160 pounds, compared to 80-pound females). The males grow beautiful, flowing moustaches and beards (and get bald spots on top of their heads); the females grow breasts where breasts belong, and cradle their babies in their arms while nursing them.

Their skeletons are basically similar to those of humans, with the exception that their arms are proportionally longer and stronger, and their legs shorter and weaker. They were the first tailless trapeeze artists, made to fly rather than run.

Lots of people have seen orangutans on television as super-cute, big-eyed, sweet-looking babies. But those same people might be amazed at how different some of the race's most impressive members look. Adult males from Borneo and Sumatra seem to be almost different species. The Sumatran adult male is thinner, has an almost-human face and a blond or white beard and moustache. The red-haired Bornean male, by age 15, has grown a huge ridge of dark-skinned soft tissue that protrudes from his forehead and cheeks, framing his face. He also grows a big skin pouch that hangs under his chin, hiding the upper chest. Orangutans are one of the most silent of animals, but when the full-grown Bornean male does decide to make a noise—when he feels the urge to call out for female company, for instance—the pouch acts as a

resonating chamber and gives his grunting call such volume and authority that no one who hears it ever forgets it.

Orangutan females, however, are not as easy to impress as human listeners. They come to visit only if they feel like it. Once they arrive, though, they'll often flirt outra-geously.

Whether this fascinating life style will continue much longer depends mainly on efforts to preserve parts of the rain forests as habitats for the orangutans. The most promising effort is being promoted by the World Wildlife Fund, which wants to establish a reserve of 168,755 hectares in the Sarawak region in north-west Borneo. It's to be called the Lanjak-Entimau Orangutan Sanctuary. The orangs are there. The trees are there. And life for both of them goes on—for now.

Reading VI

Sanctuaries May Be Rhino's Last Hope

Name:
   Great Indian Rhinoceros
Formal name:
   Rhinoceros Unicoris Linnaeus
Habitat:
   Tiny shrinking ranges in Nepal
   and northeast India's Assam area
Size of Litter:
   One is enough
Size at Birth:
   Up to two feet tall and 125
   pounds
Adult size:
   Up to six feet tall at shoulders, up
   to 6,900 pounds
Surviving numbers:
   An estimated 1,000 to 1,100

By JACK MILLER
Toronto Star

The biggest mammal that ever walked the earth—the greatest land animal to give birth to its babies as humans do—was a rhinoceros.

It was as long as a school bus and its shoulders were as high as two school buses stacked one on top of the other and it may have roamed where Toronto is now.

This was not like any rhinoceros we can find in the world today. But then, hundreds of kinds of rhinos were like nothing we can find today. They started 60 million years ago in North America, roamed from Alaska down to Mexico, from the Atlantic Ocean to the Pacific and all around the Great Lakes. And they spread in time (probably by way of the ancient Bering Strait ice bridge) to almost all of Asia, Europe and Africa. But now they've all vanished from the scene except for five fading varieties on a few pinpoint ranges in Africa and south-central Asia.

Yet even what little is left of this once-magnificent family of creatures is second in size, among land animals, only to the elephant, which its long-ago cousin could dwarf.

The great Indian rhinoceros stands 6 feet, 6 inches tall (almost 2 metres) and, like all rhinos, it's much longer than it is high. It weight a massive 3,130 kilograms (6,900 pounds). It's the tallest surviving cousin, but the white rhino of Africa, which stands 1.8 metres (6 feet), is even heavier at 3,600 kg (8,000 pounds).

Incredibly, for all this bulk, for all their ungainly look, stumpy legs, and oversized heads, these beasts walk almost delicately on their toes (three on each foot) and can run as fast (though not as long) as a racehorse. They can chase down anything that annoys them at a terrifying 60 kilometres an hour (40 miles per hour).

It's no surprise that most things try not to annoy them. Even giant Bengal tigers have been gored on the long, rock-hard horns of mother Indian rhinos, then tossed aside like rag dolls, when the rhinos thought their babies were threatened.

Unless they feel threatened, though, the rhinos don't go picking fights. They're not man-eaters, or even meat-eaters. They just like to browse, eating grass and leaves. The females are among the animal world's best mothers—they keep their babies with them for years, sometimes until they're almost as big as themselves, teaching the kids everything they'll need to know to survive.

Great Indian rhino babies are born 2 feet tall and up to 125 pounds. Considering the ordeal such a delivery must be, the mothers could not be blamed for turning on the kids—but they don't.

The two-horned black rhinocer-

Reprinted with permission—The Toronto Star Syndicate.

os of Africa is the most plentiful variety left, which hardly seems fair, since it's the meanest of them all: It hates every other living creature so much that it even shuns its brothers and sisters and roams alone.

The white rhino, which used to be found in a few spots in north and south Africa, has not been seen lately in the north, and may be on the way to joining its hundreds of old-time cousin species as a memory.

The little Sumatran rhino (the only one with hair) is rare now and the small Javan variety has almost disappeared.

And far to the east, in a few tiny enclaves squeezed up against the Himalayas in Nepal and in the Assam region on India's far northeast frontier, somewhere around 1,000 great Indian rhinos are fighting to keep alive the most distinctive branch of this once-huge family tree.

Living tank

Most rhinos have smooth skins, but the great Indian looks like what humanity has come to expect a rhinoceros to be—a living tank, built for battle, almost a visual relic of the dinosaur age.

Massively thick skin covers its sides and shoulders and haunches, looking like overlapping plates of heavy armor, with bumps along the "seams" that look like rivets. Its eyes are shielded behind folds of that skin. Its legs look too strong and thick to be deflected in their charge. And the great spear-like horn projecting from the top of its long snout may be the most unstoppable weapon in all the arsenals of the animal kingdom—a blow from it, with a charging rhino behind it, can bowl over a car or small truck.

Rhinos have the hardest horns anywhere. Other animals' horns have a hard outer shell of a substance called keratin (like fingernail tissue), with a core of softer material. But the rhino horn is all keratin—the tight-packed fibres as hard as stone and a lot tougher.

Roaring into battle, the great Indian rhinoceros looks invincible.

But it's not. The skin may be thick but it's soft enough to be scratched easily. The eyes see so poorly through their armored slits that an adversary can get within a few metres of it unseen.

Maybe the least known of all the rhino's weaknesses, that giant horn is attached almost loosely to the big hump on the snout end of the skull—a hard enough blow has been known to knock it off. If this happens, the rhino can grow a new one.

But the poachers who ignore conservation laws to hunt the great animals never seem to think of somehow drugging the animal and stealing this weapon and leaving it to grow another. Instead, they kill for rhinoceros horn, which can be ground up and sold for twice the price of gold per ounce, because it's supposed to be a magic cure for almost every malady, including sexual failings. (It's not, but the buyers go on believing and paying and encouraging the hunters.)

Human tormentors

Stiff laws in India and Nepal now are silencing most of the poachers' guns, but farms and their grazing cattle keep cutting into the Great Indians' feeding lands. Now and then, when one of the animals wanders hungry into a farmer's greenery for a snack, the people can get excited and shout and startle it.

The question now is whether eight sanctuaries set up in India and a big 900-square-kilometre one in Nepal can keep the Indian breed from vanishing like the others. The two governments are trying to make it work and at last word, the numbers at least had stopped shrinking.

Appealing to the Reader

In all these readings, the writer tried to appeal to your sympathy for the endangered animals. In this activity you will examine how he did this. You have twenty minutes to complete questions 1 and 2 below and twenty minutes to complete questions 4 and 5.

1. Find two or three other people who read the same article as you.
2. Together, reread the article, highlighting any places in the text where the writer's information or particular choice of words appears directed at the reader's emotions or feelings. In each case, discuss what feelings you think the writer wanted to elicit in the reader. How effective was the attempt, do you think?
3. Regroup with your partners from the previous activity and tell them about your article.
4. In your magazine article, do you think you might find it useful to appeal to the sympathies of your readers? Explain. Can you think of any situations in which this technique might *not* be suitable?

Library Research Assignment

This assignment will give you more information for your article. It will also better acquaint you with the resources in the library. In groups of three or four, read your instructions carefully.

1. Go to the library. If there is a science museum nearby, or a branch of the World Wildlife Fund, you might be able to use those resources as well. Choose an endangered animal, perhaps one in your own country. Find out the same kind of information about this animal that you have found out about all the others, in enough detail to make it useful for the magazine article. Also, bring any other related information you would consider useful or interesting, such as a description of the animal and its usual habitat. If possible, try to bring a picture.
2. Prepare a six-to-seven-minute talk on this animal. Your talk should be well prepared, with an inform-and-focus section that prepares your reader for your information. Your classmates will be taking notes, so you will need to organize your presentation for their benefit.
3. To take notes, you'll need to set up charts like the ones you've used before. You should have these ready when you come to class.
4. Take turns giving your presentations. Remember to talk (not read) to your audience. You may use cue cards, but write only a few words on each one; otherwise you'll be tempted to read.

Questions for Discussion

Individually, consider the following questions. If you wish, jot down key points you want to make. In your groups, discuss your responses.

1. Judging from what you have learned over the last few classes, how serious is the problem of animal endangerment?

2. Which animals are endangered as a result of natural causes?

3. Which animals owe their precarious situations directly to overkilling by humans? For what reasons have people killed these animals?

4. In what ways do humans indirectly threaten the lives of animals? Categorize these ways. Think of examples of animals whose existence has become endangered as a result of indirect methods.

5. Is this endangerment not just the natural result of population growth or the advancement of civilization?

6. What do you think of this view: "People are more important than animals. Why should people in Madagascar go short of food or possibly face starvation so that lemurs can continue to exist?"

WRITING THE ARTICLE

Prewriting

Analyze Your Task

1. Reread your writing task on page 129. Highlight the key words and discuss them with your teacher.
2. With two or three partners, discuss the following questions. You have fifteen minutes.
   a. Consider your audience: Who are they? How much are they likely to know about the topic? How interested are they likely to be? Why is this age group an important audience to reach now?
   b. Consider your purpose: What are you trying to *accomplish* with your article?

c. On the basis of your answers for (a) and (b), consider the kind of support you'll need to include.

Support for Thesis Statements

Do this activity in your groups. Reread the second paragraph from "Endangered Wildlife—Mammals" in order to answer the questions below.

1. What is the thesis of this section?
2. How many subtheses support the central one? How do you know?
3. A writer might support a thesis in a number of ways. Which of the following did this writer use?

- short examples
- an extended example
- statistics
- an explanation of the thesis or terms in it
- a conclusion that restates the thesis
- a conclusion that recommends
- an analysis of the causal relationships involved

4. Can you explain why he chose to use the ones he did?

Discuss your answers to these questions with your teacher.

5. In your groups, reread the interview with Peter Raven, on pages 130 to 133. What kinds of support did he use in his answers to questions 2 and 5?

Select Your Information

1. What main point or thesis will you try to prove in your article? Write your central thesis statement in the space below.

2. How will you prove this thesis; that is, what subtheses will you need to prove in order to prove the main thesis? Put each subthesis at the top of a new page.
3. Go over your readings and notes. Using a highlighter, boxes, circles— whatever you prefer—isolate any information you think you'll need.

When you finish, take notes in your own words on the information you want to include to support each point in your article. Use the pages you've just prepared.

Organize Your Information

1. Work on one page at a time. Decide how the ideas are connected and how they should be sequenced. On each page, draw a tree sketch showing the information you intend to include and the relationships involved. Use key words to help you remember each idea. Look over your sketches to see if you've left out any information that your audience might need in order to understand. Also check to ensure that all information in each section is relevant to that point.
2. Put the pages together in the order you want for your article.

Rehearse Your Article With a partner, take turns telling each other the information outlined in your trees. As you listen, try to place yourself in the position of a teenage reader in some other part of the world. If you think your partner needs to add, delete, or move information to clarify or support the ideas, be sure to say so. When you finish, revise your sketch as you wish.

Draft One: Focus on Information and Organization

Now you're ready to write the first draft. Write your central thesis and then the body of your article. As usual, double-space so that you have room to revise.

Conference and Revise

1. Work with a partner. Exchange articles and read each other's. As you read, draw a sketch of the article, including the main thesis statement and the subtheses.
2. Now look closely at the subthesis statements. Ask yourself

   if they all support the central thesis;

   if combined together, they prove it; and

   if they're sequenced in a logical and effective order.
3. Read each section carefully to ensure

   that everything is relevant,

   that there is enough information to substantiate the subthesis, and

   that you understand clearly what the writer is saying.

4. Mark any problem with an asterisk (*).

5. Assign a mark out of 15 for content and effective organization.

6. When you finish, discuss your evaluation with your partner.

7. Revise your own article as necessary.

Draft Two: Organize for Your Reader

The Inform Section

1. Reread your main thesis. Then consider these questions:

   How can I establish the importance of what I am about to say?

   What background information do my readers need to understand my article?

   How can I lead them step by step from the opening to my central thesis statement?

2. Write the inform section of your article.

3. Exchange with a partner, and comment on each other's work.

4. With your teacher, discuss the differences between the inform section in this essay and the inform section you would write for your professor in an academic essay.

The Conclusion

1. Consider these questions:

   What is the purpose of my article?

   How might I use the conclusion to help me achieve this purpose?

2. Write the conclusion of your article.

Use scissors and tape to put all the parts of your article together. Read it over carefully to make sure the ideas flow logically and coherently from one to the next. Listen to the ideas as you read. Add any transition words or phrases to help your reader see the connections between adjacent ideas. Revise as you wish. Rewrite any illegible sections; your partner will need to be able to read your article.

Draft Three: Focus on Language

Expressing Causal Relationships   As you write your article, you'll likely need to use expressions of cause and result. English has many ways of expressing such relationships. The purpose of the next set of activities is to help you practice using a few of them.

A. "Because. . ." Do this activity with a partner. Read sentences a and b to answer the questions below:

> a. The forests themselves are productive only because the trees have the ability to lock up nutrients.

> b. Instead they kill for rhinoceros horn, because it's supposed to be a magic cure for almost every malady.

1. In each sentence, circle the cause and underline the effect.
2. Formulate rules about where to put "because" and what kind of structure follows it.
3. What other words can replace "because"?

Discuss your answers with your teacher.

B. "Because of. . ." Do this activity with your partner. Read the following sentence to answer the questions below:

> The Rocky Mountain Bighorn is now restricted in its distribution because of the encroachment of habitation.

1. Again, circle the cause and underline the effect.
2. How is the cause constructed differently from the one in the earlier sentence?

C. "As a result of. . ." Alone, read the following sentence to answer the questions below:

> The black-footed ferret suffers the same fate as the prairie dog as a result of poisoning campaigns.

1. What is the cause? the effect?
2. What construction follows "as a result of"?

Check your answers with your teacher.

Practice Use "because of" or "as a result of" followed by a noun phrase to combine each cause-and-effect pair below into one sentence that clearly shows the relationship between the ideas.

1. Cause: increased hunting
   Result: the wood bison population has declined.

2. Cause: excessive hunting practices
   Result: sea otters were practically exterminated.

3. Now use these two pairs of ideas to write sentences using "because." You will have to change the forms of some of the words. Check your answers with a partner, then with your teacher.

D. "So...that"

1. Do this activity with two partners. In the sentences below, find both the cause and the effect. Then check your answers with your teacher.

   The leatherback's head grows so big that the creature can't pull it back inside its skull.

   The eastern cougar is so secretive that only unconfirmed sightings from scattered points throughout Eastern Canada indicate that it may still exist.

2. With your partners, formulate rules about how the expression "so... that" operates in an English sentence.

3. Listen as your teacher reads the two sentences aloud. For what reason might a writer choose the "so...that" construction over another causal structure? What sort of information is used with "so...that"?

4. Read the sentence below. What other kind of word can be used between "so" and "that" besides an adjective?

   And when a baby dies, sea otter mothers are known to grieve so deeply that they'll keep the little body clutched on their chests for weeks, trying vainly to coax it back to life.

5. Together, construct "so {adjective / adverb} that" sentences using the following information:

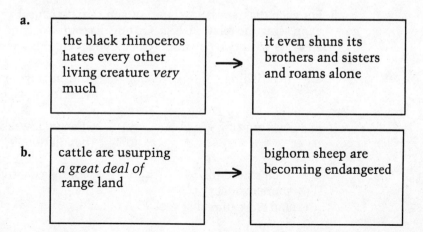

   a.

   | the black rhinoceros hates every other living creature *very much* | → | it even shuns its brothers and sisters and roams alone |

   b.

   | cattle are usurping *a great deal of* range land | → | bighorn sheep are becoming endangered |

Causal Verbs

1. In English, verbs are also used to express causal relationships. Sometimes the verb does only that. For example:

> The precarious situation of most of the species has been caused by excessive exploitation or by the demands of an uninformed public.

What are the causes? What is the result? How do you know?

2. Other causal verbs, however, can indicate both the relationship and the effect. For example:

> The moose, introduced in 1904, further depleted food supplies.

What is the cause? the effect?

The word "depleted" carries two meanings: that the moose *caused* the food supplies to be *used up*.

3. Look over your readings. Find at least two examples of causal verbs that express both the relationship and the effect. Write the complete sentences below.

4. Share your answers with two partners. In each sentence, find the cause and the result. Then think about why the writer chose to use a causal verb rather than any other causal expression.

5. For each diagram below, use an appropriate causal verb in a sentence expressing the relationship. Do one diagram at a time, discussing your answers with two partners. Check your sentences with your teacher.

    a.   overfishing   ⟶   the endangerment of several species of whales

    b.   overhunting   ⟶   drastic decrease in sea otter population

    c.   man's need for more residential and recreational space   ⟶   animals deprived of available habitat

    d.   fur hunters   ⟶   extermination of sea otter
                                                                    in Canadian waters

Whenever you read, note the cause and effect structures writers use. Ask yourself why they chose those particular ways to express the causal relationships involved.

To write your final draft, do the following:

1. Read your article aloud, one section at a time, as if you were giving a speech to the high school students. Listen to the sound of your words. Try to imagine their effect on an audience. Make any revisions you consider advisable.
2. Check your expression of causal relationships.
3. When you've finished, write the final draft.
4. Exchange papers with two partners. Edit one another's for spelling, punctuation, and grammar. Discuss any problems. Make necessary corrections.
5. Hand in your article.

Chapter 6

Child Labor

*T*his chapter is a test. The topic is child labor. You will likely have at least one day to read the texts carefully before you answer the questions. You might want to predict some of the questions, but the test situation will be more authentic if you don't do the questions ahead of time. As you do the test, you'll practice writing answers in a given amount of time.

The test takes about three and one-half hours to complete. The schedule is as follows:

Component	Points	Time
Introduction: Think About the Topic	0	15 minutes
Reading I: "Work in a Sawmill"	5	10 minutes
Reading II: "Child Labour" (30 +3)	10	30 minutes
Reading III: "Employment Legislation, Part I"	10	20 minutes
Writing		
Analyze the Question	0	15 minutes
Gather Your Information in Your Own Words	0	45 minutes
Reading IV: "Employment Legislation, Part II"		
Plan Your Essay	0	20 minutes
Write the Essay and Edit	25	45 minutes
Total	50	3 hr, 20 min

THINK ABOUT THE TOPIC (Points: 0; Time: 15 minutes)

In Canada today, children under sixteen spend approximately five and a half hours per day in school, five days a week, forty weeks a year. Such conditions, however, were not always the norm. In nineteenth century Canada, a child's life was much more rigorous. Children were frequently required to work long hours in appalling conditions for little or no pay. Child labor in Canada, particularly in the nineteenth century, will be the focus of this chapter.

A. Write brief answers to the questions below. You have five minutes.

1. In your country, at what age are children usually considered old enough to be left at home alone (a) when the parents go out at night? (b) during the day?

2. Did you have a job when you were between ten and fifteen years old? If so, what was it? What were your responsibilities? How many hours per day did you work? How much were you paid?

3. Did you ever look after your brothers and sisters? If so, were you paid, and how much?

4. Does your country/province have any laws against employing children to work in factories, mines, or stores? If so, what are they?

5. In North Carolina in the United States, school-age children may legally stay home from school to help with the tobacco harvest, tobacco being the state's leading industry. Would a similar practice be allowed in your country/province? If so, under what circumstances?

B. In groups of three or four, discuss your answers, noting the similarities and differences. You have ten minutes for discussion.

READING I: "WORK IN A SAWMILL" (Points: 5; Time: 10 minutes)

Read the text entitled "Work in a Sawmill." It is the testimony of a child laborer interviewed about his accident. The place, Canada; the time, the late 1880s. What can you conclude about the conditions under which children worked in Canada in the late nineteenth century? On a separate sheet, write your answer, both the conclusion and the support.

Reading I

Work in a Sawmill

*A Montreal newspaper in 1903
reports on an accident involving
child labour.*

Part of the testimony of John Gale before the Royal Commission on the Relations of Labour and Capital in the 1880s:

Q: I see that you have lost one of your arms?
A: Yes, my right arm.
Q: How did that occur?
A: It was an accident in a sawmill.
Q: How old were you then?
A: Between eleven and twelve years of age.
Q: Were there any other boys working there, at the time you met with this accident, about your age?
A: Yes.
Q: What were you getting at the time you worked there?
A: I was only getting 25 cents a day.
Q: What were you engaged at when you lost your arm?
A: Taking blocks away from the circular saw.
Q: These were large saws? How large were they?
A: About two feet (60 cm) in diameter.
Q: Your employer did not do anything at all for you?
A: No.
Q: As you are now, can you earn a living?
A: No; not unless I learn something—not unless I get an education.
Q: Do you know of any other boys having received accidents?
A: Yes; about two months after a boy was working in the mill, where I was, and he got both his legs and arms taken off.

Reprinted with permission—the National Library of Canada. Excerpt from *Horizon Canada*, Volume 1, No. 3, 1984.

READING II: "CHILD LABOUR" (Points: 30 ÷ 3 = 10; Time: 30 Minutes)

Use the information from this reading (pp. 159–161) to answer the nine questions below. Write your answers on a separate sheet. Please answer in your own words; do not copy from the text.

1. State the two main disadvantages of being a child of a large farming family in the late nineteenth century. (2 points)

2. List five conditions of apprenticeship: two for the master craftsman, three for the trainee. (5 points)

   Craftsman   **Apprentice**

   1.   1.

   2.   2.

                               3.

3. Outline the process by which industrialization decreased the wages paid to skilled adult male workers. (5 points)

4. Why were immigrants essential to the Canadian economy in the nineteenth century? (3 points)

5. This question is worth 5 points. Read statements (a) to (h) below. Write the letters of the ones you would include to support the following thesis:

   In the last half of the nineteenth century, child labor in Canada was extremely common.

   a. Parents frequently placed their children in the charge of a master craftsman.
   b. Thirty-three thousand worked in Ontario; twenty-two thousand in Quebec.
   c. After 1815, many immigrants poured into Canada.
   d. The 1891 census showed that approximately 75,000 children between the ages of ten and fourteen were employed in Canada.
   e. Some children attended school.
   f. Many children worked at home taking care of younger siblings while their parents worked.
   g. The weekly salary for children was about $1.50.
   h. While some sold newspapers or shined shoes, others worked as messengers or servants.

6. Using the information you selected in question 5, draw a tree diagram showing how you would organize these statements to support the

thesis. Use key words or letters; you do not have to write out all the sentences. (3 points)

7. Can you think of any reasons why the parents of a child worker might not object to having their child punished for being careless on the job? (3 points)

8. What evidence is there that employers discriminated against both women and children? (3 points)

9. This question is worth 1 point. Write the appropriate letter. The main idea of paragraphs 21 to 24 is

   a. that churches and progressive movements were involved in ending child labor.
   b. the importance of mandatory primary school attendance.
   c. the fact that social reforms regarding child labor took so long to achieve.
   d. that the laws regarding child labor were not strictly observed.

Reading II

Child Labour

The Industrial Revolution in Canada had some ghastly side effects. One was the employment of thousands of children, some of them less than ten years old, in mines and factories, working at dangerous machines for barely more than a dollar a week.

By FERNAND HARVEY

1   These days, it goes without saying that children must attend school. But the situation was very different during the last century. School attendance was not compulsory and parents often preferred to have their children work in order to increase the meagre family income.

2   It would be wrong to think, however, that child labour appeared only with industrialization and the development of factories. In reality child labour existed much earlier in Canadian history.

3   Without doubt, child labour was most widespread on the farm. This was true from the beginning of New France up until the first third of the twentieth century. Farming in eastern Canada was traditionally organized around the family. The father, mother and children all had to help out and for this reason large families were considered a necessity. However, as they grew older, rural children had to leave home to find new land to settle on, or to try their luck in the city, because not all of them could inherit the family property.

4   Child labour on farms continued well into the twentieth century, when farm mechanization and compulsory schooling finally brought an end to this old family tradition .

A Different Kind of Childhood

5   In pre-industrial society, child labour was not restricted only to agricultural work. It existed also in the practice of apprenticeships. At the outset of the nineteenth century, when there were no real technical schools, parents who wanted their children to learn a manual skill placed them with a master craftsman who signed a legal agreement to teach them the various branches of his trade. The craftsman also agreed to feed and lodge his apprentice and sometimes even to clothe and wash him. As for the apprentice, who was seldom younger than twelve years old, he agreed to obey his master and not leave him without permission.

6   The apprentice signed a contract for three years, during which time he agreed to work eleven hours a day during the winter and twelve hours a day in summer. In certain cases, the contract stipulated that the child must also perform household chores asked for by the master.

7   Whether it was a matter of working on a farm or serving an apprenticeship, children in pre-industrial society were compelled to put in long hours of work. There was virtually no time for school or recreation. Few primary schools existed and very few children had the opportunity to attend school even on an irregular basis.

Children and Industrialization

8   Industrialization began slowly in eastern Canada around 1850 and accelerated in the 1880s. Several factors explain the country's industrial development. The influx of immigrants after 1815 created a domestic market for the consumption of goods and services. The construction of canals, then railways, made transport and trade easier. Tariff policies instituted by the government of Prime Minister John A. Macdonald in 1879 also favoured the setting up of factories and created thousands of

From *Horizon Canada*, Vol. 1, No. 3, 1984. Reprinted with permission.

jobs. Cities like Montreal, Quebec and Toronto were filling with immigrants, as well as people from rural areas. This shift to the cities contributed to the birth of a new social class which had not existed in pre-industrial society: the working class. It was this class that formed the labour supply in the development of capitalist enterprise.

9   From the point of view of technology, the Industrial Revolution involved two great changes. Traditional energy sources in the big factories were replaced by the steam engine, greatly increasing production capacity which until then had been fairly limited. Moreover, the traditional tools of the artisan gave way to machinery which could produce manufactured goods effortlessly, with much more precision and speed.

10   It is not hard to guess the effect of these technological changes. If physical strength was no longer required to fulfill certain tasks, if the artisan's skills could be replaced by a machine, workers no longer needed to be adult males to perform certain jobs.

11   The employment of children in manufacturing offered obvious advantages for business people, not only in Canada but in all industrialized nations at the time. Employers could afford to be more independent with their skilled workers who as a result lost their negotiating power. By replacing them whenever they had the chance with women and children, employers were able to dominate the passive, non-unionized work force and pay drastically reduced salaries.

What a Workday!

12   In Canadian cities during the last century, manufacturing was not the only place children worked. Many also were found in the service sector. Some were employed in stores; others selling newspapers, or as messenger boys or shoeshine boys; and others, especially young girls, as domestic servants.

13   The 1891 census revealed that there were about 75,000 children between ten and fourteen years of age on the job market in Canada, 33,000 of them in Ontario and 22,000 in Quebec. These statistics are probably on the conservative side and do not take into account children who stayed at home during the day to look after their young brothers and sisters while their parents were out working.

14   Government investigations of working conditions, along with newspaper reports, give us a picture of the life of working children in the nineteenth century. The time had passed when a twelve-year-old child was placed as an apprentice to a master-craftsman for three or four years. In the mechanized factories, children often were hired at nine or ten years of age. They were no longer learning every aspect of a skill, as they once did. Instead they carried out simple, repetitive tasks which required no special skill or training. As a result, employers had everything to gain by hiring young children.

15   Within the factories, working conditions for children were very hard. Because children belonged to the same work teams as adults, they had to work the same long

hours. According to testimony heard by the Royal Commission on the Relations of Labour and Capital in 1888, workers, including children, were working ten hours a day, sixty hours a week in the manufacturing sector; and twelve hours a day, 72 hours a week, in the service sector. Sunday remained the only day off during the week and the idea of an annual vacation was still a dream.

16   As for salaries, they remained very low for children. When you consider that the average weekly salary in a factory was around $8.50 for men and $4.00 for women at the end of the last century, the meagre $1.50 a week paid to children demonstrates the considerable spread between workers in terms of age and sex. It also demonstrates how much money employers were saving by hiring children.

17   But one of the most astounding aspects of child labour concerns factory discipline. In order to assure production, hundreds of workers had to be organized, and disciplined. Children presented a special problem simply because they were so young and inexperienced.

18   Factory regulations covered a wide range of behaviour, including lateness, absenteeism, insubordination, rudeness and negligence. Foremen were given the authority to discipline workers and when it came to children, corporal punishment was not out of the question. If a rule were broken, the employee might be fired or given a fine which would be deducted from his salary. Children in particular were

penalized for absenteeism, rowdy behaviour or faults in their work.

19 Child labourers were at times the object of physical violence. The hearings of the Royal Commission on the Relations of Labour and Capital revealed scandalous cases at the Fortier cigar factory in Montreal. Several young employees who had been found guilty of theft or absence from work admitted to having been beaten. Others told of being locked in the "black hole" in the basement of the factory by a former police officer, acting as a special constable for the owner.

20 While child labour in the nineteenth century can be explained by technological changes and the economic interests of business people, the financial circumstances in which families found themselves also played a role. Fathers of families working in industry, as well as the service sector, counted on supplementary income from work done by their wives and children. Small as it might be, the financial contribution from children was important, considering how little financial leeway most working class families had.

Social Reforms

21 Reforms were slow in coming to meet the problem of child labour and the marginal existence of children. The first to react were the churches and charitable organizations. In Toronto at the beginning of the twentieth century there were 55 charitable organizations and more than two hundred churches involved in helping indigent families and individuals.

22 But these efforts proved insufficient. A progressive movement gathered strength, demanding social reforms which included the protection of children. Newspapers also published stories denouncing the working conditions and the lives poor children had to lead. Public opinion then went in two directions. One group favoured reducing the hours of work and raising the minimum age for child labour; another group favoured compulsory public education.

23 However, governments were slow to react. Because matters of work and education fell under provincial jurisdiction, it was in the provinces that legislation was adopted to protect children from the abuses of industrial society. In 1884 Ontario became the first province to adopt a law prohibiting manufacturers from employing boys of less than twelve years of age and girls less than fourteen. Quebec passed a similar law a year later. However, because of a lack of inspectors, the laws were seldom respected. It was not until the beginning of the present century that legislation limiting child labour was observed .

24 At the same time, provinces started to pass legislation making primary school education compulsory. Ontario adopted such a law in 1891. Other provinces followed suit, and by the end of the First World War, Quebec was the only province without such legislation. With most children now in school instead of the factory, one of the worst excesses of Canada's Industrial Revolution was over.

READING III: "EMPLOYMENT LEGISLATION, PART I"
(Points: 10; Time: 20 minutes)

The next reading, from a text on personnel management, deals with employment legislation in Canada, particularly the aspects of human rights legislation, statutory school-leaving age, and minimum age for employment.

Read each of the following statements. Then read the text to see if it is true or false. Write "True" or "False" in the blank accordingly. Record your answers on a separate sheet.

_____ 1. The purpose of human rights laws regarding employment is to prevent discrimination in the areas of deciding whom to hire, how much to pay, and whom to promote to a higher position.

_____ 2. In Canada, legislation regarding employment is restricted to the federal government; the provinces have no say whatsoever in these matters.

_____ 3. In Quebec, a child must usually remain in school until the age of fifteen, whereas in Ontario the age for leaving school is sixteen.

_____ 4. A fourteen-year-old living in Alberta may be legally permitted to stay home for two weeks to help with harvesting the grain.

_____ 5. The provincial leaders in minimum-age-employment laws were Ontario, Quebec, and Nova Scotia.

_____ 6. Even after "minimum age for employment" legislation had passed, the practice of hiring younger children continued.

_____ 7. By 1900, enforcing the Factory Act was considered as important as enforcing liquor-related crimes.

_____ 8. Today, all provinces have identical minimum age laws but the age may depend on the job.

_____ 9. Whereas a seventeen-year-old youth may legally work in an Alberta coal mine, he may not be able to work legally in a Nova Scotia coal mine.

_____ 10. It could be legal for twelve- to fifteen-year-old youths in British Columbia to work after school in a restaurant or grocery store, yet illegal in another part of Canada.

Reading III

Employment Legislation, Part I

HUMAN RIGHTS LEGISLATION

Human rights legislation is intended, in the words of the Canadian Human Rights Act, "to ensure that every person should have equal opportunity with others to make a life without being hindered by discriminatory practices, and to protect the privacy of individuals and their right of access to records containing personal information concerning them. Insofar as employment is concerned, the purpose of human rights legislation is to prevent people from being treated differently because of their race, religion, sex, marital status, and so on when it comes to decisions about hiring, pay, and promotion. Rather, these decisions should be made on the basis of *individual* qualifications.

In Canada, the jurisdiction for the protection of human rights, sometimes called civil liberties, is shared between the federal and the provincial governments. The result is separate federal and provincial legislation in the field of human rights. Each of Canada's 13 jurisdictions forbids a slightly different set of discriminatory acts. Moreover, since enforcement and interpretation are the preserves of commissions and courts within each jurisdiction, there are considerable differences in actual practice.

STATUTORY SCHOOL-LEAVING AGE

All the provinces and territories forbid the employment of a child of school age during school hours, unless the child is excused for some reason provided in the relevant school attendance act. School-leaving age is 16 in Alberta, Manitoba, Nova Scotia, Ontario, Saskatchewan, and the Yukon, and 15 in the other six jurisdictions. Work exemptions are provided for a variety of circumstances. In five provinces (Manitoba, New Brunswick, Newfoundland, Nova Scotia, Quebec), a child may be exempted temporarily from school attendance, on the application of a parent or guardian, if his or her services are required for employment or farm or home duties. Alberta and Saskatchewan have provisions for work experience programs.

MINIMUM AGE FOR EMPLOYMENT

The desire to establish minimum ages for employment was a goal of trade unions and social reformers in the 19th century. Developments were slow: factory legislation developed cautiously from the 1880s, caught between the more generous impulses of the age and the employers' firm grip on legislatures and party finances. By 1888, children were banned from smaller factories in Ontario, and shopkeepers could not employ boys under 14 or girls under 16 for more than 12 hours a day or 74 hours a week. Quebec and Nova Scotia, then eventually the other provinces, followed this humanitarian lead at a cautious distance. Enforcement in all provinces lagged even more. At the turn of the century, Ontario critics noted that while Toronto employed three inspectors merely to hunt out liquor offences, the entire province employed only three inspectors to enforce its Factory Act.

Today the minimum age for employment varies so greatly, by province and by type of work, that employers and PAIR professionals are well advised to investigate the regulations for each specific situation they face. For example, in most jurisdictions, a person must be 18 to work below ground in mines, but in Alberta it is 17 and in Nova Scotia it is 16 for metal mines but 18 for coal mines. Above ground, the standard minimum age is 16, as it is in factories, but a few jurisdictions permit certain kinds of work at 15 and forbid others, particularly heavy kinds, until 18.

Many jurisdictions permit younger youths to work outside school hours or on vacations in shops, hotels, and restaurants and in such occupations as messenger, newspaper vendor, and shoe shiner. Many acts prohibit young people's working at night. For example, Alberta forbids the employment of persons under 15 between 9:00 P.M. and 6:00 A.M., while those between 15 and 18 can work from 9:00 P.M. to midnight on retail premises selling food or beverages only in the continuous presence of someone 18 years of age or over.

CHAPTER 6 WRITING TASK: TIMED ESSAY

Situation You are a student in a second-year labour relations course. Your final examination contains the following essay question:

> In the nineteenth century, Canadian children were exploited—taken advantage of for financial gain—by both their employers and their families to an extent not possible today.
>
> In an essay of two to three pages, support this statement.

Writing the Essay

You will have approximately two hours to complete this writing task, following a series of four steps:

Step 1: Analyze the Question (15 minutes) Read the question carefully, highlighting the key words. What is your main thesis statement, the statement you have to prove in your essay? Write it at the top of a separate sheet of paper. What sections should your answer contain in order to prove this thesis? How does the professor expect them to be sequenced? With two partners, discuss your answers to these questions.

On the sheet with the thesis statement, begin a tree diagram of your answer. Use one heading for each of the sections you decided you would need.

Step 2: Gather Your Information in Your Own Words (45 minutes) This step allows you time to gather your information for your essay. You will use your earlier three readings as well as a fourth reading—"Employment Legislation, Part II"—on pages 166–168. Quickly read over all four texts, highlighting information necessary for your essay. Make key-word notes in the margin. Be sure to select only *relevant* information.

Step 3: Plan Your Essay (20 minutes) Use the information from your margin notes to complete the tree sketch. Be sure not to copy from the text but to restate the ideas in your own words. Use enough key words to remember the ideas; include statistics where necessary. Go over your sketch, adding transitional phrases that will help your reader see how the ideas are related.

Reading IV

Employment Legislation, Part II

EQUAL PAY FOR MEN AND WOMEN

All jurisdictions prohibit an employer from paying different wages to male and female employees who perform the *same or similar work* under the same or similar conditions (usually in the same establishment) that requires similar skill, effort, or responsibility.

In the Greenacres Nursing Home case (1970) and the Riverdale Hospital Case (1973), the Ontario Court of Appeal ruled that job comparisons should be based on work actually performed rather than on formal job descriptions. In the latter case, the court also ruled that as long as some men do the same work as women, equal pay is justifiable for the whole occupation.

Because of the difficulties in making comparisons among jobs, the Quebec and federal jurisdiction now require equal pay for *work of equal value*; the criterion applied to assessing the value of work performed by employees in the same establishment is the composite of the skill, effort, and responsibility required for performance and the conditions under which the work is performed. In other words, the requirement is the comparison of dissimilar jobs in terms of their value to the employer. One commentator says that these provisions create serious problems of implementation because "it requires the development of job-content evaluations. . . and this will lead to fundamental questions about who runs the enterprise."

The concept and implications of equal pay provisions are further discussed in Chapter 12.

HOURS OF WORK

Hours-of-work provisions relate both to the maximum number of hours of work permitted per day and per week and to the number of hours per day or week after which an overtime rate must be paid. Eight hours of work per day and 40 hours per week are the most common standards (the federal jurisdiction, B.C., Manitoba, Newfoundland, Saskatchewan, and Yukon), but there are other combinations: Alberta, eight and 44; New Brunswick, nine and 48, Ontario, eight and 48, the Northwest Territories, eight and 44. Nova Scotia and Prince Edward Island have only a standard work week of 48, and Quebec 44 hours.

The accepted rate for overtime is 1.5 times the regular rate but it comes into effect at different points in different jurisdictions and even after a different number of hours in the same province for different industries. For example, in Alberta overtime generally begins after eight hours in a day and 44 in a week, but for ambulance drivers and cab drivers it starts after ten hours in a day or 60 hours in a week. There are so many variations in the different jurisdictions that PAIR professionals must consult the relevant employment standards branch.

They are also well advised to peruse the provisions themselves. Every jurisdiction permits exceptions to the general rules to allow for differences in production periods, seasonal variations, and customary standards and also provides for changes to accommodate special problems. (A common feature is the possibility of averaging hours over a number of weeks.) Familiarity with the regulations may suggest grounds on which the regulatory body may grant exemptions. It can also alert personnel officials to any need to obtain a permit for hours beyond a stated maximum.

WEEKLY REST DAYS

All jurisdictions require employers to provide at least one full day of rest each week, on Sunday wherever possible. Exceptions are allowed for farm workers, domestics, and various other categories of workers in different provinces. Special provisions are made for the accumulation of days of rest for workers in highway and railway construction, geophysical exploration, and oil-well drilling in Alberta, for bus operators and truck drivers in B.C., and for watchmen, janitors, and superintendents in Ontario.

ANNUAL VACATIONS WITH PAY

Every jurisdiction except Saskatchewan requires two weeks of vacation with pay after one year of employment; in Saskatchewan, the figure is three weeks after one year. Many labour laws increase the amount of vacation after a stated number of years of service with the same employer.

The usual rate for vacation pay begins at 4 per cent of annual earnings (again, Saskatchewan is more generous with 3/52 of annual earnings) and rises as an employee becomes entitled to more vacation. Pay must be given one to fourteen days before the vacation begins, depending on the jurisdiction.

HOLIDAYS

Only Prince Edward Island lacks legislation dealing with paid general holidays. The number varies from five in Newfoundland to nine in the federal jurisdictions. All the lists include New Year's Day, Good Friday, Labour Day, and Christmas Day; frequently added are Victoria Day, Dominion Day, Thanksgiving, Remembrance Day, and Boxing Day. Newfoundland has Memorial Day, while Quebec has la fête de Dollard des Ormeaux and la fête de St. Jean Baptiste. Other special provincial days are British Columbia Day, New Brunswick Day, Saskatchewan Day, and Discovery Day (Yukon). In all jurisdictions, employers must provide regular pay for holidays not worked and two to two and one-half times regular pay (or another day off with pay) for holidays worked. Most laws make special provision for work in continuous operation and other selected industries, such as construction.

MINIMUM WAGES

Generally, minimum wage provisions cover almost all workers—excepting only most farm labourers and, in some jurisdictions, domestic workers. A lower minimum rate is usually set for young workers, student trainees, and the handicapped and, in some provinces, for employees who serve alcoholic beverages (Manitoba, Ontario, Quebec) and for domestic workers (British Columbia, Newfoundland, Ontario, Quebec). Ontario provides a higher rate for construction workers.

The interprovincial differences in minimum rates can be sizeable. In July 1981, for example, there was an almost one-dollar difference between the country's highest minimum wage rate (Quebec and Saskatchewan, at $4.00 per hour) and the lowest (New Brunswick at $3.05 per hour). Since the minimums change at different intervals in each province, the PAIR professional should keep a table with the relevant rates and the dates of change, which can normally be obtained from the local employment standards branch of the department or ministry of labour.

Step 4: Write the Essay and Edit (45 minutes) Using your sketch as a guide, write the essay. When you finish, edit it for clarity and accuracy. Hand it in when your teacher says that time is up.

Exam Strategies

After you've handed in your papers, form groups of four or five to discuss the questions below.

1. Did highlighting the key words help you focus on what you were asked to do?
2. Did it help to discuss your ideas with a partner? If so, how? If not, why not, do you think?
3. How helpful was the time spent preparing to write? What other strategies did you use or might you have used to help you prepare more efficiently and effectively?
4. Did you find it useful to write down the thesis before you started collecting your information? How else might you keep yourself on track?
5. How much did you use your sketch as you wrote? Would you take time to sketch out an answer in another essay question? in a short answer question?

Chapter 7

Earthquakes

*I*n this chapter you'll learn about earthquakes. You'll focus on why some earthquakes cause more destruction than others and examine ways to decrease the death toll and damage caused by major quakes. You'll also practice the following skills and strategies:

- reading for specific, relevant information and ignoring the irrelevant
- highlighting and note-taking
- reading and interpreting nonlinear text
- interviewing
- generalizing from data and writing such generalizations
- selecting and writing inform-and-focus sections
- recommending
- writing a letter of concern

THINK ABOUT THE TOPIC

A. Do the questions below, which focus on what you already know about earthquakes.

1. Have you ever been through an earthquake? If so, when and where? Was it considered major or minor?

2. In your country, do earthquakes happen (check one)
   a. frequently?
   b. occasionally?
   c. rarely?
   d. never?

3. If earthquakes do occur there, are they generally (check one)
   a. major?
   b. minor?
   c. sometimes major, sometimes minor?

4. Is there any particular area in your country where an earthquake is likely to happen? If so, where?

5. What major earthquakes do you recall hearing or reading about in recent years?

6. Can you think of any reason why people might be reluctant to move to the state of California in the United States?

7. Which of the following scales are used to measure the magnitude or strength of an earthquake?
   a. Fish
   b. Mercalli
   c. Music
   d. Richter

8. The *epicenter* of a quake is (check one)
   a. the total area damaged by an earthquake,
   b. an epidemic of disease caused by pollution from an earthquake,
   c. the point on the earth's surface directly above the place where an
      earthquake breaks out.

9. A *foreshock* is (check one)
   a. an earthquake of lesser strength, directly following the major quake.
   b. an earthquake of lesser magnitude, directly preceding the major quake.
   c. a series of four earthquakes.
   d. a feeling of dread or fear prior to an earthquake.

10. What is the difference between an earthquake rated "7" and one rated "8"?

B. In groups, compare and discuss your answers.

READING I: "QUAKES SOW DEVASTATION IN MEXICO"

On September 19, 1985, two major earthquakes hit Mexico, causing thousands of deaths and massive damage to parts of the country, especially Mexico City.

A. Read the article "Quakes Sow Devastation in Mexico" in order to answer the questions below. Highlight the answers in the text and put the question numbers in the margin. Ignore all irrelevant information. Work as quickly as you can; you have only three minutes.

1. What caused the earthquakes?
2. How large were the quakes on the Richter scale?
3. What were at least five effects of the earthquakes?

B. Check your answers with two partners.

Reading I

Quakes Sow Devastation in Mexico

A gigantic shift on the Pacific Ocean floor jarred Mexico's west coast last week, causing devastation in Mexico City, 230 miles away. Preliminary reports from the Mexican Government said the earthquake had killed 3,000 people, leaving thousands more injured and homeless. Yesterday, a White House official said the final total of dead and injured could reach 10,000.

A powerful second earthquake compounded the destruction, much of it in the capital's historic center, which rises above an ancient lake-bed, an insecure footing that made the destruction worse.

Streams of people ran weeping through the streets, waving wedding photographs and calling the names of missing relatives. Tens of thousands of rescue workers—many of them volunteers—picked through rubble seeking survivors. The sky was darkened by dust and the smoke from dozens of fires fed by broken gas lines. Water service, inadequate for the sprawling city's 18 million residents in the best of times, was cut off. Electric power was also out across half the city. Army and police patrols attempted to prevent looting.

Schools, hospitals, churches, apartment houses, hotels and Government offices were among the destroyed buildings. Houses plummeted down hillsides. At sea, two freighters and 19 fishing trawlers were feared to have sunk in 65-foot waves. At least three Americans, a mother and her children, were killed, the State Department said.

The first earthquake registered 7.8 on the Richter scale and was felt 1,000 miles away in Houston. It was followed by 25 lesser aftershocks and the second quake, which registered 7.3. Apparently unrelated smaller jolts were felt in Santa Barbara, Calif.

The United States and other countries in the hemisphere and Europe as well as international relief organizations offered help. President Reagan said he was "stunned and saddened." In his radio address yesterday, he said Mrs. Reagan would stop in Mexico tomorrow to express American support.

A Mexican official said reconstruction costs would be "astronomical"—in the tens of billions of dollars, according to a White House estimate. The Reagan Administration said a worldwide relief effort would be required to cope with "a historic catastrophe."

READING II: "MEXICO QUAKE DEVASTATION"

A. The map on page 175 indicates the areas affected by the earthquake in Mexico. Use it to answer the questions below. Jot down key words to help you remember. You do not need to write complete sentences.

1. Where did the earthquake break out (that is, where was the epicenter) in relation to Mexico City?

2. Which Mexican state suffered the highest death toll? Why is this not surprising?

3. Is it true that the distance from the epicenter is not the only factor that determines the extent of the damage from a major earthquake? Justify your answer using evidence from the map.

B. When you finish, check your answers with three or four other people. Resolve any problems by referring to the text.

Reading II

Mexico Quake Devastation

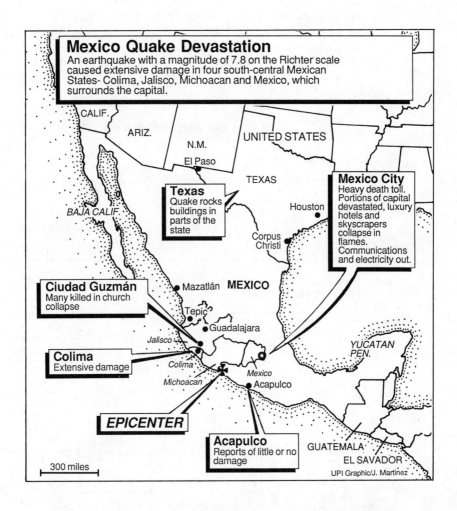

Mexico Quake Devastation
An earthquake with a magnitude of 7.8 on the Richter scale caused extensive damage in four south-central Mexican States- Colima, Jalisco, Michoacan and Mexico, which surrounds the capital.

CALIF.
ARIZ.
N.M.
El Paso
UNITED STATES
TEXAS
BAJA CALIF.

Texas
Quake rocks buildings in parts of the state

Houston
Corpus Christi

Mexico City
Heavy death toll. Portions of capital devastated, luxury hotels and skyscrapers collapse in flames. Communications and electricity out.

Mazatlán   **MEXICO**

Ciudad Guzmán
Many killed in church collapse

Tepic
Guadalajara

Jalisco

YUCATAN PEN.

Colima
Extensive damage

Colima
Michoacan
Mexico
Acapulco

EPICENTER

Acapulco
Reports of little or no damage

GUATEMALA
EL SAVADOR

300 miles

UPI Graphic/J. Martinez

READING III: "CRASH OF CONTINENTS TO BLAME?"

Now you'll turn to the topic of why earthquakes occur. As you do this activity, you'll practice reading only for required information and ignoring the irrelevant. Do not read any further than you have to in order to answer the questions. Work as quickly as you can; you have only ten minutes.

1. Reread the lead paragraph in Reading I: "Quakes Sow Devastation in Mexico." What caused the quakes there? How will this reading likely extend your information?

2. Use information from Reading III, "Crash of Continents to Blame?," to complete the following diagrams showing how three events strained the earth's crust, making the region vulnerable to earthquakes.

STRAINS ON THE EARTH'S CRUST

ORIGINAL STRAIN

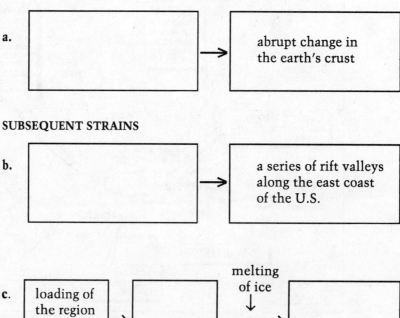

a. [ ] → abrupt change in the earth's crust

SUBSEQUENT STRAINS

b. [ ] → a series of rift valleys along the east coast of the U.S.

c. loading of the region by icy sheets → [ ] → melting of ice → [ ]

3. How certain are the scientists about the validity of their explanations? Highlight any sentences in the text that tell you this.

4. In groups of three, compare and discuss your answers. Resolve any differences by referring to the text. Discuss your answers with your teacher.

5. As a class, consider this question: How much of the article did you need to read?

Reading III

Crash of Continents to Blame?

By WALTER SULLIVAN

The earthquake and foreshock that hit the New York area yesterday originated about two miles west of Cameron's Line, which marks an abrupt change in the earth's crust that resulted from a collision between North America and a European-African land mass 400 million years ago.

Geologists suspect that earthquakes in this region may in some way mark the release of strain accumulated in that collision and in subsequent stresses on the landscape.

In particular the later splitting apart of the continents to form the Atlantic Ocean created a series of great rift valleys along the East Coast, one of which crossed what is now Westchester County, the Hudson River at Tappan Zee and northern New Jersey.

More recently—within the last 100,000 years—the region was heavily loaded with ice sheets, causing the crust to sink and then rebound after the ice melted.

Whether these factors or more current activity within the earth set the stage for yesterday's quake and foreshock is uncertain.

Soon after yesterday's quake, Columbia University's Lamont-Doherty Geological Observatory, based in Palisades, N.Y., near the quake site, dispatched a team to record tiny aftershocks in the hope that they would indicate the nature of the rupture, four miles underground near Ardsley, N.Y.

Dr. Margaret Anne Winslow of City College, reached at the observatory, with which she is also affiliated, said yesterday that two other quakes had been recorded this year in the vicinity of yesterday's quake and foreshock. They occurred on Jan. 26 and May 10 and were probably too weak to be felt by residents.

Cameron's Line was identified in the 1950's by Eugene N. Cameron of the University of Wisconsin. It has been traced from the eastern flank of the Berkshire Mountains of Western Massachusetts through western Connecticut, Westchester County, along White Plains Road to the west of Bronx Park.

Rocks to the west of the line are thought to include some from the continent's coastline before its collision with another land mass. Those to the east are believed to consist largely of sea-floor formations pushed against the continent during the collision.

Cameron's Line itself is a zone 50 to 300 feet wide showing ample signs of crushing and slippage.

According to Dr. Winslow, the foreshock yesterday , of magnitude 2.0 on the Richter scale, occurred 47 seconds after 6:05 A.M. The main shock, of magnitude 4.0, occurred at 6:07:41.

The Richter scale is an index of ground motion and thus reflects the amount of energy released. On the modified Mercalli scale, which estimates the local damaging effect of an earthquake, yesterday's main shock was about magnitude 4, according to Dr. Winslow. That would be sufficient to awaken light sleepers, tilt hanging pictures, jostle parked cars and rattle dishes but not break them.

Dr. Winslow said the observatory had received reports on the quake from Dix Hills, L.I.; Sussex County, N.J.; and western Massachusetts. She added that the pavement of a highway in Sparkill, N.Y., two miles north of the observatory, had been cracked, apparently by the tremors.

The main shock yesterday, she said, was the 16th earthquake in the New York City region in the last 250 years estimated at magnitude 3.5 or greater. The strongest, in 1884, is thought to have been about magnitude 5 and centered in Brooklyn, but no detailed records are available.

The 1884 quake, sometimes called the Amityville earthquake, was felt as far away as Burlington, Vt., and Baltimore. One in 1893 appears to have been centered between 10th and 18th Streets in Manhattan, creating consternation in local pool halls.

Maps of earthquake activity tend to show clustering of events near large cities.

CHAPTER 7 WRITING TASK: A LETTER OF CONCERN

You are a group of citizens living in a medium-sized town 150 miles from a fault in the earth's crust. Your area has recently experienced several earth tremors, measuring 4.5 to 5.2 on the Richter scale. You are concerned about the possibility of a major earthquake and want the town council to adopt measures to minimize the death and destruction that could result if one occurred. There are two or three measures you consider particularly vital.

You've decided that if you all write letters to the council members, you might be able to move them to act. Your task is to convince the council that these measures are necessary. You will prepare for and write your letters over the next few classes.

INTERVIEWS

This activity will tell you what people know about earthquakes. You'll interview people outside your class in order to find out the following information:

1. when people think of earthquakes, which ones, if any, come immediately to mind,
2. whether people are concerned about the possibility of an earthquake in your area,
3. if they are aware of any tremors or quakes that have occurred there in the past,
4. if they know what to do if an earthquake occurs.

You'll work with one partner. *Each* of you will interview at least *two* people. You will have twenty-five minutes to conduct all four interviews.

Find a partner. To prepare to interview, you need to carry out the following steps:

Step 1: Write the questions you will ask in order to elicit the required information. Check them with another pair of classmates.

Step 2: Plan where you will go to conduct the interviews.

Step 3: Decide how you will get people to stop and answer your questions.

Step 4: Set up a sheet for recording your information.

Note: Remember to thank people for their time, even those who do not stop to talk. Keep within your time limits.

Interview Follow-Up: Generalize from Your Data

In order to do this next task, both you and your partner will need identical copies of the information you collected. Take time now to make these copies.

One partner will be A; the other, B. The class will form two groups: one of A's; the other of B's. In your new groups, combine your data to come to general conclusions about the questions you asked in the interviews. Then write complete sentences to answer the questions.

Question 1: Which earthquakes were most frequently remembered by the people you interviewed?

Question 2: Generally speaking, how concerned are people about the occurrence of an earthquake in this area?

Question 3: In general, how well informed are people about earthquake history in this geographical area?

Before you do the fourth question, do Reading IV, on page 182, which tells you what to do in the event of an earthquake. Then answer the fourth question.

Reading IV

If an Earthquake Occurs

Stay calm. Don't panic.

If you are indoors, stay there. Do not run outside; you might be hit by falling debris. If you are in a house, store or high-rise building, take cover under a heavy desk, table, or bed; or stand in an inside doorway away from windows. (A door frame or inner core of a building are its strongest points and least likely to collapse.) Do not dash for exits, as stairways may be broken and jammed with people. Do not use elevators as power may fail.

If you are outside, stay there. Move away from buildings to avoid crumbling walls and falling debris. Stay away from power lines and dangling electric wires.

If you are driving, stop quickly and stay in your car. If possible do not stop on a bridge, overpass, or where buildings can fall on you. Your car can provide protection from falling debris.

From *Earthquakes*, Emergency Preparedness, Canada. Reprinted with permission.

Question 4: On the whole, do people know what to do if an earthquake occurs?

Present your findings to your teacher, including the statistical support for each of the generalizations you stated in your answers.

Quiz: Do You Know What to Do After an Earthquake?

Below you will find a list of suggestions about what to do *after* an earthquake occurs. In each blank, write "True" or "False," depending on whether or not you consider it sound advice.

_____ 1. Phone your friends and relatives to see if they're safe.

_____ 2. Wear shoes to protect your feet from debris or broken glass.

_____ 3. If the water is off, use emergency water from water heaters, melted ice cubes, and canned vegetables.

_____ 4. If you live near the ocean, go to the shore. You will be safe there.

_____ 5. If the electricity is off, light a match to find your way safely around your house.

_____ 6. Don't go sightseeing. Drive your car only if necessary, and then with caution. Keep the roads free for rescue and emergency vehicles.

_____ 7. Listen to your battery-operated or car radio for instructions. Follow them.

_____ 8. Reenter damaged buildings only to retrieve your valuable possessions.

Discuss your reasoning with two partners; try to arrive at a consensus for each question. Then look at the answers at the end of the chapter to see if you were correct.

READING V: "MEXICANS LINK DAMAGE IN QUAKE TO BREACHES OF CITY BUILDING CODE"

This reading will examine one reason why the earthquake in Mexico caused so much devastation: new buildings did not meet legal construction standards. The information includes both a short-term and a long-term approach to preventing death and destruction.

A. Read the headline of the article on pages 185–186 to predict the content.

B. Read the five statements below. Decide if each is "Probably True" (PT) or "Probably Not True" (PNT). Write the appropriate letters in the blank beside each statement. When you finish, quickly scan the text to check your answers.

_____ 1. If builders had not tried to cut corners on safety standards, more newer buildings might have been saved.

_____ 2. If newer buildings had been built as well as the older buildings, there would have been less damage.

_____ 3. If government supervisors had strictly enforced the building codes, more buildings might have withstood the earthquake.

_____ 4. If building codes had been strictly enforced, there would have been no damage.

_____ 5. If the earthquakes hadn't been so severe, the death toll from collapsed buildings wouldn't have been as high.

C. Discuss your answers with two partners. Refer to the text to resolve differences.

D. Quickly scan the article to find answers to the questions below. As you scan, highlight the required information and put the question number in the margin. Again, ignore irrelevant information.

1. According to this article, how much of the damage was probably preventable and due to improper construction?
2. What recommendations did Eduardo Matos Moctezuma make about the materials, foundations, and construction techniques?

In groups of three or four, check your answers.

Reading V

Mexicans Link Damage in Quake to Breaches of City Building Code

By JOSEPH B. TREASTER
Special to The New York Times

MEXICO CITY, Sept. 24—A group of intellectuals and many architects here say they believe that a number of buildings that were destroyed or heavily damaged in two earthquakes last week had been constructed in violation of the city's building codes.

"It was a combination of corruption and a lack of efficiency," said Homero Aridjis, a 45-year-old writer and former diplomat who founded the intellectuals' group, known as the Group of 100.

The assertions came as residents began to look at the damage as somewhat less catastrophic than many had feared in the immediate aftermath.

There was heavy destruction and the death toll, now at 4,200, continues to rise as rescue teams reach the lower levels of crushed buildings. But in an urban area of 18 million people, the loss of life, residents agree, could have been worse.

Reports from Architects

Juan Gurrola of the College of Architects, a professional organization, said that based on reports from 200 to 300 members, there appears to be a "very high possibility" that many of the buildings "were poorly built with not the right materials."

"If the building codes had been followed in very minute detail, damage would have been avoided in 50 percent of the cases in these earthquakes," said Agustín Escobar, a civil engineer who specializes in building earthquake-resistant foundations.

Mr. Escobar said he did not think that corruption was involved. But he said contractors and Government inspectors were "very lax."

The owner of a construction company said the Government had adopted a strict building code after the earthquake of 1957, which until last week had been the most devastating in Mexico.

But he said the codes were often not followed.

"It is up to the individual contractor," he said. "The jobs are not well inspected."

Mr. Aridjis, the writer, said that as an "act of elementary justice" the Government must conduct a "deep and honest investigation" into the destruction.

"Otherwise," he said, "the inhabitants of this city will be living in fear and permanent insecurity."

Government officials say that at least 400 buildings were destroyed and 700 others seriously damaged.

Insurance company officials quoted in El Universal, a leading newspaper, said more than 7,000 buildings had suffered some damage.

More than 100 of the destroyed buildings were either owned or rented by the Government, including the buildings used by the Ministries of Commerce and Communications and Transportation. Several large public housing buildings were also destroyed as were two hospitals and more than 30 schools.

Mr. Aridjis and others in the Group of 100 noted that none of the more than 450 of the city's historic buildings had been seriously damaged.

"The old ones were built to last," Mr. Aridjis said. "Many of the new ones were built only for profit, without concern for the people who were going to live and work in them."

2,000 to 4,000 More Dead Expected

The government believes that, in addition to the 4,200 dead already counted, 2,000 may yet be found buried in rubble. Others expect as many as 4,000 more bodies to be recovered.

On the quality of construction, Raúl Ferrera, a partner in an architectural firm, said:

"We have very good techniques for building here as you can see in the very high buildings that are still standing. But some owners and contractors do not pay attention to building codes, and the Government does not enforce them."

He said Government inspectors "give attention to building plans, but rarely supervise construction."

"Getting approval to build, all the licenses, is very difficult in Mexico," he said. "It is a real mess for architects and contractors. But after that they very rarely pay attention to the construction."

Eduardo Matos Moctezuma, an archeologist and member of the Group of 100, said an investigation must look carefully "into building materials, foundations and into the whole range of techniques used in construction."

He said experts should determine whether builders cut corners by doing such things as skimping on concrete and steel reinforcing rods.

Some architects said that among the building code violations were the use of walls and floors thinner than required by Government standards and supporting columns smaller than specified.

Some architects said they believed building practices had become increasingly lax as more than a quarter of a century passed without a catastrophic earthquake.

"Builders began following 'soft practices' because they did not suppose such a huge earthquake would happen in this country," Mr. Escobar said.

READING VI: "WHY SO MANY BUILDINGS FELL"

This reading, an illustration, is on page 188. Read the headline. Do you think the reading will contain information relevant to your writing task? Why or why not?

1. Identify the four different kinds of buildings in the diagram on page 188. Write the names in Column A below. In Column B, briefly describe what happens to each design in a large earthquake.

A
Kinds of
Buildings

B
Their Fate During
an Earthquake

a.

b.

c.

d.

2. Read the statements below. Then examine both the illustration and the accompanying text, "Why So Many Buildings Fell." If the statement is true, write "True" in the blank; if false, write "False." When you've finished, check your answers with two partners. Use the text to clear up any disagreements.

_____ a. If more buildings had been built on rollers, there might have been less damage.

_____ b. If Mexico had been built on an old lake bed, fewer buildings would have collapsed.

_____ c. If tall buildings hadn't been built close together, some damage could have been avoided.

_____ d. Twisting might not have caused structural collapse if T-shaped buildings had been built symmetrically.

_____ e. If the adobe structures hadn't been built to withstand earthquakes, they might have fallen apart.

Reading VI

Why So Many Buildings Fell

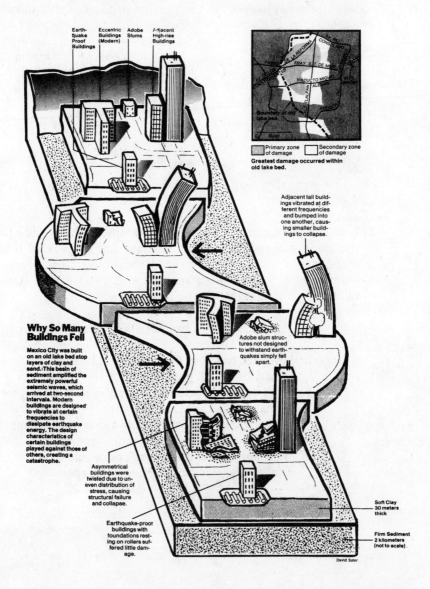

Why So Many Buildings Fell

Mexico City was built on an old lake bed atop layers of clay and sand. This basin of sediment amplified the extremely powerful seismic waves, which arrived at two-second intervals. Modern buildings are designed to vibrate at certain frequencies to dissipate earthquake energy. The design characteristics of certain buildings played against those of others, creating a catastrophe.

Earthquake Proof Buildings

Eccentric Buildings (Modern)

Adobe Slums

Adjacent High-rise Buildings

Primary zone of damage   Secondary zone of damage
Greatest damage occurred within old lake bed.

Adjacent tall buildings vibrated at different frequencies and bumped into one another, causing smaller buildings to collapse.

Adobe slum structures not designed to withstand earthquakes simply fell apart.

Asymmetrical buildings were twisted due to uneven distribution of stress, causing structural failure and collapse.

Earthquake-proof buildings with foundations resting on rollers suffered little damage.

Soft Clay 30 meters thick

Firm Sediment 2 kilometers (not to scale).

David Suter

READING VII: "CLUES SOUGHT FOR SAFER CONSTRUCTION"

READING VIII: "CALIFORNIA IS STEPPING UP ITS EARTHQUAKE PREPARATIONS"

Read the headlines for these next two news stories. Do you think they could be helpful for your writing task? Why or why not?

1. To read these news stories, you'll work with a partner. First you'll divide the readings. Then you'll read your story to answer the questions. Next, you'll check your information with others reading the same one. Finally, you'll share your information with your original partner. You have one hour and thirty-five minutes to complete the entire task.
2. First, find a partner. Decide who will read which story. Reading VII begins on page 191; Reading VIII, on page 195.

READING VII: "CLUES SOUGHT FOR SAFER CONSTRUCTION" (pp. 191–192)

A. Prepare to Read (5 minutes)

1. Read the first three paragraphs. What peculiarity of Mexico City made the earthquake damage even heavier? How?

2. The news story has been divided into three subsections, each with its own heading, to help the reader organize the subtopics of this fairly complex idea. What are the three subheadings? What do they mean?

B. Read and Highlight (20 minutes)   Read the questions below and then read the article, highlighting the relevant information. Make notes in the margin, but wait until you get to Part C before you write your answers below.

1. Section 1: "Sediment and Shaking"

   a. If a city is built on an area that was once covered with water, what two factors could increase the damage of any sizeable earthquake?

b. How has the writer tried to make the second factor understandable to the naive reader?

2. Section 2: "Buildings Already Weakened"

    a. In what way can being built on sediment cause problems for buildings?

    b. How might such problems be overcome?

3. Section 3: "Buildings That 'Float'"

    a. In the first paragraph of this section, you learn of two methods of making large buildings earthquake resistant: (i) building on piles, and (ii) allowing the building to float, including one design called "base isolation." Find out what this term *base isolation* means and how it works.

    b. In the last paragraph, the writer again helps the reader to understand by giving him a very clear example of base isolation. On a separate sheet of paper, draw a diagram to show the foundation of the Imperial Hotel in Tokyo.

C. Check Your Information (30 minutes)   Compare and discuss your answers with two other people doing the same news story. Take brief notes in the spaces provided.

D. Prepare Your Presentation (10 minutes)   Prepare a ten-minute oral summary of the information you selected. Make sure you have enough information to make the ideas very clear to your partner. Remember to use your own words as much as you can. Also remember *not* to read your information; instead, talk to your partner. You may use cue cards with a few words on each.

E. Share Your Information (30 minutes)   With your partner, take turns presenting your information. Take notes on any information you think you'll need for your letter. Ask and answer questions if necessary for full understanding.

Reading VII

Clues Sought for Safer Construction

By WALTER SULLIVAN

To specialists in earthquake-resistant construction, the heavy damage inflicted upon Mexico City in the disaster Thursday will provide the most valuable demonstration they have ever had of what design features in a modern city are most resistant to such an onslaught, particularly when structures are built on a deep accumulation of sediment.

It has long been known that the central part of Mexico City, resting on a prehistoric lake bed, is particularly vulnerable to shaking. David Harlow of the United States Geological Survey, a specialist in the geology of that region, said yesterday that in previous, less violent earthquakes the city center had been shaken "much more than surrounding areas."

The sediment accumulation on which the city was built is believed to be from 500 to 1,000 feet deep and such material, in an earthquake, "would shake like crazy," Mr. Harlow said yesterday in a telephone interview from Menlo Park, Calif.

Sediment and Shaking

It is widely believed that the most severe earthquake to strike North America in modern times was centered at New Madrid on the Mississippi River in southern Missouri in 1811. It is suspected, Mr. Harlow said, that its shaking was especially violent because of the valley's deep sediment accumulation. The same, he added, may be true of the 1886 earthquake in Charleston, S.C.

Another hazard in such situations is known as liquefaction. It can be demonstrated by placing an object on sand in a bowl and adding water until it almost reaches the sand's surface. As soon as the bowl is shaken the object sinks. Such an effect has been blamed for much of the damage inflicted on buildings resting on landfill near the bay during the San Francisco earthquake of 1906.

According to Dr. Thomas L. Holzer, a specialist in soil mechanics at Menlo Park, much of the sediment under Mexico City, being a lake bottom deposit, is probably too fine-grained for liquefaction. An exception, he said would be in areas where sand was laid down by inflowing rivers.

Buildings Already Weakened

Dr. Holzer pointed out that, according to early reports from Mexico City, most of the damage appeared to be from collapse caused by severe shaking, rather than from the subsidence that follows liquefaction. Whether liquefaction had actually played a role, he said, could only be determined by direct inspection. In 1977 he did a walking tour of the city's central area and found that many older buildings seemed "structurally stressed" by long-term settlement into the soft sediment. Thus, he said, they were "already weakened" and prone to collapse.

Buildings can be built on such deposits, he said, if precautions are taken. One measure is to drive pipes deep into the sediment and fill them with coarse material through which water can rise to the surface. This prevents the accumulation of water pressure between grains, making the deposit less subject to liquefaction.

Buildings That 'Float'

In some cases large buildings are built on piles driven into the sediment, whereas others are allowed to "float" on the deposit. A number of Federal and academic specialists in quake-resistant construction are heading for Mexico City to see which methods were most successful.

Another focus of interest is the resort city of Acapulco, whose towering waterfront hotels for years have rivalled those fronting Miami Beach. According to Mr. Harlow, shocks recorded following the main quake on Thursday indicated that, after the rupture began deep under Playa Azul, it progressed southeast down the coast for 60 or more miles—possibly beyond Acapulco.

Perhaps the most widely discussed aspect of quake-resistant engineering is the use of what is known as base isolation to minimize damage to a structure. The foundation is designed so that the structure is not firmly attached to the ground, allowing the building to remain relatively stationary while the land beneath it shakes.

An example is a recently completed government building in San Bernardino, Calif. It rests on flexible bearings designed by Dr. James M. Kelly, professor of civil engineering at the University of California's Earthquake Engineering Research Center in Berkeley . He is a leading champion of base isolation.

About two years ago, he said yesterday, he received a brochure from an architect-owned construction company in Mexico City offering an "Anti-Seismic System" that used base isolation. He believes at least one building was built to this design.

"Two of my colleagues leave for Mexico City tonight," he said, carrying the brochure in the hope of finding the building and learning how it fared. According to Dr. Holzer, however, it is "almost impossible" to use such construction for buildings more than 10 or 15 stories high.

A famous example of base isolation was the Imperial Hotel in Tokyo, designed by Frank Lloyd Wright to survive severe quakes. He placed the hotel on an eight-foot layer of firm soil that covered a deep deposit of shaky mud. Piles were driven into the soil, but not deeper, so that the building would not be coupled to the mud. The hotel, now demolished, withstood the great Tokyo earthquake of 1923, in which buildings around it collapsed.

READING VIII: "CALIFORNIA IS STEPPING UP ITS EARTHQUAKE PREPARATIONS" (pp. 195–196)

A. Prepare to Read (5 minutes)

1. This article begins on page 195. Before you start to read it, reread your writing task on page 180 to remind yourself what kind of information you're looking for.
2. Now read the date and the headline of this article. What probably happened in California in the month after the quake in Mexico? Why?

B. Read and Highlight (20 minutes) The preparations discussed in this story can be divided into two kinds:

- those which reduce the potential damage before the earthquake actually happens, and

- those that deal with the emergency immediately after the earthquake.

Read the article carefully, highlighting the important information in both categories. Label each item "damage" or "services," as appropriate. This will help you classify the information later.

C. Check Your Information (30 minutes)

1. With two other people who read the same news story, discuss the information you highlighted. Then, on a separate sheet of paper divided into two columns (see below), make any notes you consider useful for your writing task. Use your own words except for specialized terms. Number the main preparations in each category.

PREPARATIONS FOR REDUCING THE POTENTIAL DAMAGE	PREPARATIONS FOR PROVIDING EMERGENCY SERVICES

2. Consider again the problem with the emergency communication system. What kinds of communication are they possibly referring to? What suggestions can your group think of to improve the survivability of these communication systems immediately after an earthquake? How might your suggestions help? Take notes on your ideas.

D. Prepare Your Information (10 minutes)   Prepare a ten-minute oral summary of the information you isolated. Remember to use your own words as much as you can. Also remember *not* to read your information; instead, talk to your partner. Ensure that you have enough information to clarify and support your points.

E. Share Your Information (30 minutes)   With your partner, take turns presenting your information. Take notes on any information you think you'll need for your letter. Ask and answer questions as necessary for full understanding.

Reading VIII

California Is Stepping Up Its Earthquake Preparations

By ROBERT LINDSEY

HOLLISTER, Calif.—Like a pincushion, the earth's crust near this rural central California town is punctured by scientific probes that measure the constant geological turbulence beneath Hollister as opposite sides of the San Andreas Fault crash and rub against one another.

So many small earthquakes, such as the tremor that shook the New York City area yesterday, and occasional bigger ones, that knock things from shelves, occur near here that a few years ago local entrepreneurs began selling T-shirts labeling Hollister "The Earthquake Capital of the World."

But after last month's devastating quakes in Mexico, others in this farming town of 16,000 have started to take their proximity to the San Andreas Fault more seriously. The city recently bought a 24-foot trailer and outfitted it as a mobile command post jammed with communication equipment and other gear designed to coordinate emergency services. Hospitals conduct drills regularly, preparing to handle large numbers of casualties from an earthquake.

In California, the risk posed to life and property by the San Andreas Fault has been familiar for more than a century. However, even as geologists began to warn a decade ago that enormous pent-up forces were threatening to unleash a huge earthquake, many Californians seemed oblivious to the danger.

But that attitude has been changing. At the University of California, Los Angeles, a commission appointed two years ago reported last week that a major quake could kill as many as 2,000 people on campus if it struck during school hours. Further, the study gave "very poor" earthquake safety ratings to 22 of the university's 90 buildings.

Clearly the Mexico City quakes, which toppled scores of buildings and killed thousands of people, have prompted officials all over California to take the threat even more seriously. Although the experts do not expect a California earthquake to follow the pattern of earth movements they saw in Mexico, scientists say there were enough chilling parallels to make the Mexican tragedy a kind of preview of what may lie ahead here. Because of the similarities, said John MacLeod, an official of the state's Seismic Safety Commission, the Mexico City earthquakes are likely to become history's most heavily studied.

Since the quakes, scores of California police and fire officials, emergency service and communications experts, geologists, physicians, hospital administrators, architects and other specialists have traveled to Mexico City in hopes of learning why damage was so heavy and how best to cope with such a disaster after it occurs.

Although some experts say they expect it to be months before they reach any conclusions, the Mexican quakes are already leading to changes. Some local officials, advised that much of Mexico City's emergency communications system was out of service for hours, are studying ways to increase the survivability of their own networks.

Gov. George Deukmejian signed legislation authorizing the upgrading of a temporary post-earthquake emergency control center at a military reserve training facility in southern California and design work on a damage-resistant command center from which emergency services would be directed.

Other legislation directed the Seismic Safety Commission to develop plans to pinpoint and reduce potential architectural hazards and required a special review of plans for police, fire and other emergency facilities built in the future aimed at enhancing their ability to withstand major earthquakes.

Citing the experience of Mexico City, an organization of structural engineers called for the establishment of tough new standards to make future buildings more resistant to the lateral motion and other forces created during a substantial earthquake.

The owners of the Huntington-Sheraton Hotel in Pasadena decided last week to close its central building, an imposing structure that has been a local landmark since 1906, on the grounds that engineering studies indicated it would not survive a major quake.

Officials of the Seismic Safety Commission, noting that many victims of the Mexican earthquakes died when unreinforced brick buildings collapsed, have called for immediate steps to strengthen more than 50,000 similarly designed buildings in California.

The Los Angeles City Council passed in 1981 a law requiring the strengthening or razing of 8,000 such buildings over a period that, with extensions, owners could stretch to a decade or longer.

A few days after the Mexican quakes, the City Council voted to accelerate the program and require that all of the buildings be reinforced or destroyed within five years. "Los Angeles has probably been the leader, outside Japan, of preparing for a major earthquake," said Hal Bernson, the Council's principal specialist on earthquakes. "What Mexico City did was remind Los Angeles that in a few years, we also are going to have a big earthquake, and it reminded us again that we should get ready for it."

WRITING THE LETTER

Prewriting

Analyze Your Task

1. Reread your writing task below, highlighting key words:

> You are a group of citizens living in a medium-sized town 150 miles from a fault in the earth's crust. Your area has recently experienced several earth tremors, measuring 4.5 to 5.2 on the Richter scale. You are concerned about the possibility of a major earthquake and want the town council to adopt measures to minimize the death and destruction that could result if one occurred. There are two or three measures you consider particularly vital.
>
> You've decided that if you all write letters to the council members you might be able to move them to act. Your task is to convince the council that these measures are necessary. You will prepare for and write your letters over the next few classes.

2. In groups of four or five, do the following:

Consider your audience—their probable knowledge about the topic and their possible reactions to your recommendations.

Consider your purpose—what you're trying to accomplish with regard to this audience.

Consider how you want the council to perceive you—as an expert in seismology? as someone concerned yet relatively uninformed about earthquakes? as a well-informed and educated citizen?

Now think about the information you'll need to include, given these considerations.

Review Your Information   Meet with a group of three or four other citizens. This first meeting will be a brainstorming session in which you come up with as many ideas as you can regarding earthquake preparations. Don't evaluate them yet; just jot down the ideas for future discussion. To record your ideas, set up a separate page with three columns (as shown on the next page), and write your ideas in Column A.

Evaluate Your Information   For each idea in turn, consider both the advantages and the possible disadvantages. During the discussion, make brief notes in Columns B and C. If you support an idea, try to think of ways to avoid negative consequences or disadvantages. This will help you practice convincing the city council members.

A MEASURE	B ADVANTAGES	C DISADVANTAGES

Select Your Information

1. Think again about your audience and your purpose; then select two or three recommendations to make to the council.

2. For each recommendation, ask yourself these questions:

   a. What will it involve?
   b. How can I make sure that my readers will understand exactly what I mean?
   c. How can I convince my audience that this measure is necessary in order to save lives and/or to protect the city?

3. Go over your readings and notes to find any information you feel you need to help convince the council. You might want to consider the following kinds of information:

   • examples of other cities that have experienced earthquakes

   • opinions/recommendations of experts

   • possible consequences if your recommendations are or are not followed

   • explanations of information/terms that might not be known to your audience

   • any objections the town council might have to your ideas and how you might counter these objections

   In some way, mark the information you want and use key words to label it.

4. Using your own words, take notes. Use a separate page for each recommendation.

Organize Your Information

1. First, consider how you will sequence your recommendations. Can you explain why?

2. Next, go over your notes on each recommendation. Decide how you will sequence the information within that section. Again, think about why you're doing it that way.

3. For each recommendation, draw a tree diagram to show both the ideas you intend to include and how they are related.

4. Work with a partner. Take turns talking each other through your sketches. Comment helpfully on both the information and the organization.

Draft One: Focus on Information and Organization

Now, using only your sketch, write your first draft, focusing on getting your information down on paper.

Conference and Revise   Work with a partner. Listen carefully to his or her letter, trying to think about the recommendations as would a member of the town council. Keep in mind the following questions:

1. What recommendations has the writer made?
2. Is each one clearly stated? well supported?
3. Have possible objections been answered?
4. If you were on the town council, would you be convinced about the need to follow this recommendation?

Make helpful, substantial comments and suggestions. Then revise your letter as desired.

Draft Two: Organize for Your Reader

Write the Inform and Focus Section   The introduction to your letter is very important. It may well decide whether or not your letter will be read. You will need to:

- attract the attention of your readers,

- establish with them a common bond that will help them feel positive toward both you and your message, and

- convince them that your ideas are worth reading.

Before you write your inform-and-focus section, do the next activity.

Evaluating Inform Sections

A. Below you will find four different introductions to your letter. Read them. Then decide which one of the four you prefer. Be prepared to explain why you chose this one and not the others. Consider both positive and negative factors.

Introduction 1. Recently, our town has experienced two tremors, both measuring around 4 on the Richter scale. As most of you who live here already know, our town is in an earthquake zone, near a sizeable fault in the earth's surface. It is possible, then, that a major earthquake could happen here. What I would like to suggest in this letter are three possible ways of avoiding the huge death toll and massive destruction that could face us if an earthquake did happen here.

Introduction 2. The purpose of this letter is to point out three possible methods of preventing thousands of people from being killed or injured and many of our buildings from being destroyed.

Introduction 3. An earthquake can be a terrible disaster. So far, our town has had only tremors, but because of the nearby fault, we could face a major earthquake in the near future. We must act now to avoid a heavy death toll and the devastation that frequently accompanies a major earthquake.

Introduction 4. In recent years, earthquakes such as those in Mexico City and San Francisco have made us aware of the death and destruction that a major earthquake can bring. We who live in this town have known for a long time that we live in an earthquake zone. The recent tremors have reminded us of the fact that we, too, could face a similar disaster. But if we prepare for such a disaster, we can avoid at least some of the usual loss of life and property from an earthquake. This letter offers three suggestions to help us protect our town and our fellow citizens.

In small groups, share and discuss your evaluations. Then, discuss your decisions with your teacher.

B. Write your own your introduction. Exchange papers with a partner and comment on each other's work.

Recommending

A. In this letter, the thesis statements will likely be recommendations. There are many ways in English of recommending. The purpose of this activity is to give you an opportunity to practice some of them.

Read the four sentences below. In each one,

- underline the recommendation itself, and

- highlight the part of the verb that indicates to the reader how important or urgent the writer considers the advice.

1. Eduardo Matos Moctezuma, an archeologist,. . . . said an investigation must look carefully into building materials, foundations, and into the whole range of techniques used in construction.

2. He said experts should determine whether builders cut corners by doing such things as skimping on concrete and steel reinforcing rods.

3. It reminded us that we should get ready for it.

4. The government must conduct a "deep and honest investigation" into the destruction. . . . Otherwise, the inhabitants of this city will be living in fear and permanent insecurity.

Discuss your answers with two partners. Then, together, do the questions below:

1. In sentence 4, how has the writer made his case stronger?

2. What phrases could replace "Otherwise"?

With your teacher, discuss other structures you can use to recommend. List them below.

B. Consider each of the following ideas in terms of its value in minimizing the death and destruction from a major earthquake. Rate its usefulness on a scale of 1 to 5, 1 being the least valuable and 5, the most valuable.

_____ 1. build emergency control facilities

_____ 2. pass stricter building codes

_____ 3. conduct research into predicting earthquakes

_____ 4. tear down buildings that might be unsafe

In small groups, briefly discuss your similarities and differences.

C. Put each idea into a recommendation that indicates how necessary you consider it as part of earthquake preparation. Try to practice a variety of structures. Write each sentence below in the space provided.

1.

2.

3.

4.

Discuss your sentences first in groups; then, with your teacher.

Reread your letter, making sure that each recommendation is clearly stated.

Transitions   Also, reread your letter to ensure that you have included bridges between sections that will help your readers make the necessary transitions.

The Conclusion   Your conclusion should clinch the arguments you've made in the body of your letter.

1. In groups of three or four, discuss different ways of doing this.

2. Write your conclusion. Exchange papers with a partner and comment on each other's work.

Using scissors and tape, incorporate your new sections and any revisions into your text. Rewrite any illegible sections. Revise your second draft, again double-spacing it, reading it aloud as you write. Listen for a logical flow of ideas.

Conference with a Partner Exchange letters with a partner. Read your partner's letter as if you were a councillor. One part at a time, consider the introduction, the thesis statements, support, transitions, and the conclusion. Mark with an asterisk any places where you feel the reader needs extra help in following the ideas.

After you've finished, discuss any problems. Revise as necessary.

Letter Format Before you write the final copy, you will want to discuss with your teacher the appropriate format for such a letter. Your discussion should include the following:

- the format on a page, including spacing
- punctuation
- appropriate ways to address your readers
- appropriate ways to close your letter
- what you would write on the envelope

Draft Three: Focus on Clear and Effective Language

Pay Attention to the Tone of Your Letter

1a. Consider your audience. Do you want them to see you as angry? afraid? concerned? knowledgeable? expert? Try to define that image for a partner.

b. Consider your purpose. What do you want the town council to *do* after they've read your letter?

2. Reread your letter aloud (quietly), one section at a time, as if you were presenting this at a council meeting. Ask yourself if the image you want to project is the one that the letter creates. Also, ask yourself if the language says what you want it to, in the way you want. If it doesn't, try other ways, again on paper and aloud. Decide which version fits better in that section of the text. If you wish, ask the opinion of a classmate.

3. Revise your letter this way, one section at a time. This is the tricky, time-consuming part. You'll probably write only a few sentences at a time.

4. When you've finished, exchange letters with two partners. With a pencil, circle any errors you find in the text. Give back the letter and discuss any problems.

5. Correct the errors, checking with a partner or your teacher.

6. Hand in your letter.

Answers to Quiz, page 183

1. False. Don't use the telephone except in a real emergency. Leave the telephone lines open for official use.
2. True.
3. True.
4. False. Stay away from waterfront areas. Large earthquakes at sea often generate tidal waves.
5. False. You may set off a gas explosion. Have an emergency flashlight and new batteries ready and use them instead.
6. True.
7. True.
8. False. Leave your valuable possessions inside. Walls may collapse after the original shaking has stopped.

Chapter 8

High Technology and You

*T*he twentieth century has seen vast and rapid technological progress. Today our daily lives are affected by machines our great-grandparents never even dreamed of. The last twenty years alone have witnessed a technological revolution. This chapter will focus on changes in our lives as a result of computerization and the two-sided nature of this technological advance.

As you work through the activities, you'll practice the following skills and strategies:

- finding the main idea of a text
- reading to find the author's plan
- making an appointment
- interviewing people in organizations using computers and recording important information
- presenting this information to a group
- selecting and organizing information in order to argue your point of view
- clarifying for your reader

THINK ABOUT THE TOPIC

A. This activity will help you recall some of your prior knowledge of computers and computerization. Answer the following questions as accurately as you can. Jot down a few key words to help you remember your ideas for the discussion in Part B.

1.   Do you know how to operate a computer/word processor?

a little.

2.   If yes, how well and what kind?

draw picture , Apple.

3.   How have computers already changed certain aspects of life in your country?

Organization, development.

4.   What other changes in your life do you foresee as a result of the high-tech revolution?

use, apply , make money.

5.   In general, how do you feel about the changes? Why?

good . save time.

6.   On the whole, what is the attitude of your parents toward the present and future effects of high technology? your grandparents?

They would see is it good for them life

B. In groups of three or four, share and discuss your answers.

READING I: "SEVEN MODERN TECHNOLOGICAL WONDERS" (pp. 208–209)

A. The first article you'll read describes seven technological innovations. Read the descriptions; then decide on their importance to society today. Rank them from one to seven; then, below, write them down in order of decreasing importance (i.e., number 1 will be the most important). You have 3 minutes.

1. personal comp.

2. Micowave oven

3. cal.

4. compact disc

5. Telep.

6. cand

7. cat. scan

B. In groups of three, compare and discuss your answers, justifying your decisions on the relative importance of each "technological wonder." Do your choices reflect differences in your values?

Reading I

Seven Modern Technological Wonders

SEVEN MODERN TECHNOLOGICAL WONDERS

1

THE CREDIT CARD
a familiar sight in wallets the world over, today's plastic credit card is a popular means of activating products of high technology such as calling card telephones and automated banking machines.

2

THE MICROWAVE OVEN
a boon to the food and restaurant industry and a welcome addition to busy households, the microwave oven cuts energy costs as well as saves time and labor. Cooking time can be cut to minutes; leftovers and frozen food can be cooked, stored and served in the same container.

3

THE POCKET CALCULATOR
basic mathematical functions, metric conversions and trigonometric equations are all performed by a portable calculator that can be conveniently carried in pockets, purses and briefcases.

4

THE PERSONAL COMPUTER
whether it's used to balance family finances, write a college term paper or play video games, the personal computer is becoming increasingly common in Canadian homes. The software market is burgeoning and the personal computer's applications are seemingly limitless.

5

THE COMPACT DISC
a hi-fi enthusiast's dream come true, this 12-centimetre, one-sided disc reproduces the full spectrum of music clearly, crisply and totally free of background noise. Finely etched grooves contain the digital information from the recording session; a laser beam then "reads" the information and circuitry inside the player translates the digits into a faithful replica of original sounds.

6

THE CELLULAR TELEPHONE
a new form of wireless mobile communications that uses radio frequencies rather than telephone wires to transmit messages in small geographic areas called "cells." As callers using a car or portable phone move from one cell to another, their transmissions are "handed off" or transferred to adjoining cells without interference or interruption.

7

THE CAT SCANNER
the CAT scanner enables physicians to scan the anatomy in successive layers by radiation. Internal organs and tissues can thus be visualized easily and painlessly. By combining x-ray equipment with computer technology, this useful tool provides doctors with the information needed to accurately diagnose otherwise hard-to-detect disorders.

CHAPTER 8 WRITING TASK: ARGUMENTATIVE ESSAY

You are a student in a philosophy of science course, where the professor has assigned you the following task:

Write a 1,000-word essay supporting one of the following statements:

1. Although computerization has the potential to improve the quality of life for present and future generations, it poses a serious threat to various aspects of society. + –

or

2. Although computerization can be a force for disruption and displacement, we should still be optimistic about the impact high technology has had and will probably continue to have on our society. – +

How are these two statements different? How are they similar? To do this assignment, you'll have to

- select information relevant to your task,
- organize it to support your thesis, and
- express your ideas in clear, effective language.

The next few activities will help you do this.

READING II: "MICROELECTRONIC APPLICATIONS: THEY'RE CHANGING ALL ASPECTS OF OUR LIVES" (p. 211)

Do this activity in groups of three. You have ten minutes.

1. Below you will find the title, summary statement, and introduction of your next reading. Read the title and the summary statement to predict the content of the article.
2. Now read the first two paragraphs—the introduction. Try to predict more specifically what the article will be about. Make point-form notes below.

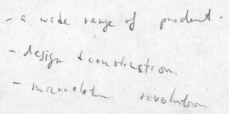

- a wide range of product.

- design & construction.

- microelectron revolution

Reading II

Microelectronic Applications

They're changing all aspects of our lives.

Computers-on-a-chip are being plugged into tiny spaces in a wide range of consumer, industrial and office products. This is where the revolution starts—not with a bang, but with a chip.

In 1976, Robert Noyce, a founder of Intel—the world's largest producer of micro-chips—wrote a widely-quoted article for *Scientific American*. In his paper, he suggested that, "by 1986, the number of electronic functions incorporated into a wide range of products each year can be expected to be 100 times greater than it is today... It is in the exponential proliferation of products and services dependent on microelectronics that the real microelectronics revolution will be manifested."

The microelectronics revolution has been triggered by significant and dramatic changes in the design and construction of electronic components over the past 30 years. Integrated circuits (which include both microprocessors—the "brain" of the computer—and microchips "dedicated" to a certain task) have produced the revolution in consumer products, industrial equipment, robotics, laboratory instruments, automobiles, communication devices, office equipment, and computers themselves.

Read for Specific Information

Now that you have a general idea of what you will read about in the rest of the article, you can focus on the information.

On page 213 you'll find a tree sketch showing the information in this reading and how it has been organized. As you read the article, you'll complete the sketch.

"Tiny Integrated Circuits"

A. The first section, which focuses on the circuits themselves is made up of the ten sentences below. Except for the first one, however, they are not in the right order.

1. Individually, read the sentences and put them in the correct order.
2. When you finish, compare your answers with those of three partners and try to reach a consensus.

"Tiny Integrated Circuits"

__1.__ "Integrated circuits have been able to spur revolutionary changes in these fields because they are tiny, inexpensive, and can be efficiently produced."

__6__ "Putting an integrated circuit such as a microprocessor into a product adds only about 5% to the product's production cost."

__3__ "The computing power of an early '60s room-size computer can today be plugged into tiny spaces in millions of different products."

__7__ "That means the decision to build an integrated circuit into a product is no longer based on economics."

__2__ "Over the past 30 years, electronic components have shrunk in size from two-inch vacuum tubes to microscopic scratches on a sliver of silicon."

__10__ "The president of Intel, George Moore, has warned the chip industry that soon the output of microchips in the world will be so huge that 9/10ths of it will just sit on the shelves unless the industry makes concentrated efforts to find new applications."

__5__ "The second factor guaranteeing the proliferation of microelectronic products is their cost."

__4__ "If there is room in a product for an electronic board measuring 1" by 1" then there is room for a highly sophisticated, programmable computer that consumes little energy and has a long lifespan."

__8__ "The power of integrated circuitry is now essentially free."

__9__ "Massive over-supply is the third factor promising widespread application of microelectronic products."

3. As a class, discuss the strategies and clues you used to discover the right sequence.
4. Fill in Part A of the sketch.

"Finding the Applications" and "Microchipping Products"

Individually, read the next two sections—"Finding the Applications" and "Microchipping Products"—in order to complete the next two parts of the tree sketch. When you finish, compare sketches with two new partners.

Microelectronic applications are changing all aspects of our lives

A. Tiny Integrated Circuits

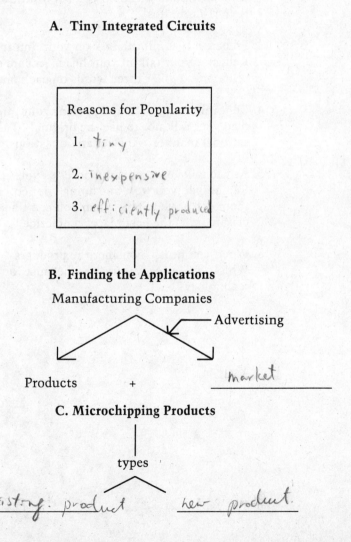

Reasons for Popularity

1. tiny

2. inexpensive

3. efficiently produced

B. Finding the Applications

Manufacturing Companies

Advertising

Products   +   market

C. Microchipping Products

types

existing product   new product

Oral Summaries

This next activity should take just under an hour. Be sure to obey the time limits in parentheses.

1. Form groups of five, if possible. Quickly look over the rest of the reading. How many sections has it been divided into?   Distribute these sections evenly among yourselves. (3 minutes)

2. Individually, read your sections, looking for what—when the article was written in 1983—were considered new advances in technology. Make key-word notes in the margin. Then turn the page over. Tell yourself the main points and the important information for each. This technique will help you use your own words, not those of the text. (10 minutes)

3. Prepare a five-minute talk on your information. Use your own words. Rehearse your talk in your head. Prepare cue cards if you wish, but write only two or three words on each one. (10 minutes)

4. Re-form your groups and present your information. Be sure neither to read your talk nor to use the original. Talk to your group in a conversational manner. Answer any questions you're asked. (30 minutes)

5. As the talks proceed, take notes as you need for your essay. (*Note:* Remember, you won't be doing your colleagues any favors if you let them continue to talk when you can't hear or understand. The classroom is the best place to practice.)

6. When you finish, consider the products you have in your notes. Which are already obsolete because of further advances in technology?

Reading II

Microelectronic Applications

They're changing all aspects of our lives.

Computers-on-a-chip are being plugged into tiny spaces in a wide range of consumer, industrial and office products. This is where the revolution starts—not with a bang, but with a chip.

In 1976, Robert Noyce, a founder of Intel—the world's largest producer of micro-chips—wrote a widely-quoted article for *Scientific American*. In his paper, he suggested that, "by 1986, the number of electronic functions incorporated into a wide range of products each year can be expected to be 100 times greater than it is today... It is in the exponential proliferation of products and services dependent on microelectronics that the real microelectronics revolution will be manifested."

The microelectronics revolution has been triggered by significant and dramatic changes in the design and construction of electronic components over the past 30 years. Integrated circuits (which include both microprocessors—the "brain" of the computer—and microchips "dedicated" to

a certain task) have produced the revolution in consumer products, industrial equipment, robotics, laboratory instruments, automobiles, communication devices, office equipment, and computers themselves.

Tiny Integrated Circuits

Integrated circuits have been able to spur revolutionary changes in these fields because they are tiny, inexpensive, and can be efficiently produced.

Over the past 30 years, electronic components have shrunk in size from two-inch vacuum tubes to microscopic scratches on a sliver of silicon. The computing power of an early '60s room-size computer can today be plugged into tiny spaces in millions of different products. If there is room in a product for an electronic board measuring 1" by 1" then there is room for a highly sophisticated, programmable computer that consumes little energy and has a long life-span.

The second factor guaranteeing the proliferation of microelectronic products is their cost. Putting an integrated circuit such as a microprocessor into a product adds only about 5% to the product's production cost. That means the decision to build an integrated circuit into a product is no longer based on economics. The power of integrated circuitry is now essentially free.

Massive over-supply is the third factor promising widespread application of microelectronic products. The president of Intel, George Moore, has warned the chip industry that soon the output of micro-chips in the world will be so huge that 9/10ths of it will just sit on the shelves unless the industry makes concentrated efforts to find new applications.

Finding the Applications

Companies such as Intel, IBM, Texas Instruments, and other corporate giants have poured billions of dollars into the design and production of chips and chip-based products. And they are not the sort to let their wares sit on the shelf. They have to discover applications for their chips and, most importantly, markets for their micro-chipped products.

Which means that the major market for micro-chips will be consumers— because advertising can create consumer demand. Advertising campaigns can very effectively manipulate consumers to "need" micro-chip products. As the advertising campaigns get into gear, department store catalogues will be crammed full of chip-powered or chip-enhanced products.

Helping this trend is the fact that the application of micro-chips enjoys a high degree of social acceptance. Chip production and the production of chip-powered goods don't have the immediate, visible consequences of some industrial processes. Microelectronic plants don't have huge stacks billowing out smoke.

Microchipping Products

Already existing products are first in line to be micro-chipped. This allows for the quick, efficient application of chips without the expense and creativity needed to develop new products. It is much easier to plug an integrated circuit into an old product than design a whole new product.

The integrated circuits will, of course, be hidden away in the product. People won't notice an integrated circuit. They'll pay attention to the product's enhanced control or added features. But, noticeable or not, there will be miniaturized computers somewhere inside.

The department store catalogues already display the first wave of micro-chipped products—the tiny calculators and digital watches. But they also offer hand-held games that simulate arcade machines, and TV computerized games. (All games will sell better if they're given an "educational" aura.) The catalogues will soon have dolls that do more than cry and wet. And they'll have little toy tanks that children can program to follow imaginary obstacle courses.

Household Goods

But it is the household goods section of the catalogue that will be most changed by the microelectronics revolution. Integrated circuits will produce a host of "intelligent" goods for gadget-hungry people who want to spend more time at home.

A microwave oven is a good example of a micro-chipped appliance. By pushing a number of buttons in various sequences, according to the directions on the door, the cook is actually programming a microprocessor inside the stove. The microprocessor stores the information in some memory chips and then calculates the time, monitors the temperature of the food, and controls the cooking cycle. It's a computerized stove.

Some fridges on the market have microprocessors that count how many times, on average, the fridge door is opened so that it can calculate the best frost/defrost cycle.

Thermostats with chips in them to remember when and how many times to turn on the furnace have been around for three or four years. The newer models can set themselves by monitoring the outside temperature, checking the barometric pressure, choosing the comfort level, and analyzing the occupancy trends of the household (How many people are in the house? Which rooms are they using?).

There are washing machines that monitor the temperature of the water so they can determine how much soap to use. Vacuum clearers are being sold that can automatically go through a house along a memorized path.

New Inventions

While most of the consumer goods that will be micro-chipped will be familiar, some will be brand-new inventions. The TV games such as Atari and Intellivision could not have been developed without the invention of microprocessors.

More new products will be designed by giant corporations in billion-dollar laboratories, and by individuals in garages. Micro-chipped goods will be hawked more than encyclopedias ever were.

Industrial Equipment

Another major field being revolutionized by the micro-chip is industrial equipment. Any product that today includes a sophisticated motor will be scrapped in favour of products that use very simple motors guided by microprocessors.

Currently, motors have to be designed to very detailed specifications to perform their tasks. They're difficult to operate and subject to numerous breakdowns, as well as expensive maintenance. In a micro-chipped product the motor will be simply designed with few parts, and it will be guided in its operations by a microprocessor that will control its every move. Longer-lasting, quieter, and more energy-efficient motors will result.

Parts Manufacturing

Machine tools will also be affected by micro-chips. It has been estimated that 75 per cent of all parts in North America are made in quantities of 50 or less. These parts have a tremendous similarity between them. This makes parts manufacturing a perfect candidate for flexible, programmable tools—tools that can be developed using the "mind" of the computer.

What's more, the flexibility and power of the microprocessor has been increasingly coupled in recent years with innovations in sensoring equipment. Sensors using thermostats and television cameras are measuring sounds, sights, and temperatures to feed into a microprocessor, which can decide on appropriate action.

Welding machines, for instance, can turn themselves on and off by measuring the heat they generate in their work. Machines with sensors, microprocessors, and lasers are now being used in textile plants to cut precise patterns in cloth.

These sorts of innovations have given further impetus to the development of robots.

Automobiles

Integrated circuits will also be built into automobiles as Detroit tries to improve its product and win back its customers. The legislatively-induced need to closely monitor exhaust emissions and improve fuel economy makes cars the perfect candidates for microchips.

Microprocessors will decide on functions such as fuel injection. Other chips will record engine performances and display their results on the instrument panel. There are now cars on the lot with the computer power of an Apple II computer built into them.

Some cars even have built-in voices to announce the opening of doors and low gas levels.

Along with remembering fuel consumption, the car's computer will remember how fast the car was driven on average and whether or not the break-in period was adhered to. Mechanics will be able to learn much about a car by tapping the car computer's memory banks.

They will also be able to learn a lot about the driver—with all that entails for loss of privacy.

Communication Devices

Another major area quickly being revolutionized by micro-chips is communication devices. Microprocessors are being married to fibre optics to produce means and methods of communicating that will change the world and its people radically and permanently. New telephone switching systems are being developed to allow for the concurrent transmission of computer data and voice—something that has up to now been impossible. Teleconferencing—the meeting of people through voice and visual communications over long distances—is now in its infancy, but about to quickly mature.

Huge computer data banks of information are being developed for people to access with their telephones or computers. Electronic mail systems are already in place and being used. Facsimile machines are communicating to each other over thousands of miles.

New forms of media, such as teletext and videotex, are being introduced. And, most significantly, two-way home communication sets which meld the characteristics of television, radio, computers, telephones and stereos are being developed. Computer communications will have significant effects on how we work, where we work and if, in fact, we work at all.

Robots

Industrial robots don't resemble R2-D2 in any way—they look more like overgrown Mechano sets. Most of them are articulated arms that can bend and twist and go through specific programmed actions.

Robots are now, with the discovery of

microprocessors and innovations in sensory equipment, much more affordable than ever before. The microprocessors built into them would have cost $300,000 a decade ago; now they cost less than $300.

Robots currently range in price from $10,000 to $120,000. And even the more expensive ones can be paid for in two or three years, because they work day and night all year round.

Robots learn the first time and forever. They're programmed by being put through a series of steps. The best welder in the plant, for instance, will take the robot through the steps involved in welding a spot, and from then on the robot will perform the task itself.

There are currently about 3,000 robots working on assembly lines in the United States. Japan has over 10,000. There are approximately 3,000 in Europe, and Canada has about 300.

Serf Labour

The term robot comes from the Czech expression for drudgery and serf labour. Which is appropriate, because robots are, at least initially, being introduced into repetitive, uncomfortable, or dangerous jobs.

Robots are used in the testing section of the St. Catherines Foundary. They are spraying paint on the GM truck line in Oshawa. Ford has 17 robots working on its assembly line in Oakville, Ontario.

Robots are very appealing to industrial employers. They can be put to work in dirty, dangerous jobs, forced to work 24 hours a day, and be relied on not to organize a union or call a strike.

About $80 million worth of robotic equipment was sold throughout North America in 1979. That figure is expected to reach $440 million by 1985.

GM of Canada expects shortly to have about 90 robots working in welding, material handling, and painting operations. About 100,000 robots will be introduced into North America by the end of the decade, and Canada will have about 1,500 of these.

The innovations in sensoring equipment and microprocessors that are now making robots more feasible are also radically transforming analytical instruments in laboratories. The number of instruments for laboratory use are increasing significantly while, at the same time, growing simpler to use. All this will spur dramatic advances in sciences such as genetics.

Offices

Another area being hit by the micro-chip revolution is the office, where almost 35 per cent of Canadians work for a living.

The office hasn't changed very much in its structure and methods of work since the turn of the century. The last really major change in the office came in 1873 when the typewriter was first produced.

The typical clerical worker in an office today is backed up by only about $2,000 worth of equipment, compared to the $25,000 investment behind the average production worker. The reason why so little has been spent backing up office workers is simply that not very much equipment to back them up has existed.

But that is all about to change. The micro-chip is making possible a large variety of office machines designed to increase dramatically the productivity of an office worker. Machinery such as word-processors can allow one worker to produce the work of two or three. Communicating computers will allow terminals to be set up in the home, and computer memory banks will do away with file cabinets. The micro-chip revolution is right now exploding in the nation's offices.

Computers

Computers themselves will be radically transformed by the discovery and subsequent improvement of the microprocessor. The world's first modern computer filled a 15,000-square-foot room at the University of Pennsylvania. Today, computers that fit into briefcases are more powerful than that first computer.

Our lives will be changed by computers in their varied forms—big mainframes, medium-mini's, and small microcomputers. And so will our workplaces, our unions, and our political institutions. We should be monitoring computers and their effects as closely as they are monitoring us.

THE INTERVIEW RESEARCH ASSIGNMENT

Newspaper and magazine articles have given and will give you background information about the impact of the microelectronic revolution. What you need now, however, is to do primary research on the issue. For this you'll need to talk to people in various institutions that have already computerized their operations. This activity will give you that opportunity.

1. Form groups of four or five.
2. Decide on a few times when you're all available. Make an appointment for the group to interview someone in an organization that uses computers. Here are some suggestions:

bank	parking garage
police department	transportation organization
library	hospital
newspaper	post office
manufacturer	supermarket

Ensure that the place you go for the interview does, in fact, use computers. To get as wide a variety of information as possible, no two groups should go to the same kind of organization.

3. Plan questions that will give you the following information:

   a. what functions computers perform in that organization
   b. why the organization decided to introduce computers *production - cost service*
   c. what benefits/advantages there are in using computers in this kind of operation
   d. what disadvantages/problems were encountered as a result of computerization
   e. how the organization has minimized the problems
   f. how many jobs were lost because of the switch to computerization
   g. how many more jobs are likely to disappear within the organization
   h. what, if any, jobs have been created because of computerization
   i. the name and position of the person interviewed

Points to Remember

1. Some of these questions should be asked very delicately. You may be asking about sensitive issues. Be very careful how you word your questions and the tone you use to ask them.
2. You'll need to get together to sort out convenient times for all of you, who will do the interviewing, etc. Some of you should take

notes during the interview. Afterwards, you should get together to complete your notes before you forget the information (recall drops by 50 percent after twenty-four hours!). For the class stipulated by your teacher, prepare a ten-minute talk based on the information you obtained during your interview, answering questions (a) through (i).

Remember, this information is to be used to help you write your essay. Pay special attention to the pros and cons of computerization.

Oral Reports

Your teacher will tell you what day you will report on the information from your interviews. To ensure that everyone has an opportunity to hear and use your information, the following procedure is suggested:

1. Re-form your groups so that each new group has one person from each of the old groups.
2. Take turns talking to your group. Answer questions at the end. You have a maximum of fifteen minutes for your talk.
3. As the others talk, take any notes you need for your essay. Ask for repetition and clarification as necessary.

READING III: "COMPUTERS IN THE HOME: ELECTRONIC HULA-HOOPS" (pp. 224–225)

READING IV: "COMPUTERS IN THE WORKPLACE: INDUSTRIAL REVOLUTION—PART TWO" (pp. 226–227)

expert

READING V: "PUNDITS WRONG, HI-TECH REVOLUTION WILL CREATE MANY JOBS" (pp. 228–229)

These readings and oral presentations will give you more information for your essay. You have one hour and ten minutes to complete both activities. Form groups of three. Each person will choose one article.

1. Individually, read your article, highlighting any information on the advantages/disadvantages of the high-tech revolution. Take key-word notes in the margin.
2. Go over the information and, in your own words, take notes on a separate sheet. Decide how to organize the points and number them according to the sequence you've decided on. You want your listeners to be able to take notes easily.

3. Prepare a ten-minute presentation of your information. Make sure you tell your listeners which side of the issue you'll deal with first and how many points you will discuss for each side. Use cue cards (with two or three words on each) if you wish, but don't read your talk. Rehearse your talk in your head.

Oral Presentations

In your group, take turns presenting your information. Be as clear as you can and give examples to illustrate your points; your listeners will need detailed support for their essays. You have thirty minutes to complete the presentations and another ten minutes to answer questions.

When you finish, think of as many other ways as you can in which our day-to-day lives have changed as a result of the technological revolution.

Evaluating Text

After you've given your presentations, work with the other people who read your article. Consider the following questions:

1. What was the attitude of the author toward the microelectronic revolution? How did he make you aware of this?
2. How easy or difficult was it to read this article? Why was this so? Would you say that your article was well organized? Why or why not?
3. Re-form your earlier groups. Take turns presenting this information to your two partners.

Reading III

Computers in the Home

Electronic hula-hoops?

Computers haven't yet become common in our homes, and freelance writer **Gordon Diver** *found there is some doubt about their potential.*

"Zap those asteroids! Halt the stellar invaders! Shoot down attacking aliens!"

So run the ads.

Harmless fun, perhaps, but is it worth the investment? At a recent computer exhibition a father was overheard saying to his ten-year-old son, "I'm not going to spend $2,000 if you're not going to use it!"

Probably, the father's idea of using it went beyond star wars. Certainly, the exhibitors were stressing more serious uses. But perhaps father had heard that the home computer was no more than an electronic hula-hoop.

Current advertising would have you believe that the home computer will improve the quality of your life beyond your wildest dreams. Students will be able to learn foreign languages without any effort. They will use the computer like a handy, one-volume encyclo-paedia with hook-ups to data sources all over the world. It's simple. Just insert a pre-pro-grammed data tape. A whole library of programs will be at your fingertips.

For those less studiously-minded, a whole new art form has been created. You can program your home computer to print any typewriter symbol, spaced accord-ing to your instructions. The result may be a picture of Snoopy asleep on top of his doghouse or a three-dimensional diagram of a space ship, depending upon your interests. There are two ways of achieving these results. One is by typing a few simple commands that the computer already understands. The other way is to buy ready-made programs at great expense and insert them, just as you would insert a cassette. But don't be fooled into thinking that this is really using a computer. In order to program similar materials you would need to study computer programming for months, perhaps years.

The adults in the family might have different uses for the comput-er. Up-to-the-minute weather forecasts would be available. If it's going to rain in half an hour, why bother watering the roses? Or, shall we cancel the family picnic?

Theatre bookings can be made, confirmed, and paid for electroni-cally in seconds if your have the right connectors. The same is true of airline tickets. The computer will even ask you your destination, what time you would like to arrive, and if you need to rent a car when you get there. But this is already being done by your travel agent.

You will be able to do the shopping without leaving the house. A list of groceries, household articles, even specials, will be displayed on the screen along with the day's prices. When the items have been selected, the cost will automatically be deducted from your bank account. No actual cash need change hands, saving time by not having to stand in line waiting for a teller. Deposits can be made in the same way, going directly from the payroll department of your employer into your account. This is already common practice.

With all this extra time, you can improve your bridge or chess game by solving problems submitted by the computer. Or, if you want to pick up a few extra dollars and still not leave home, you can work a little on your word processor. A word processor is a computerized typewriter that can correct errors, save letters for future use, and recall them as needed. Any number of copies can be made.

The home computer can compile and save a mailing list of friends that can be recalled as needed. Names can be added or deleted. The computer can even be programmed to remind you of upcoming birthdays.

People will be able to read the entire newspaper, including advertisements, on the screen. If any permanent records are required, a print-out can be made.

Mother and father can see at a glance the condition of the family budget. In April, the family's income tax returns can be done in minutes. Complicated decisions and calculations that might take hours could be done instantaneously.

So far, the applications described have been for the average Canadian home. For some, the home computer could be of even greater use. Many business people, for example, need not go to the office every day. With a direct line to the office, and even branch offices, much of the day's business could be done at home. Only occasional visits to the office might be necessary. Travel would be cut considerably, resulting in a much more time-efficient workforce and a less crowded transit system. Flights to out-of-town offices would also be reduced, thereby lowering costs.

Permanently handicapped or temporarily ill students could study at home. A teacher could be in constant electronic contact to check progress. The same advantages apply to students living in remote areas.

An ordinary person's portfolio of stocks and bonds could be analysed on an hourly basis as a matter of course, or more frequently if the stock market is extremely active. Various choices regarding buying and selling could readily be programmed and recalled as needed.

Many self-employed people have been using computers for some time. Certain farmers, for example, have large tracts of land which might be widely separated. By putting sensors in strategic locations, a computer in the farmer's living room can tell him when to irrigate the crops and how much water to use. It can even shut the water off when the correct amount has passed through the pipes. It can warn if there is going to be a frost. It can even tell which damaging bugs are active and which insecticides to use.

As more people work at home, there will be a great change in family life. Nowadays, in many households, both parents go out to work. This means, of course, a great deal of time is spent outside the home. With about one third of an adult's time spent in sleeping, and another third in working, little time remains for the family. With computers in the home, we could be on the verge of a return to the closely-knit family unit.

There can be no question about the impact of the computer on our society. By the year 2,000, experts predict that home computers will be as commonplace as colour televisions are today. By 1990, less than ten years away, 50 per cent of Canadian TVs will have computer attachments.

Already there are huge centralized databanks storing incredible amounts of information. To draw from this bank $450 worth of extra equipment is required. Hooking into the source costs another $100. Whenever anyone uses this source, the central computer calculates the cost. At todays prices the cost is $15 per hour during business hours. At other times the cost is $4.50 per hour.

Remember the father talking to his son: $2,000 is a lot of money for a toy that may just stay on the shelf.

Consider once more the average family. Computers are improving rapidly. People, though, are remarkably slow to change in any basic way. The computer industry advertises by appealing to our higher goals: culture, education, etc. But we can't overlook human nature.

You may improve your bridge with the home computer, but you would probably rather play cards with a real person. You can handle the family finances with a pencil and a small notebook—total cost $1.85. If necessary, you can splurge on a $9.95 pocket calculator. And, would you rather study a foreign language for months on end or zap asteroids?

Honestly, now—would you?

Reading IV

Computers in the Workplace

Industrial revolution—
part two

More automation in the workplace will bring greater efficiency. However, as freelance writer **Bruce Gates** *discovered, the computer revolution might involve some big social costs.*

"Take that, machine breath!" Carol exclaimed, as she whacked Henry with her shoe. Henry showed no emotion. Carol collected herself, picked up her shoe and fled the office.

Downstairs in the cafeteria, she ordered a coffee and Danish from the automatic dispenser, slumped into a chair and began talking to the stranger next to her.

"I've been a good secretary all my life, and now I'm just a button pusher for that darned word processor my boss calls Henry.

"My boss treats that machine as if it were human—I'm surprised he doesn't bring it flowers, the way he carries on about it. Henry this, Henry that. Always Henry.

"'Tell Henry to get my expense account out of the files. Tell Henry

to deposit my cheque with the bank. Get Henry to search the library's data banks for an article written in *Maclean's* last December on calculators.' All I do is answer the phone and plug Henry into the receiver. Henry does the rest—I just watch.

"I'm jealous. I'll admit it. I feel my job slipping away from me— Henry does all the things I used to do, and he does them faster with no spelling mistakes or adding errors.

"I no longer feel in control of my job or my life. Everything's done by these stupid computers.

"It used to be that my boss would ask for my opinion on a contract—now it's all programmed into Henry and the dozen other Henrys in our office.

"Finally, it happened. I watched Henry whip off another 1,000-word memo in a minute flat. But it was the wrong memo! I could have killed myself. I punched in the wrong code, and I couldn't get Henry to stop. I got the sudden urge to scream and belt that machine. And I did ..."

Forgive Carol for her temper— by 1990, she and five million other "Carols" in Canada, male and female, will feel the same cool efficiency of computers in their workplace. Few professions will escape the invasion—doctors, lawyers, bank tellers, dictatypists, and secretaries will find their work has either changed or disappeared. Some experts predict that 10 years from now, 90 per cent of today's secretaries, dictatypists and file clerks will either be doing something else or standing in unemployment lines. Most of their jobs will have been taken over by word processors linked to telephones and computers. And, when the voice-activated typewriter is on the market, the takeover by machines will be complete.

Technically, we've come a long way fast. Too fast, perhaps—our ability to deal with the social problems created by our technological brilliance hasn't kept pace.

"What microelectronics has done is allow work to be done with fewer people," says the Ontario

Federation of Labour's Education Director Ray Hainsworth. "It has also increased productivity greatly.

"We already have something like a couple of hundred thousand video display terminals, and that's only been within five years," he says. Hainsworth wonders what we'll do with all the displaced people, mostly women, who will be hardest hit by office automation.

More women will find themselves competing with men in traditionally male professions, such as engineering. But engineers and architects must also cast a wary glance behind them—computers are already major tools in design and construction.

It seems even computer programmers, repairmen, language interpreters and middle managers may not be strangers to unemployment offices. Researches are working on the fifth generation of computers that can repair themselves, be simple enough for use by any person, and yet complex enough to control workplaces like hospitals and factories. There will even be a computer that will instantly translate what you say— you could talk to a Japanese without knowing a word beyond *sukiyaki*.

That doesn't mean there won't be any jobs. If you're high on computers, there will be jobs for you—we can't turn out enough of these people now. The *Montreal Gazette* reports that each computer science graduate gets up to six job offers. The computer industry needs 5,000 more experts than our colleges and universities produce each year. By the year 2000, our computer industry could need 100,000 more highly-trained people.

What this means is a massive change for our education system. But it will be a slow process. And there are those who say it isn't wise to ignore general arts in favour of technology.

More than ever, some argue, courses in ethics will take on greater importance. And the social costs of replacing people with machines can't be ignored. Do we really save money by increasing productivity if we have to put out more in unemployment and welfare? Is the dollar sign the only measure of success?

We may see a two-day week or office shift work, giving us more leisure time. This means possible job growth in the travel and leisure industries. But, says Hainsworth, "We're going to have to find new ways to redistribute income. Otherwise people are not going to be able to afford these leisure activities."

Until we do find answers, it may be wise to delay the office of the future to prevent the Carols of the world from taking out their frustrations on the machines.

Reading V

Pundits Wrong, Hi-Tech Revolution Will Create Many Jobs

By NICHOLAS J. PATTERSON
The writer is an economic analyst and communications consultant in Ottawa.

There is a remarkable amount of unfounded pessimism today about unemployment effects of the upcoming electronics revolution. It is reflected everywhere, not just among labor leaders and the NDP, but also in Mr. Lalonde's budget and even in the Science Council, which should know better.

Despite the repeated lessons of history, they have all overlooked the large impending new job creation, inherent in the wide-scale commercial application of the microcomputer and electronic technology.

Rather than displacing workers, this revolutionary technology will create far more jobs than it eliminates, just like every other major new technology without exception, through history, from the invention of the wheel, right through to the internal combustion engine, the automobile, and the mass-production assembly line.

Each one was supposed to create massive unemployment. Each instead created millions of new jobs and greater prosperity.

Even in recent years, we have had a prime example of how this works in practice—a pertinent one, since it involves computers. It is the experience over the last 20 years with the old-fashioned large-sized mainframe computer and its impact on the workforce.

When these computers were first introduced in the early 1960s, the naysayers predicted, as they always have, that large numbers of workers, in this case clerks, would be displaced and massive unemployment would ensue. In fact the opposite happened.

In 1960, there were 10 million clerks in the U.S., accounting for 15 per cent of the labor force. By 1980, the number of clerks had grown to 18 million and they now account for 19 per cent of the labor force. The massive installation of computers during the 1960s and 1970s was accompanied by a substantial growth in the number of clerical jobs, and moreover, a 25 per cent increase in their share of the total

job market—rather than a reduction.

This is surprising only to those who ignored the huge information output of these machines and the need for increased staff to handle the output. This, along with the large increase in the volume and diversity of information, created more jobs within existing industries. But more important, from an employment standpoint, is the fact it gave birth to entire new industries. For example, the introduction on a widescale, of credit cards is only one large, entirely new industry, created from scratch.

Pessimists claim that workers displaced by automation will be unqualified to assume the new positions created by electronics technology. This may be true, insofar as displaced workers will likely take up the less skilled positions, vacated by other younger workers, who become qualified and gravitate toward the new hi-tech jobs. Such critics forget that the labor market is a constantly simmering mass, seething and shifting with constant change. Most people

Reprinted by permission—Nicholas. J. Patterson, Executive Director, Canadian Development Institute (CDI) of Ottawa, Canada.

change jobs frequently these days.

The reason why technology increases jobs and prosperity, instead of reducing them, is that automation cuts costs, while at the same time permitting increased production and higher wages and profits. This constitutes a source of new wealth and hence a demand for new products, which can be supplied by new technology. In turn, the new production and new products create new jobs.

Perhaps the experience of agriculture is the most striking example of how the economy deals with automation and absorbs its displaced workers, while society becomes richer in the process. In 1933, it took 1.1 million workers, out of a labor force of 2.7 million, to produce food and other farm output for domestic use and export. Agriculture workers accounted for 40 per cent of employment in those days. Now farm workers number only 465,000, a mere 4.4 per cent of a much larger labor force of 10.5 million. Less than half the number of workers feed almost four times as many people.

The main factor behind this remarkable transformation was farm mechanization, the introduction of the tractor and the combine, each a by-product of the automotive revolution and the internal combustion engine. Lest we forget, this was the revolutionary technology which, according to some, was supposed to create a whole new generation of unemployed workers, in the displaced horse and buggy business.

The problem is that among those studying this question, the shrill cries of the amateur futurists have drowned out the factualists, who look at history and the actual case experience with technology and unemployment.

READING VI: "ELECTRONIC OFFICE CONJURING WONDERS, LONELINESS AND TEDIUM" (pp. 231–233)

The following news story will provide you with more information for your essay.

1. Read the story, looking for advantages and disadvantages of computerization. As you read, make notes in the margin. When you finish, take notes on two separate pieces of paper: one for advantages and one for disadvantages.
2. Form groups of three or four. Compare your notes. Add any information you might have missed.

Reading VI

Electronic Office Conjuring Wonders, Loneliness and Tedium

By WILLIAM SERRIN

Rebecca Alford arrives each weekday at 7 A.M. for her job processing health claims at a life insurance company in Syracuse. For the next nine hours, except for breaks and lunch, her day is dominated by a computer.

Mrs. Alford says her job at the Equitable Life Assurance Company is monotonous and is paced by strict output standards, and that workers are intensely scrutinized by superiors. "If you stop working, they ask you what you are stopping for," she says. "Pinning you to a computer, I don't like that at all."

She works at a video display terminal alongside some 55 workers in the department, processing 70 claims a day. She gets a 15-minute break in the morning and an hour off for lunch.

The Electronic Office

Mrs. Alford, who is 30 years old, earns $217 to $400 a week, depending on production. She says the pay standards, a form of piece work, are so complicated that workers do not know how much they will earn each week.

Her work environment is a manifestation of the electronic office, in which many tasks are performed with the help of computers and other new technologies.

As typewriters and other office equipment are replaced by video display terminals all over the country, clerical workers and, to an increasing extent, professional and management workers are feeling the effects. Many, like Mrs. Alford, find the work monotonous and boring. But many others are pleased and say the new technologies make the work less time-consuming by removing tedious tasks of the past.

The technologies, which many experts say constitute one of the more important developments in the workplace in the 1980's, are bringing fundamental changes in the way office work is organized and performed in general business offices, insurance companies, brokerage houses, banks and the like.

The new machines offer huge productivity improvements in office work, which has expanded explosively in recent decades but has long escaped the intensive efforts to improve productivity that occurred in the factory.

Spirited Debate on Effects

Experts spiritedly debate the positive and negative effects of the technologies. Their arguments include these:

Some experts say the technologies often mean that jobs are broken up into less skilled, lower paid jobs and often mean the elimination of jobs.

Others say the technologies generally make work more creative, often mean higher responsibilities and pay, and ultimately mean expanded employment.

Advances in telecommunications and satellite transmissions are allowing the shifting of office work from central cities to rural or suburban areas or even out of the country.

Computers are having a significant effect on women, who make up 80 to 95 percent of typists, secretaries, bank tellers and keypunchers.

The technologies could mean difficulties for unions, which have organized only about 10 percent of private office workers.

In recent years, the number of electronic work stations in use has risen markedly, and it is expected to increase substantially, authorities say. Today some 12.7 million video display terminals, personal computers, word processors and the like are in use in the United States, with the number expected to rise to 41 million by 1987, according to International Data Corporation, a market research company in Framingham, Mass.

Some experts fear that a push for productivity will mean elimination of many jobs women hold, among them file clerks, secretaries, claims processors and some management workers. Eleanor Holmes Norton, professor of law at Georgetown University, who is president of the National Council on the Future of Women in the Work Place, says the technologies offer "the clear prospect of permanent displace- ment" of much middle-echelon work.

Factories in the Office

Yet a major concern of some experts is that the technologies are transferring characteristics of factory work to the office, including the creation of jobs that are routine, interchangeable and strictly monitored and paced; extensive use of time-and-motion studies and strong reliance on part-time, temporary or off-peak period workers.

The computerization, some experts say, means a continuing decline in what has been called the social office. Doris McLaughlin, a technology specialist at the University of Michigan, says the technologies "are making work a lot more lonely."

"It's tedious, it's boring,"

Gladys Hunter, 45 years old, says of her clerical job at a Cleveland bank. She works from 1 P.M. until the work is done, anywhere from 8 P.M. to midnight, entering data from checks into an electronic coding machine so the transactions can be handled by a computer. "We sit all day and process these checks," she says. She is expected to handle 1,600 checks an hour.

"Some girls are bringing in radios, with headphones, to get them through the night," she says.

Praise for New Devices

Others praise the technologies. "We're not talking about eliminating the human factor," says Randy J. Goldfield, a computer consultant with Omni Group. "All we can do is have the machines do the grunt work a lot faster. We're talking about removing a lot of the low-level work from the desks of secretaries and even professionals and having it automated, and presumably providing a bonus factor of available time in which people can be more creative and productive."

Some executives have little experience with the machines and consider using them to be clerks' work. Some office workers and executives find it difficult, says Kenneth J. Koenke, New York area director for Wang, to break the paper habit.

But this is changing. "Before executives were calling up Data Processing and saying, 'I need such and such figures,' " Mr. Koenke says. "Now they are saying, 'I can punch the data myself.' "

Five office workers at Harvard University said they enjoyed a number of aspects of the new technologies. "It's a joy not to have

to retype," said Christina Knapp, a Harvard secretary.

Anne Miller, a worker at the Widener Library, said the machines offered explosive gains in the collection of information and making information available to scholars and the general public.

But the workers, members of Harvard-United Automobile Workers, a labor group trying to organize office workers at the university, said there were numer- ous fears: that there is little opportunity for advancement with the new technologies, that employ- ers do not consult workers about how the machinery is designed, installed and used, and that often the work pace is expected to increase.

Barbara Lewis, a secretary at Harvard, said, "I feel I'm doing six days' work in five."

May Roe, another Harvard secretary, said the technologies offered little chance for advance- ment. "Once you have the skills, they want you to use the skills all the time," she said, rather than having the opportunity to advance to new jobs.

Threat to Jobs Disputed

The women contended that many university workers feared job loss because of the technologies.

Miss Knapp said, "If you're not quick, you're shunted to other work." She says the issue is participation. "We would welcome the technologies if we felt we could feel some control over what happens to us, " she said.

Daniel D. Cantor, Harvard's director of personnel, concedes the office technologies are "new and somewhat scary," but he says Harvard, which is resisting the union organizing drive, is working to see that the systems are installed with the least disruption. He says the technologies pose "no job threat" to workers and that the reaction of most employees has been positive.

"I don't think the electronic office reduces employment a bit," says Charles A. Jortberg, president of Jortberg Associates, an office automation consulting concern in Peabody, Mass. "It makes much more efficient use of the current labor force. It gives more satisfaction to people who work in the electronic office, except for some poor person who has to sit in front of a C.R.T. eight hours a day." A C.R.T. is a cathode ray terminal, another term for video display terminal.

Jon A. Turner, assistant professor of computer applications at New York University, says the computers can enrich work, making it more enjoyable and challenging and increasing wages, or make work less desirable, with reduction in skills, less opportunity for promotion and less pay.

Experts say the technologies have explosive potential. The costs are continually dropping and the capabilities constantly being increased. New developments, like computers that can transcribe the human voice, might arrive within five years, says John Patrick Hefferon, a Wang vice president. Already some computers that can understand simple voice commands are in use at numerous companies.

The inventions that improved office efficiencies and in some cases made office work more pleasant and rewarding, such as the telephone, typewriter, adding machine, and copying machine, were generally installed without much thought to maximizing productivity.

This was because office work for so long constituted a comparatively small part of the economy. Moreover, as office work began to expand in the late 19th century and early in this century, women were brought into the office work force, and by World War II, 90 percent of office workers were women.

Melvin Kranzberg, professor of the history of technology at Georgia Institute of Technology, says this was because "women would do this work more cheaply than male clerks."

But in the last decade or so, with the mushrooming growth of office work—about one-half of the nation's work force is now employed in handling of information—it has become clear to business that office productivity was lagging significantly, and that vast productivity improvements in office work must be achieved if profit levels were to be achieved and office costs, rising at 15 percent a year, reduced.

Some experts see an advantage in addressing such issues now, when the installation and use of the technologies are still at a relatively early stage.

"Looking at these technologies today is like having an opportunity in 1880 to sit down and say, "What do we want to do about the assembly line?' " says Harley Shaiken, a work and technology specialist at Massachusetts Institute of Technology.

Mr. Kranzberg of Georgia Institute of Technology and others say few examples exist to show that the nation thinks through the impact of new technologies, like the automobile, the tractor or the superhighway, even though these technologies have profound effects not only upon workers but on how the nation develops and functions.

QUESTIONS FOR DISCUSSION

A. Prepare to discuss your answers to the following questions, supporting your position. Jot down points to help you remember what you want to say.

1. What appear to be the major advantages of the microelectronic revolution?

    — improve / human life   — create job.

    — save time   - (creative)

    — convient.   - (productive)

    — good for economie   - high pay.

        a) product more   —enrich work.

        b) inexpensive.   —higher responsibility.

    — more efficiently.   — ~~creat~~ expand employment.

    — help on communicate

2. What do you consider to be the major disadvantages?

    ~~improve humanbif~~   —worse loss job.

    - dominate by computer.   Jor-95%

    - job lost.   — lonely, boring

    - less pay

    - less oppurtinity & promotion

        - change work.

3. On balance, does the high-tech revolution seem to be displacing jobs or creating them? Why do you say so?

    both. displace a little.
        creating a lot.

4. Who (industry? government? society? the individual? no one?) should assume the responsibility for retraining those who are displaced by computers? *Yes*

5. How dependent do you think we are on the various chip-based products, including computers themselves? Explain.

B. Exchange views with three or four colleagues. Together, list new industries or jobs that have been created by the high-tech revolution; for example, the manufacture of labels to put on floppy disks or special dishes for microwave ovens. List as many as you can.

READING VII: "ELECTRONIC EPIDEMIC: COMPUTER VIRUSES CAN PUT WHOLE NETWORKS UNDER THE WEATHER"

The next news story you will read examines various forms of computer mischief—ways of disabling computers and disrupting the services they provide. Find answers to the questions below. Read all the questions before you read the news story so that you'll know what information is required.

1. In the case described, what was the mischief?
A kind of destructive program, as a devastating instrument of electronic warfare or terrorism.

2. According to the article, computer mischief comes in four forms: Time Bomb, Rabbit, Virus, and Trojan Horse. As you read the definitions, fill in the blanks in the news story with the correct term chosen from this list.

3. Add spokes to the circle below to indicate the areas of our lives dependent on, and consequently potentially threatened by, computers. The first one has been done for you.

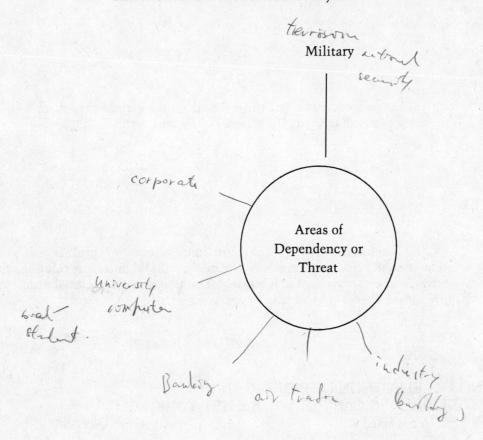

terrosun
Military *national security*

corporate

Areas of
Dependency or
Threat

University computer

local student.

Banking   *art trades*   *industry (building)*

4. Beside each area you add, write one or two key words to help you *more, taxation,* remember the examples provided by the news story.
5. In groups of three or four, check your answers.
6. Next, try to add to the examples presented in the news story, especially current examples. The examples you include may be either true or hypothetical.

Reading VII

Electronic Epidemic: Computer Viruses Can Put Whole Networks Under the Weather

By ROBIN LUDLOW
Southam News

Anyone who's had a computer "crash" knows the sinking feeling of disbelief when files are zapped into the cosmos never to be seen again.

It's annoying enough if it's an accident. But deliberate sabotage is reaching epidemic proportions.

U.S. computer and defence experts were working feverishly late in the week to stop a computer software "virus" from disabling about 6,000 military, corporate and university computers at dozens of locations.

By Friday, they appeared to have gained the upper hand. "As far as we know, the virus is now dead," said Stephen Wolff, director of networking and communication research at the National Science Foundation in Washington.

Computer security experts were calling it the largest and most extensive assault on the U.S. computer system. And it all started with a prank by a computer-science student.

It wasn't the worst form of virus—the kind that destroys data—but it was bogging down computers by rapidly multiplying and engorging memory capacities.

Dr. David Parnas, professor of computing and information science at Queen's University in Kingston, Ont., says the U.S. experience "is very good evidence of the vulnerability of all the computer networks upon which we depend."

Computer viruses can breed more quickly than cockroaches and are more difficult to eradicate. They can scramble data into electronic confetti or wipe out files.

"Once you can cause a program on somebody else's computer to execute with data that you supply, you have a lot of power," Parnas says.

"We should think about the implications for the tremendous defence networks we're building up."

Computer mischief comes in several forms:

• A sort of electronic chain letter that multiplies its own malignant message, consuming memory and processing time and overwhelming the system or network. This is what was happening in the U.S. this week.

• A program hidden within another. The main program does what it is supposed to do but the concealed hitchhiker usually does harm.

• Just what it sounds like. It waits for a specified date or event to detonate and kill data. Time bombs can come as Trojan Horses.

• The worst because it changes existing programs at a basic level and scrambles or erases data.

It is a hidden, destructive, parasitic program that usually makes its way to the computer's central operating system, where it orders its host to make more copies of itself.

It can lie dormant until triggered by some event, duplicate itself and spread its nastiness to other computers through networks, bulletin boards or shared disks.

A high-tech sort of germ warfare, computer viruses are a

relatively new and dangerous development.

Society has become irrevocably dependent on computers from corner cash machines and personal computing to taxation, military and defence systems.

Almost every aspect of life is controlled in some way by computers—banking and air traffic control systems, universities, the life insurance industry, personnel, payroll and tax records, pension funds, medical treatment—the list is almost infinite.

So is the potential of computer mischief as a devastating instrument of electronic warfare or terrorism. Catastrophic collapse is especially feared in military networks and the highly automated banking system.

A destructive program could be inserted into a computer by a terrorist, white-collar criminal, bored student or malicious vandal.

Spies could disrupt vital research or endanger national security. A virus could cripple a major weapons system, send a missile off course or wipe out intelligence data.

Industrial spies could plant subtle programs to alter quality control and create billing errors or equipment failures.

Like people, computers are sociable—they call each other and exchange information. But the very quality that makes them so valuable also makes them vulnerable.

Where information can go, viruses can go and the explosion of computer networks has multiplied the pathways by which they can spread.

David Gamey, a computer security consultant with Coopers and Lybrand in Toronto, says most companies are concerned about access, errors and omissions from within a system.

There are numerous stories of low-level clerks embezzling funds, disgruntled employees sabotaging computers, and competing executives tainting each others' work.

But viruses and rogue programs from the outside "are a new kind of threat that must be considered in security terms."

Gamey says personal computers are much more susceptible to

subterfuge because there are so many and they usually lack even rudimentary safeguards.

Most desktop computers and some larger systems have the equivalent of a sleepy guard at the door. Larger corporate and government systems are usually better protected.

Computers connected to networks and bulletin boards are the most vulnerable. Viruses can enter a computer's memory piggybacking on innocent game programs or electronic mail.

As such episodes increase and receive more publicity, they tend to encourage copycat efforts, with egotistical programmers trying to design more elegant and sophisticated mischief.

Some experts hope the novelty of software viruses will pass, like letter bombs and poisoned Tylenol. But the threat will remain.

Computer security seems to be a career with depressingly bright prospects—perhaps for the perpetrators who know so much about it.

READING VIII: "CIVILIZING THE HIGH-TECH REVOLUTION"

This article is your final reading. It 's fairly long and complex.

1. Before you start, prepare to read using any of the strategies you've practiced in this book.
2. Read the article, making margin notes on any information relevant to your writing task.
3. Note also why people fear high-tech, and any suggestions the writer makes for "civilizing" the high-tech revolution.

Compare your notes with those of two partners.

Reading VIII

Civilizing the High-Tech Revolution

So many familiar institutions have been affected by micro-electronic technology. The traditional service station is giving way to the self-service outlet that offers lower prices because of computerized pumps that record the gasoline sales at a central cash desk. The neighborhood hamburger stand has been supplanted by chain operations that use computerized systems to speed through orders and control inventory. The time-honored institution of banking hours has been effectively abolished by electronic terminals that offer round-the-clock service. The post office has been challenged by the private transfer of letters and documents via word processors—electronic mail. Word processors and electronic calculators are as common in our offices and homes today as typewriters and mechanical adding machines used to be. And in a reversal of form, the old penny arcade has been revived in the form of electronic video games.

The revolution has been brought about mainly by the development of microchips, little bits of silicon that can be made to count, memorize functions, recognize symbols and respond to instructions. They have made possible such wonders as the telephone that answers itself and the cash register that "knows" what to charge for a bunch of grapes and by reading those mysterious stripes on the sides of packages, whether a can contains tomato soup or chicken noodle soup.

The chips have a remarkable ability to store information. They can squeeze the contents of books by at least 10,000 times. Using a combination of microchip and laser technology, all the words in the 435 kilometres of bookshelves in the Library of Congress in Washington, D.C., could be contained on one wall of a large living room. And the capacity of microchips is expanding all the time.

Too Fast for Some

However, that expansion may be happening too quickly for many of us. It's one thing to pop a casserole into a microwave oven, quite another to confront high technology in the workplace. Charles Barsony understands those fears and believes they are natural. Barsony is acting program director for computer-integrated manufacturing at Toronto's Ryerson Polytechnic Institute. "Today we are where science fiction was 20 years ago," he says. "Young people have no trouble with high technology and in fact are very much attracted to these new frontiers. But the older segment of the population very quickly realizes that it generally doesn't have enough technical background to handle this stuff."

Just what is it about high technology that worries us? Barsony says that "people are normally afraid of the unknown. High technology, by its very nature, is a great unknown and requires a lot of specific expertise to understand it."

According to Peter Frost, an organizational behaviorist at the University of British Columbia, people in organized groups develop subcultures, each with its own beliefs and value systems. "And some subcultures are more predisposed towards technology than others," says Frost. "In the past, for example, the human resources departments of companies were much more comfortable dealing with social issues than with technical questions. Science and research groups, on the other hand, were more open to technology. So whatever technological device is being introduced," explains Frost, "the subculture must be able to relate to it and recognize it. The manner in which it is introduced can determine how positively or negatively it is received by the subculture."

Frost also believes that while it is seldom openly admitted, many people view computer systems "in terms of power. Those who introduce and control the technology also control the information, and it is often that centralization of information and power that is resisted."

Allaying Fears

How can our fears about high technology be allayed? Peter Frost suggests that the issue must be looked at from a social as well as a technical perspective. "What we want is productivity but we don't want to lose humanity either. For that reason, it is vital that we remember the social humanism dimension," he says.

Another organizational behaviorist, Philip Mirvis of Boston University, agrees, and he believes the critical question to ask is, "Can we make better use of ourselves in the adaptation to new technology?" We are familiar with the terms *computer hardware* and *software*, but Mirvis speaks of a new buzzword that has been coined by organizational behaviorists: *orgware*. Orgware implies that we need to "help people think about how to organize so they can make use of the technology and manage the organization as it undergoes a technological change."

One thing Mirvis and his colleagues are discovering in organizations is that "while computer technology may alleviate certain technical problems, it doesn't make organizational problems go away. The notion of orgware is that it will sensitize people to the organizational consequences of high technology."

Mirvis feels that we are seeing a "greater sensitivity to the human factor at work today but that there is plenty of room for improvement." He wishes, for instance, that computer companies, instead of simply selling hardware and software to clients, would dedicate themselves to helping organizations adjust to the new technology. Besides giving classes in computer operation, Mirvis says, "these companies should be discussing centralized versus decentralized computing systems with their clients. They should be addressing clients' concerns about safety and health, the physical design of offices and factories, and new career possibilities opening up to employees."

High technology offers a fine opportunity for managers to learn how to improve the running of their organizations but first they must learn about the new technology and its applications. They must also be willing to allocate some resources inside the firm to that end. "But instead of presenting high technology in this way," says Mirvis, "too many computer companies simply try to sell their equipment as solutions to problems. We've got to start helping people use technology more effectively."

However, in Mirvis' opinion, it is not only the purveyors of high technology who must shoulder the responsibility. He would like to see "politicians and ministers address the broader implications of high technology. Just how are we able as a society to make technological judgments? I think that question should be debated in the community far more than it has been."

Mirvis insists that introducing technology into broader society must be done slowly and sensitively. His research supports that belief, indicating that "when users of technology understand why the company has brought it in, feel they'll be given the needed support to learn it and are convinced it will benefit everyone, not just the powers that be, they are much more receptive to the technology and make better use of it." Proof, indeed, of the importance of frank communication.

Deciding Who Takes Control

To gain wisdom through technology, we must treat it wisely. The servant could well become the master if we, as a society, give way to our fears about technology or regard it as a force we cannot handle. If, on the other hand, we think of what we can do with it with human values in mind, it can be made to serve us magnificently. This is what it is meant to do; whether it does or not is entirely up to us.

WRITE THE ESSAY

Prepare to Write

You'll now work on the essay, going through a series of steps.

Analyze Your Task   Reread your writing task on page 210. In groups, consider the following questions:

1. How many parts are there to each sentence?   2
2. What does this tell you about the kind of information your professor expects in the essay?
3. What does this tell you about the necessary organization? *Serial connection*
4. What thesis statement will your professor expect? *from question*
5. Which thesis are you going to support? Why?

Gather Your Information   Now you will need to go back over your readings and notes, highlighting information you need for your essay. Before you start to take notes, however, do the following activity.

Clarifying Ideas

A. Good writers are aware of the needs of their readers. They understand that what might be perfectly clear to them might not be at all clear to others. So good writers pay attention to clarifying their ideas with details, statistics, examples, and illustrations, or the comparison of the unknown to the already familiar.

In this activity you'll examine how the writer of "Civilizing the High-Tech Revolution" helped his readers understand exactly what he meant. The relevant paragraph is noted at the beginning of each question. Write point-form answers.

1. *Paragraph 1:* How does the writer make sure that the reader understands exactly what he means about the micro-electronics industry affecting institutions that we are already familiar with?

   example → benefits.
   → everyone use.
   → any kind of job.

2. *Paragraph 3:* How does the writer ensure that the reader knows exactly what he means by a "remarkable ability to store information"?

   example. → store 430 km of bookshelves in library of congress in Washington

3. *Paragraph 11:* How do we learn what the author means when he says that Philip Mirvis believes that companies need to help organizations adjust to the new technology?

- lot of room

- Indicate company should
give classes, central or decentr

B. In groups of four or five, compare and discuss your answers. Then discuss them with your teacher.

Select Your Information

1. On separate pages for advantages and disadvantages, take point-form notes on the information you need for your essay: main points, clarification, examples—anything you feel should be there.
2. For each page, group related ideas. What kinds of chunks of information are developing? Will you need all the information you have gathered?

Plan and Rehearse Your Essay

1. On a separate page, draw a tree sketch, showing your information and how you intend to order it. Include your central thesis, your subtheses, and any clarification, examples, comparisons, or statistics; that is, your support.
2. As before, talk your sketch through with a partner, telling him or her what you're going to say in your essay. Discuss any problems. Revise as you wish.

Draft One: Focus on Information and Organization

Write your first draft.

Conference with a Partner   Read your essay aloud twice to your partner. The first time, he or she will evaluate your arguments, including the support. Discuss any problems with the content: gaps, irrelevancies, lack of support—whatever your partner identifies. The second time, he or she will listen for organization—thesis statements and the logical flow of ideas. Revise as necessary.

Draft Two: Organize for Your Reader

1. Write your inform section.
2. With two partners, discuss the purpose of the conclusion to this essay. Then write your conclusion.

3. Reread your essay, adding transition sentences where necessary.
4. Using scissors and tape (or a word processor if you have one), incorporate into your essay all the new text you've just written.

Conference with a Partner Exchange drafts with a colleague. Have your partner skim your essay and tree the main ideas. Check this sketch with what you intended to write. See if the two agree. If not, revise as necessary. Then read carefully for the progress of ideas through each small section.

Draft Three: Focus on Language

1. Read your essay aloud as if you were on stage in front of an auditorium full of people. As you read, listen for any problems with clarity, grammar, or vocabulary. This is the time to ensure that your language does not interfere with the communication of your ideas.
2. Exchange papers with a partner. Edit each other's essays.
3. Correct your errors, checking with a friend or your teacher.
4. Hand in your essay.